The Language Police

☆

THE LANGUAGE POLICE

*How Pressure Groups Restrict
What Students Learn*

Diane Ravitch

ALFRED A. KNOPF   NEW YORK   2003

THIS IS A BORZOI BOOK
PUBLISHED BY ALFRED A. KNOPF

Copyright © 2003 by Diane Ravitch
All rights reserved under International and Pan-American
Copyright Conventions. Published in the United States by Alfred
A. Knopf, a division of Random House, Inc., New York, and
simultaneously in Canada by Random House of Canada Limited,
Toronto. Distributed by Random House, Inc., New York.

www.aaknopf.com

Knopf, Borzoi Books, and the colophon are registered trademarks
of Random House, Inc.

Library of Congress Cataloging-in-Publication Data
Ravitch, Diane.
The language police : how pressure groups restrict what
students learn.—1st ed.
p.   cm.
Includes bibliographical references.
ISBN 0-375-41482-7
1. Textbooks—Censorship—United States.   2. Test bias—United States.
3. Censorship—United States.   I. Title.
LB3045.7 .R38 2003
371.3′2—dc21   2002040622

Manufactured in the United States of America
First Edition

For Mary

Contents

Acknowledgments

THIS BOOK began as an essay for *Daedalus,* commissioned by its editor, James Miller. When I finished the essay, I realized that I had only scratched the surface of a huge scandal in American education, and the essay quickly grew into a book.

Many people helped me as I searched for examples of censorship codes in action. I thank Francie Alexander for her files on censorship issues in California; Glen W. Thomas for background on California's social content guidelines; Commissioner David Driscoll of Massachusetts for examples of that state's bias and sensitivity reviews; Commissioner Richard Mills of New York for that state's bias and sensitivity guidelines; Sandra Stotsky for explaining bias and sensitivity review in Massachusetts; David Alexander of the Texas Education Agency for describing that state's current practices; Darvin Winick and John Stevens for bringing me together with Texas education officials; Mary Crovo of the National Assessment Governing Board for information about the bias review process for federal tests; Buzz Ellis, Julie McGee, and Charlotte Frank of McGraw-Hill for explaining a big textbook publisher's dilemmas; Blouke Carus of Open Court for his files on censorship issues; Stephen Bates for sharing the Holt files from the 1980s; William Bennetta Jr. of the Textbook League for materials about bowdlerization of textbooks; Brooks Mather Kelley for sharing his experiences as a textbook author; Jonathan Rosenbloom of Time for Kids for current examples of censorship; Paul Holland, Howard Wainer, and Paul Ramsey of the Educational Testing Service for explaining DIF analysis; Michael Zieky of the Educational Testing Service for that company's bias and sensitivity guidelines; Jennifer McDougall of the Foundation for Education Reform and Accountability for gathering state standards for this project; Judith F.

Krug of the American Library Association for information about its policies related to intellectual freedom; and Hannah Richman for her energetic research assistance. I thank Lisa Wolfe Ravitch for her steadfast support. I am indebted to Rodney Atkinson, children's literature expert extraordinaire, for his sensitive collaboration on our reading list at the back of the book.

I am grateful to Jeffrey Mirel, Chester Finn Jr., Paul Zoch, Rita Kramer, Joseph Viteritti, Daniel Hurewitz, and Michael Ravitch for reading an early draft of the book. Any errors of fact or interpretation, of course, are mine.

As ever, I thank my good friend Mary Butz for her constant support, partnership, and encouragement. My very special thanks and love to my wonderful grandchildren, Aidan Ravitch and Nico Ravitch, who might one day enjoy a world in which schoolbooks and tests are not sanitized and censored.

My work on this book was generously supported by the John M. Olin Foundation.

I heartily thank my editor, Ashbel Green of Knopf, his assistant, Luba Ostashevsky, and my agents, Lynn Chu and Glen Hartley of Writers' Representatives.

A Note to the Reader

This book describes the regime of censorship that has quietly spread throughout educational publishing in response to pressure groups from both the left and the right. I have sought to document the pervasiveness of this phenomenon by obtaining materials from publishers, testing agencies, state boards of education, and professional associations. Occasionally an insider from a state education department, a test development company, or a publishing company provided documentation of these practices that was otherwise unavailable. I am certain that I have not uncovered every censorship code that is now in active use. I invite readers who have encountered other instances of censorship to contact www.languagepolice.com. This Web site will be active at least until 2007.

The Language Police

★

ONE

Forbidden Topics, Forbidden Words

The greatest dangers to liberty lurk in insidious encroachment by men of zeal, well-meaning but without understanding.

—Justice Louis D. Brandeis

I DECIDED to write this book as a way of solving a mystery. After many years of studying the history of education and writing about the politics of education, I discovered some things that shocked me. Almost by accident, I stumbled upon an elaborate, well-established protocol of beneficent censorship, quietly endorsed and broadly implemented by textbook publishers, testing agencies, professional associations, states, and the federal government. I did not learn about this state of affairs in one fell swoop, but one step at a time. Like others who are involved in education, be they parents or teachers or administrators or journalists or scholars, I had always assumed that textbooks were based on careful research and designed to help children learn something valuable. I thought that tests were designed to assess whether they had learned it. What I did not realize was that educational materials are now governed by an intricate set of rules to screen out language and topics that might be considered controversial or offensive. Some of this censorship is trivial, some is ludicrous, and some is breathtaking in its power to dumb down what children learn in school.

Initially these practices began with the intention of identifying and excluding any conscious or implicit statements of bias against African

Americans, other racial or ethnic minorities, and females, whether in tests or textbooks, especially any statements that demeaned members of these groups. These efforts were entirely reasonable and justified. However, what began with admirable intentions has evolved into a surprisingly broad and increasingly bizarre policy of censorship that has gone far beyond its original scope and now excises from tests and textbooks words, images, passages, and ideas that no reasonable person would consider biased in the usual meaning of that term.

The story that I now tell began in 1997, when President Bill Clinton delivered his State of the Union address. On that occasion, Clinton declared his support for national tests, and said that the states should test fourth-grade children in reading and eighth-grade children in mathematics, to make sure that they could meet national standards of proficiency. Soon after the president gave that speech, the U.S. Department of Education contracted with test publishers to develop voluntary national tests of reading and mathematics for those grades. The goal was to provide individual test scores to parents of specific children, to their teachers, and to their schools.

As someone who had been active in supporting the movement for academic standards during the 1980s and 1990s, both as a private citizen and as an assistant secretary in the U.S. Department of Education during the administration of President George H. W. Bush, I applauded Clinton's proposal. When Bush launched his education reform initiative in 1991, he too called for national achievement testing for individual students. His plan never got off the ground, however, due to the inherently controversial nature of involving the federal government in decisions that usually belong to state and local governments; his fellow Republicans opposed it, as did the Democrats in Congress.

I supported Clinton's program for national testing, but feared that it would falter unless it was strictly nonpartisan. If it remained under the control of political appointees in the Department of Education, it would lose credibility; whatever they did, their decisions would be criticized by members of the other party in Congress, and the testing program would come under a cloud. I made that argument in an op-ed article in the *Washington Post*, urging the administration to transfer responsibility for the new tests from the Department of Education to the National Assessment Governing Board (NAGB), a nonpartisan federal agency that had been supervising national testing since 1990.

Why, you might wonder, was there a controversy over national test-ing if there was already a federal agency giving national tests? Let me explain.

Since 1969, the federal government has administered a test called the National Assessment of Educational Progress (known as NAEP, or "the nation's report card"). NAEP tests are given to national and state samples of students in reading, mathematics, writing, science, history, and other academic subjects. NAEP periodically reports on the aggregate achievement of American students in the fourth, eighth, and twelfth grades, but by law it cannot measure the academic perfor-mance of any particular school district, school, or individual student. NAEP is the only regular, consistent national measure of achievement in the United States (the SAT and ACT test only college-bound stu-dents). In 1990, Congress created NAGB as a nonpartisan citizens' board to supervise NAEP; NAGB is composed of a score of indepen-dent members, appointed by the secretary of education. NAGB has a reputation for integrity, and it seemed the right place to assign control of the new national tests that might eventually be given to millions of individual children, not just statistical samples of students. Putting the two testing programs into the same organization would also assure that the new tests proposed by Clinton for individual students would be as academically rigorous as the NAEP tests.

After my op-ed article appeared, advocating the transfer of control of the national tests, Clinton nominated me as a member of NAGB (and announced it on his weekly radio broadcast). He also accepted my suggestion to assign responsibility for his testing proposal to that board. When I joined the board at its first meeting in 1998, I dis-covered that Clinton's proposed voluntary national tests (VNT) had become an important agenda item. The board spent many hours dis-cussing the development of the new tests, trying to figure out for whom they would be voluntary (for states? for school districts? for schools? for students?), how they would relate to the established stan-dards of NAEP, what time of year they would be given, how long they would last, how to accommodate students with special needs, whether to offer them in any language other than English, and a variety of other prickly issues.

Congress never approved the VNT. The tests were controversial from the start. Many Republicans feared that any national test com-missioned by the government was the first step on a slippery slope toward federal control of education. Many Democrats objected to the emphasis on testing as opposed to new general-purpose funding. By the time Clinton left office in January 2001, his VNT proposal was dead, even though it consistently ranked high in public-opinion polls. For nearly three years, however, NAGB and the test publishers who won the federal contract worked faithfully to bring the idea to fruition, keeping a watchful eye on Congress to see whether it would eventually be authorized. It never was.

During the time that the VNT was a live possibility, the first priority was to create test questions. As a new member of the board, I was assigned to a committee that reviewed reading passages for the fourth-grade test. The committee included experienced teachers and a state superintendent of education. All of us read the passages submitted by the test contractor, a major publisher that had won a multimillion-dollar contract from the Department of Education. The committee approved passages that seemed appropriate for fourth-grade students and rejected passages that seemed dull, obscure, or incoherent. Our goal was to find short reading passages of about one to three pages, both fiction and nonfiction, written in language that was clear, vivid, and engaging, as well as test questions that gauged children's comprehension of what they had read.

Our committee evaluated many passages for fourth-grade students. The passages had been previously published in children's magazines or anthologies; before they reached us, they had been thoroughly vetted by the original publisher's in-house experts. We too read them with care. As stewards of the VNT, we knew that we had to exercise extreme caution, since parents, teachers, and the media in every part of the United States would complain if anything inaccurate or contested were to slip through unnoticed.

Most of the stories were unobjectionable; none was great literature, but for the most part, they were fairly engaging stories about children, animals, science, or history. Nearly two years later, I was surprised to learn that the passages approved by our committee had subsequently been evaluated yet again by the test contractor's "bias and sensitivity review" panel. This panel, it turned out, recommended the elimination of several stories that we had approved. I learned that it was standard operating procedure in the educational testing industry to submit all passages and test questions to a bias and sensitivity review. Typically those who serve on these review panels are not drawn from academic fields such as English or history. Usually they have a professional background in bilingual education, diversity training, English as a second language, special education, guidance, or the education of Native Americans or other special populations. Such panels are hired by publishers, as well as by state education agencies, to screen every test and every textbook for potential bias. In the case of the voluntary national tests, the panel that scrutinized the items found biases that none of us—neither test experts nor members of NAGB—had perceived.

When publishers of textbooks and tests conduct bias and sensitivity reviews, these reviews are never released to the public; they are proprietary materials, and they belong to the company. I could not find a publisher willing to release them. State education departments guard the results of their bias reviews with equal zeal, even though these should be available for public scrutiny as public documents. I saw the bias and sensitivity reviews for the VNT only because I was a member of NAGB's reading committee; having reviewed the passages, I had the right to know why bias reviewers wanted to eliminate some of them.

When I read the panelists' reasons for rejecting passages, I realized that their concept of bias was not the same as the common understanding of the term. As far as I could tell, they did not actually find any examples of racial or gender bias as most people understand it. There were no stories in which girls or children who were members of a racial or ethnic minority were portrayed in a demeaning way. Some of the panel's interpretations were, frankly, bizarre. When NAGB's reading committee convened by teleconference to discuss the recommendations of the bias panel, there was first an embarrassed silence. Then, one by one, each of us chimed in and expressed our own disagreement with the bias reviewers. We eventually agreed, by unanimous vote, to reject their recommendations.

There are always other test passages to use, so the acceptance or rejection of these particular passages is hardly a cause for alarm. What is alarming, however, is the absurd reasoning that was invoked to justify the elimination of these readings. Consider that the test contractor, Riverside Publishing, is responsible for one of the most esteemed tests in the nation, the Iowa Test of Basic Skills; consider that it assembled a reputable and experienced group of people to conduct the bias and sensitivity review. The judgments expressed by this panel were not idiosyncratic; they represented state-of-the-art thinking in the practice of bias review. The reviewers acted in compliance with what are considered industry standards. The process of analyzing text that I will describe is now being applied routinely to other tests and textbooks used in American schools. The bias and sensitivity reviewers work with assumptions that have the inevitable effect of stripping away everything that is potentially thought-provoking and colorful from the texts that children encounter. These assumptions narrow what children are exposed to, at least on tests and in textbooks. Parents, teachers, and the public need to be aware of these assumptions and the reasoning process behind them, because they are reducing the curriculum in the schools to bland pabulum.

So what did the bias and sensitivity reviewers recommend? The only way to explain their strained interpretations is to give actual examples. I cannot reproduce the stories, because some of them may yet appear one day as test passages. But I will paraphrase the story sufficiently so that the reader may judge whether the charge of bias is persuasive. The examples, I believe, will demonstrate that the concept of bias has become detached from its original meaning and has been redefined into assumptions that defy common sense.

The History and Uses of Peanuts

Two of the stories that the bias reviewers rejected were short informational passages about peanuts. One passage described peanuts as legumes, in the same family as peas and beans, and lauded them as nutritious. The bias panel recommended the elimination of this selection because it asserted that peanuts are a healthy snack. It was wrong to describe peanuts as nutritious, said the panel, because some people may have a severe allergic reaction to them. At first glance, this judgment would seem to lie outside the scope of a bias and sensitivity review. The reviewers apparently assumed that a fourth-grade student who was allergic to peanuts might get distracted if he or she encountered a test question that did not acknowledge the dangers of peanuts. The NAGB reading committee recommended keeping the passage and adding an acknowledgment that some people are allergic to peanuts.

The second passage was a brief history of peanuts. It said that peanuts were first cultivated by South American Indians, especially the Incas. After Spanish explorers conquered the Incas, and Portuguese explorers defeated many Brazilian tribes, it said, the peanut was shipped to Europe for cultivation. Later, in the United States, African slaves planted and developed peanut crops. The famed scientist George Washington Carver discovered hundreds of uses for the peanut. This was not the world's most exciting story, but the NAGB reading committee concluded that it contained some interesting historical information as well as praise for an African American scientist, all of which were pluses. However, the bias and sensitivity panelists opposed the passage for two reasons: first, it used the term *African slave,* and second, it stated that Spanish and Portuguese explorers defeated native tribes. To the NAGB reading committee, these were puzzling judgments. Why was it wrong to use the term *African slave?* (Apparently the correct usage now is *enslaved African.*) Nor did we understand why the panel wanted to kill the passage for saying that some Brazilian tribes had been defeated by European explorers. The bias reviewers did not challenge the historical accuracy of this statement, but they did not want it to appear. They must have concluded that these facts would hurt someone's feelings. Whose feelings would be wounded? Children of Spanish descent? Children of Portuguese descent? Children descended from Brazilian tribes? Perhaps the word *tribe* was offensive. None of this was clear. What was clear, however, was that the passage did not express anything that a reasonable person would consider biased toward any group.

Women and Patchwork Quilting

The bias and sensitivity reviewers rejected a passage about patchwork quilting by women on the western frontier in the mid-nineteenth century. The passage explained that mothers in that time taught their daughters to sew, and together they made quilts for the girl's dowry when she married. Quilting was an economic necessity because it saved money, and there were no factory-made quilts available until the end of the nineteenth century. The passage briefly explained how quilts were assembled and described them as works of art. The information in the passage was historically accurate, but the bias and sensitivity panel (as well as the "content expert panel") objected to the passage because it contained stereotypes of females as "soft" and "submissive." Actually, the passage did nothing of the sort. It was a description of why quilting was important to women on the frontier and how it was done. Nothing in the passage excluded the possibility that mothers and daughters were riding the range, plowing the fields, and herding cattle during the day. The reviewers objected to the portrayal of women as people who stitch and sew, and who were concerned about preparing for marriage. Historical accuracy was no defense for this representation of women and girls, which they deemed stereotypical.

THE BLIND MOUNTAIN CLIMBER

One of the stranger recommendations of the bias and sensitivity panel involved a true story about a heroic young blind man who hiked to the top of Mount McKinley, the highest peak in North America. The story described the dangers of hiking up an icy mountain trail, especially for a blind person. The panel voted 12–11 to eliminate this inspiring story. First, the majority maintained that the story contained "regional bias," because it was about hiking and mountain climbing, which favors students who live in regions where those activities are common. Second, they rejected the passage because it suggested that people who are blind are somehow at a disadvantage compared to people who have normal sight, that they are "worse off" and have a more difficult time facing dangers than those who are not blind.

"Regional bias," in this instance, means that children should not be expected to read or comprehend stories set in unfamiliar terrain. A story that happened in a desert would be "biased" against children who have never lived in a desert, and a story set in a tropical climate would be biased against those who have never lived in a tropical climate. Consider the impoverishment of imagination that flows from such assumptions: No reading passage on a test may have a specific geographical setting; every event must occur in a generic locale. Under these assumptions, no child should be expected to understand a story set in a locale other than the one that he or she currently lives in or in a locale that has no distinguishing characteristics.

Even more peculiar is the assumption by the panel's majority that it is demeaning to applaud a blind person for overcoming daunting obstacles, like climbing a steep, icy mountain trail. It is not unreasonable, I believe, to consider blindness to be a handicap for a person facing physical danger. By definition, people who are blind cannot see as much or as well as people who have sight. Is it not more difficult to cope with dangerous situations when one cannot see? Yet, perversely, the bias and sensitivity panel concluded that this story celebrating a blind athlete's achievements and his heroism was biased *against* people who are blind. Blindness, apparently, should be treated as just another personal attribute, like the color of one's hair, or one's height. In the new meaning of bias, it is considered biased to acknowledge that lack of sight is a disability.

Gender Bias in a Fable of Aesop

The bias and sensitivity reviewers did find a reading selection that had the earmarks of gender bias. It was Aesop's familiar fable "The Fox and the Crow." In the story, Master Fox spies Mistress Crow sitting on a tree branch with a piece of cheese in her beak. He flatters her, tells her that she has a beautiful voice, and when she opens her beak to sing, the cheese falls to the cunning fox. The panel, of course, spied gender bias at work since the crow—a female—is vain and foolish, while the fox—a male—is intelligent and clever. The crow represented the stereotypical depiction of women as overly concerned about their appearance and easily deceived by flattering men. The fact that this gender relationship had been part of the Aesop story for generations was irrelevant. The NAGB reading committee did not want to lose the Aesop fable, because it was all too rare to find any instances of classic literature on national tests of reading. So, to ameliorate the concerns of the bias committee, we proposed to switch the gender of the fox and the crow, either to make them both the same gender, or to make Mistress Fox the flatterer of Master Crow. Aesop might be startled to find a woman flattering a man or a guy flattering another guy or a woman flattering another woman, but at least we were able to hang on to a classic fable.

A Story Condemned by Association

Another passage suggested for deletion by the bias reviewers was an animal fable taken from an anthology edited by William J. Bennett, the former secretary of education, author, and political commentator known for his conservative views. The fable, attributed to Native Americans, told about animals emerging from the darkness to "find" sunlight. Several members of the panel suggested that Bennett's name alone would be sufficient to distress many teachers and parents. They did not suggest that fourth-grade children taking the tests would be distressed, since Bennett's name would be unknown to them. The panel also rejected the fable because it implied that "darkness" and "blackness" were synonymous with fumbling around or not being able to see. The members saw this linkage as bias, presumably suggesting racial bias. Only one of the bias experts on the review panel argued that it was censorship to delete this passage simply because of the political views of its anthologist. However, even this member agreed with the other panel members that the fable should be removed because of its unfortunate references to darkness. So far as the panel was concerned, to show a preference for light over darkness was a manifestation of bias.

Deleting Mount Rushmore

Perhaps the most startling analysis by the bias reviewers concerned a short biography of Gutzon Borglum, who designed the monument at Mount Rushmore. This monument, consisting of gigantic heads of Presidents George Washington, Thomas Jefferson, Abraham Lincoln, and Theodore Roosevelt, is located in the Black Hills of South Dakota. It is one of the most famous, most widely reproduced images in the United States. Millions of tourists have traveled to South Dakota to see it. Whether one likes it or hates it, it is there. For most people, the monument has positive connotations, suggesting a sense of history and patriotism.

The bias panel recommended that the biography of Borglum be dropped because Mount Rushmore is offensive to Native Americans. The panel maintained that the monument "is an abomination to the Black Hills because many Lakota people consider the Black Hills to be a sacred place to pray." This is surely a dilemma. The Borglum sculpture on Mount Rushmore exists; it is an acclaimed national monument. Yet American children should not be allowed to read about it or its sculptor on a test because this might offend Lakota Indians, who wish that the sculpture were not there. The desire to rewrite history is one that continually plagues bias reviewers, as we shall see.

Class Distinctions in the Ancient World

The bias panel did not like a story about growing up in ancient Egypt. The story contrasted how people's ways of living varied in accordance with their wealth and status. Some lived in palaces, others were noblemen, others were farmers or city workers. The size and grandeur of one's house, said the story, depended on family wealth. To the naked eye, the story was descriptive, not judgmental. But the bias and sensitivity reviewers preferred to eliminate it, claiming that references to wealth and class distinctions had an "elitist" tone. The fact that these class distinctions were historically accurate was irrelevant to the reviewers. In the world that they wanted children to read about, class distinctions did not exist, not now and not in the past, either.

An Environmentally Sound Dwelling

One of the most charming informational stories that our committee reviewed was about a rotting stump in the forest that provided shelter and food to a succession of insects, birds, plants, and animals. The story probably would have passed muster with flying colors in light of its environmentalist emphasis on nature's ways of recycling except that it made the fatal mistake of comparing the rotting stump to an apartment house for the many different creatures of the forest. The twenty members of the bias committee voted unanimously to reject this passage because, in their view, it contained a negative, demeaning stereotype of apartments and people who live in them. If this passage were included on a test, the panel claimed, poor inner-city children would be upset: "Youngsters who have grown up in a housing project may be distracted by similarities to their own living conditions. An emotional response may be triggered."

This was a strained reading of the story. First, it is untrue that only those who are poor live in apartment houses. There are luxury highrise apartment houses, as well as apartment buildings occupied by middle-income people. Second, the story tried to show the environmental beauty of the rotting tree stump, to describe the stump as a gracious and inviting home, as well as a restaurant, to all sorts of creatures. The story did not portray either the tree stump or the insects and forest animals in a negative light. Yet the bias committee imagined that poor children who had grown up in a housing project would see themselves as insects living in a rotting tree stump if they read this passage. Following the logic of the bias reviewers, every story had to be read literally, with no allowances for simile, metaphor, or allusion.

THE SILLY OLD LADY

The bias panel rejected a passage about a silly old woman who keeps piling more and more gadgets on her bicycle until it is so overloaded that it tumbles over. The language was clever, the illustrations were amusing, and the story was higher in literary quality than the other fourth-grade reading passages proposed for the test. But the bias panel rejected it. They felt that it contained a negative stereotype of an eccentric old woman who constantly changed her mind; apparently women, and especially women of a certain age, must be depicted only in a positive light. Why would it upset or distract fourth-grade children to see an older woman acting eccentrically or changing her mind? The bias panel thought that children would get the wrong idea about older women if they read such a story. They might conclude that all women of a certain age behaved in this way.

THE ARROGANT KING

This story, a folktale from Asia, was about a king who had a marvelous elephant. The king is jealous because his subjects admire the elephant more than they admire him. He tells the elephant trainer to command the animal to do more and more difficult tricks, until the elephant ascends into the air with the trainer and flies away to a better kingdom. In the original story, the wise king in the next kingdom eventually reduces the worthless king to ashes, but that "violent" conclusion was deleted by an earlier bias review. The bias panel rejected the passage because the king was portrayed as mean and jealous. The panelists did not like this negative characterization, even though the king was indeed mean and jealous. Furthermore, the king used harsh language; he yelled, he roared, he screamed, and he shouted at the elephant's trainer. Of course, if the king had been a mild and friendly fellow, the story would not have made any sense at all, but the bias panel did not approve of such behavior. The panelists also objected because the trainer had called the king "a worthless fool" when he flew away with the beautiful elephant. But the trainer was right: the king *was* a worthless fool. I could not imagine what any of these complaints had to do with bias and sensitivity. Was the passage biased against arrogant and jealous kings? Were they afraid that children would be upset to read about a king who yelled and screamed at an underling?

THE EVEN EXCHANGE

This story came from a children's book by an African American author. It was about an African American girl who wanted to learn how to jump rope like the other girls in her neighborhood. She meets a neighbor who is an expert at jumping rope, but who is attending summer school because she is not very good at math. The new girl is good at math, so the two agree to teach each other what they do best. The bias reviewers did not like this story at all. They found that it had serious bias problems because it showed an African American girl who was weak in math and was attending summer school. The fact that this character thought of herself as not very good at math was also deeply offensive and stereotypical, the bias reviewers believed. Even though the author was African American and her book was intended to bolster the self-esteem of black girls, that did not carry any weight with the bias panel. African American children could be portrayed only in a positive light. Anything that showed weakness suggested negative stereotyping. In this case, one African American girl was good at math, and the other was not. So far as I could tell, the story showed human variability, not negative racial stereotyping, with each girl displaying different weaknesses and different strengths.

THE SELFISH RICH BAKER

This tale was about a rich baker who got angry when a poor traveler sniffed his wares. The baker goes to court to demand that the poor fellow pay him for the smells he had "stolen." The judge, however, rules in favor of the poor man and fines the rich baker for his meanness. The bias committee unanimously opposed the passage on grounds of socioeconomic bias. The panelists claimed that the story set up an antagonism between the rich baker and the poor traveler. It presumed the poor traveler to be guilty of doing something wrong because of his poverty. Of course, the story did no such thing. The rich baker was rebuked and fined for his arrogance and hostility, begrudging the poor traveler even a whiff of his baked goods. He was judged harshly for his lack of charity and his greed. I could not understand how reviewers could regard this passage as biased against the poor traveler unless they failed to grasp the point of the story.

The Friendly Dolphin

This passage was about dolphins and what wonderful creatures they are. It told the story of a legendary dolphin that guided ships through a dangerous channel. Perhaps in anticipation of a bias review, the story left out the part of the legend in which a passenger on one ship shoots the faithful dolphin, which survives but never guides that particular ship again. Fourth graders would probably enjoy reading about dolphins, particularly ones that befriend humans. No matter; the bias reviewers unanimously rejected the story for having a regional bias in favor of those who live by the sea. Once again, the concept of regional bias presumes that any story that takes place in a singular location—the sea, the mountains, the desert, a forest, the jungle—is inherently inaccessible to those who don't live in the same location.

No More Owls

The passage about owls was like a children's encyclopedia entry. It described how their keen eyesight and hearing enabled them to hunt at night for rodents. When I saw that this passage was rejected, I imagined that it was because of the violence associated with hunting (although that's how owls survive). I was wrong. The passage was rejected because a Native American member of the bias committee said that owls are taboo for the Navajos. Consequently the entire committee agreed that the passage should be dropped. The test publisher added a notation that the owl is associated with death in some other cultures and should not be mentioned anymore, neither in texts nor in illustrations.

Here is a classic problem presented by today's bias and sensitivity review process. If any cultural group attributes negative connotations to anything, or considers it taboo or offensive, then that topic will not be referred to, represented, described, or illustrated on tests. But owls exist. They are real birds. They are not creatures of the imagination.

Nevertheless, to avoid giving offense, the tests will pretend that owls don't exist. Owls are to be deleted and never again mentioned to the highly vulnerable and sensitive American schoolchild.

An African American Hero

This passage, which was enthusiastically endorsed by the NAGB reading committee, should have been an easy selection. It told the heroic story of Mary McLeod Bethune, who opened a school for African American girls in Daytona Beach, Florida, in the early twentieth century. Her school, the Daytona Educational and Industrial Training School for Negro Girls, opened with five girls and her own son Albert as pupils. Bethune had a dream but not much money. Residents of the neighborhood helped out, and students raised money for their tuition. Bethune proved to be a masterful fund-raiser, gaining the support of several wealthy white philanthropists who wintered in Daytona Beach, as well as the National Association of Colored Women.

The bias reviewers disliked the story. They wanted no reference to Bethune's son, because the story couldn't mention the son without mentioning his father. If it mentioned the father, it would have to acknowledge that Bethune and her husband had separated when she moved to Florida; to avoid mentioning separation or divorce, the reviewers wanted no mention of the son. Next, the reviewers objected to the name of the school because it included the word *Negro.* Ditto for the reference to the National Association of Colored Women. These references, the bias reviewers asserted, would be meaningless to the students and objectionable to adults who might see the test. Last, the bias reviewers strongly opposed any mention of Bethune's successful fund-raising among the wealthy white residents of Daytona Beach, which they considered patronizing. The fact that she did receive substantial funds from men like John D. Rockefeller was irrelevant. The bias committee objected to Bethune's need to "turn to" such people.

These objections, on their face, are absurd. To leave her son out of her life story as a way of avoiding the reality that she separated from her husband assumes that today's children would find this shocking; surely they are sufficiently acquainted with women who are single parents to accept this unexceptional fact. Further, the name of Bethune's school is historically accurate. It is difficult to tell a story about her school without using the name that she gave it. And why treat as an embarrassment Bethune's remarkable skills as a fund-raiser? Anyone, black or white, who could convince some of the richest men in America to support her endeavors deserves commendation. This is not an admission of weakness, but evidence of skill in the arts of persuasion. In the tightly constricted world of the bias reviewers, Bethune created a successful institution by conducting neighborhood bake sales. It would be admirable if true, but it was not true. Truth and historical accuracy, however, are not important values to the bias reviewers.

Since the voluntary national test proposed by Clinton was never authorized by Congress, it slowly disappeared as an administration proposal and eventually sank from public view. The reader might wonder why the bias reviews of questions on a test that was never given should matter. It matters because these reviews offer an unparalleled insight into the process that publishers use to evaluate reading passages and test items today. This process of review by bias and sensitivity experts is not unusual. It is customary. It did not break any new ground. Publishers of tests and textbooks today routinely engage similar panels of bias and sensitivity experts to screen their products. This is a process that effectively removes everything from tests and textbooks that might be offensive to any group or individual. It is designed to strip away words and ideas that offend anyone. Bias and sensitivity review has evolved into an elaborate and widely accepted code of censorship that is implemented routinely but hidden from public sight.

Where did these strange ideas about bias come from? How did the sensible principle of removing racist and sexist language turn into this effort to delete whatever might annoy or offend the most agitated imaginations? This was the mystery that I wanted to solve.

TWO

The New Meaning of Bias

Do you know that Newspeak is the only language in the
world whose vocabulary gets smaller every year?
                                    —George Orwell, *1984*

FOR MONTHS after I participated in the appraisal of President Clinton's proposed voluntary national test, I continued to reflect on the experience. I could not comprehend how a group of educated and presumably thoughtful adults could have become so priggish, humorless, and censorious. How had they reached their judgments? How could they find bias in apparently innocent language? Why were they willing to dismiss historically accurate facts so blithely? Something was going on that I did not understand. The bias and sensitivity reviewers saw insult in words and ideas that most people would find unexceptional. They employed a set of assumptions that were outside the realm of what seemed to be common sense.

As I tried to understand the reasoning of the reviewers, I remembered that in 1998 the president of Riverside Publishing had met with our committee to explain how reading passages for the voluntary national test would be selected. We expressed our hope that the test would be of high quality, that it would be more than just a basic skills test. We wanted the publisher to include passages based on good literature. We thought that children should read something worthwhile when they took the test, not just banal selections. We asked whether his company would choose some readings drawn from myths and fables and other classic literature. He said that they would try, but we had to bear in mind that "everything written before 1970 was either gender biased or racially biased." He said this very casually, as though he was uttering a truth too well known to need explanation or defense. This belief provided the backdrop for the document that he gave us that day, titled "Bias and Sensitivity Concerns in Testing."

When I first read this document, I was astonished by the list of topics that the test publisher considered out-of-bounds, and I filed it away. Two years later, in 2000, when I saw the results of the bias and sensitivity review, I retrieved this document and found that it held the key to the reviewers' assumptions. "Bias and Sensitivity Concerns in Testing" explained how the concept of bias had been redefined. It contained rules for self-censorship that most Americans, I believe, would find deeply disturbing.

The Riverside guidelines are a mixture of sensible general reminders about the unacceptability of bias, as well as detailed lists of words and topics that must be avoided on tests. "Bias," it declares, is anything in a test item that might cause any student to be distracted or upset. Bias is the presence of something in a test item that would result in different performance "for two individuals of the same ability but from different subgroups." So, for example, a test question that is upsetting to a member of group A (for instance, a girl) would prevent her from doing as well as someone who was from a different group (for instance, a boy). Bias, says the publisher, can cause inaccurate scores and measurement errors. It seems to be a settled principle that tests should not contain anything that is so upsetting to certain students that they cannot demonstrate what they know and can do. Presumably a very graphic description of violence, for example, would be so disturbing to some students that they would not be able to answer test questions. Presumably students would be upset by a test question that contained language that demeaned their race, gender, or religion. Riverside says that its tests "are designed to avoid language, symbols, gestures, words, phrases, or examples that are generally regarded as sexist, racist, otherwise offensive, inappropriate, or negative towards any group." In addition, tests should not contain any subject matter that anyone might consider "controversial or emotionally charged." Such things would distract test takers and prevent them from showing their true ability. It would be unfair, certainly, and the goal of a bias and sensitivity review is supposed to be fairness.

But then look at where the logic of fairness leads. There are three ways, the guidelines assert, to ensure fairness in testing. One is by "representational fairness," another is by reviewing "language usage," and a third is by removing "stereotypes." In addition, certain inflammatory topics must be avoided. Each of these versions of "fairness" leads the publisher to specify precisely what language and which ideas will be allowed and which will be banned. As I read through the guidelines, I began to understand why the publisher advised us that everything written before 1970 was biased. Few writings before that date could possibly meet the specifications laid out in the guidelines.

The bias guidelines list certain topics that are so controversial or "emotionally charged" that they must be avoided on a test unless they are directly relevant to the curriculum (in a test of reading, no particular subject matter is directly relevant, so all of these topics must be avoided). Such topics are:

Abortion
Creatures that are thought to be scary or dirty, like
    scorpions, rats, and roaches
Death and disease
Disrespectful or criminal behavior
Evolution
Expensive consumer goods
Magic, witchcraft, the supernatural
Personal appearance (such as height and weight)
Politics
Religion
Social problems (such as child abuse, animal abuse, and
    addiction)
Unemployment
Unsafe situations
Weapons and violence

The guidelines advise that accuracy should be the goal when dealing with historical information, but on a reading test (as we saw in the first chapter) historical accuracy may be sacrificed when it involves stereotypes.

In addition to the list of banned controversial topics, there is an exhaustive description of "negative" and "sensitive" material that cannot appear on a test. Negative material includes (but is not limited to) parents quarreling, children mistreating each other, children acting disobediently toward their parents, and children showing disrespect for authority. Sensitive material includes paganism, satanism, parapsychology, magic, ghosts, extraterrestrials, Halloween, witches, or anything that might conjure up such subjects, even in the context of fantasy. Anything related to Halloween, such as pumpkins and masks, must be avoided. Gambling must be avoided, as must references to nudity, pregnancy, or giving birth, whether to animals or people. "Controversial" styles of music like rap and rock and roll are out.

But that is not all. Religious and political issues must be avoided. Reading passages must not contain even an "incidental reference" to anyone's religion. There must not be any mention of birthdays or religious holidays (including Thanksgiving), because some children do not have birthday parties and do not share the same religion. In any material about Native Americans, care must be exercised to steer clear of religious traditions.

There must be no reference in any test passage to evolution or the origins of the universe. Writers must avoid any mention of fossils or dinosaurs. Their very existence suggests the banned topic of evolution. However, it is acceptable to refer to "animals of long ago" if there is no mention of how old they are and no suggestion that the existence of these animals implies evolution.

Still more topics are banned as upsetting to sensitive children. There is some overlap with the first set of banned topics, but this list adds some additional caveats. These include:

> Someone being fired or losing their job
> Rats, mice, roaches, snakes, lice
> Cancer or other serious illnesses
> Death
> Catastrophes such as earthquakes and fires (natural events like tornados or hurricanes may be okay if the context is not too frightening)
> Unnecessary violence (reference to guns or knives is forbidden except in a historical context)
> Gratuitous gore, like animals eating other animals

Serious social problems, like poverty, alcoholism, divorce,
   or addiction of any kind
Slavery and racial prejudice

The bias guidelines require that test questions "model healthful personal habits." Any references to smoking, drinking, or junk food must be eliminated. Writers must be cautious when depicting someone drinking coffee or tea and must take care not to mention even aspirin. Children must never be shown doing dangerous things, "no matter how good the moral of the story is."

The test passages must avoid beliefs, attitudes, or values that are not embraced by just about everybody. Fables are a particular concern, because they often conclude on a cynical note or have "a pragmatic moral" that someone may find offensive. Particularly taboo, the guidelines warn, is anything that suggests secular humanism, situation ethics, or New Age religion.

The people who select reading passages for tests are directed to seek out "uplifting topics." Anything depressing, disgusting, or scary should be eliminated.

Many topics are prohibited because testing experts agree that any less than ideal context will be so upsetting to some children that they will not be able to do their best on a test. But would children really be distracted if they read a story in which someone was fired or unemployed? Would they be disoriented if they read a story in which someone was seriously ill or parents were divorced? No educational research literature supports these prohibitions. There are no studies that show that children were unable to finish a test or do their best because they were asked to read a story in which the characters were rich or poor. Farewell then to *Great Expectations, Little Lord Fauntleroy,* and "The Little Match Girl," with their unacceptable images of wealth and poverty.

The prohibitions are there not because of research findings, but because the *topics upset some adults,* who assume that they will upset children in the same way. Some adults sincerely believe that children will project themselves into everything they read and that they will be deeply disturbed to read that someone else is taller than they, or that other children had a birthday party or live in a big house when perhaps they are not similarly privileged. It is hard to imagine that a fourth-grade student would be paralyzed by dread by reading a story that included descriptions of mice. Clearly forbidden by such a prohibition is any excerpt from books like E. B. White's *Stuart Little* or Robert Lawson's *Ben and Me,* not to mention stories of Mickey Mouse, Mighty Mouse, and other fictional mice beloved by generations of children.

Most of the prohibitions are a direct response to long-standing complaints from the religious right. Many of the banned topics are intended to avert the controversy that might erupt if the test referred to evolution or witchcraft or religion. Spokesmen for the religious right consider any description of behavior they do not like as an endorsement of that behavior. They reject depictions of magic, witchcraft, and the supernatural; they don't want education materials to show people engaging in bad behavior, like children disobeying their parents. They have gone to court in several jurisdictions to protest against "secular humanism," "situation ethics," and "New Age" religion, because such ideas conflict with the moral code that is fixed in the Bible.

Test publishers have found that the best way to avoid controversy is to eliminate anything that might cause controversy. As the bias guidelines of Riverside Publishing show, quite a large number of topics are avoided (i.e., censored) because of fear of complaints by the religious right. But the bias guidelines try to mollify not only conservatives, but also feminists and advocates for multiculturalism, the handicapped, and the aged. The publishers want everyone to be happy, or at least not to be unhappy. Whereas the right gets topic control, the left gets control of language and images. To see how this works, we must consider what the test publisher describes as the three types of fairness: representational fairness, language usage, and stereotyping.

The Riverside guidelines define "representational fairness" to mean that no group will be overrepresented or underrepresented. Thus, with few exceptions, reading passages are supposed to include equal numbers of males and females, and proportionate representation of all groups in terms of ethnicity, age, socioeconomic background, gender, community setting, and physical disabilities. Another way that Riverside defines "representational fairness" is that the materials on tests should be "relevant" to the life experiences of those taking the test. For example, southern students should not be expected to understand the "concepts" of snow and freezing winters, which are outside their own personal life experience. To expect them to know about such weather conditions when they have not experienced them is considered regional bias.

Language usage refers to the specific words in a test passage or test question, and here the bias guidelines become strongly proscriptive. Gender bias is implied by any use of the term *man,* as in "mankind" or "man in the street" or "salesman." All of these are now forbidden terms that must be replaced by "the human race," the "average citizen," or a "sales representative." Bias against people with a disability occurs whenever a disabled person is identified by that disability. For example, it is biased to refer to "the blind"; one must say instead, "a person who is blind." It is biased to say that someone is "wheelchair bound"; one must refer instead to "a person who uses a wheelchair." It is biased to say that someone was "a victim of polio"; one must refer instead to "a person who had polio." Then there is elitist bias, which is also unacceptable. An example of this bias is the sentence "Even though she was a poor, Hispanic woman, Maria was able to start a successful company." The sentence must be reworded as "Through hard work and determination, Maria Sanchez started a successful company."

It is easy to see how publishers might well conclude that everything written before 1970 is racially biased or gender biased. Certainly John Steinbeck's *Of Mice and Men* makes racial references that are inappropriate under the guidelines (even its title, referring to both mice and men, is unacceptable); so does Mark Twain's *Adventures of Huckleberry Finn;* so do the novels of Richard Wright, Zora Neale Hurston, and James Baldwin. The novels of Jane Austen, Edith Wharton, and Charles Dickens contain what the bias reviewers consider gender stereotypes. The publisher of Riverside was right: Most classic literature is unacceptable when judged by the new rules governing references to gender, ethnicity, age, and disability.

In addition to representational fairness and language usage, the bias guidelines warn against stereotyping. In the early years of the feminist movement, activists complained that women were shown only as housewives and mothers, rather than as scientists, professionals, and business leaders. African Americans complained that they were portrayed only in subservient roles, rather than as scientists, professionals, and business leaders. The effort to eliminate stereotypes was intended to banish any notion that certain high-status careers and activities were closed to women, blacks, and other minorities.

The definition of stereotyping, like the definition of bias, has become far more elaborate and refined as time has gone by. Educational publishers know that they must avoid showing people of a certain gender, race, ethnicity, age, or disability group in roles that might contribute to a stereotype. What was once a fairly sensible notion of fairness—don't always show women as homemakers—has turned into a presumption that they should never be shown in that role. The bias guidelines suggest that it is stereotypical to depict women as wives and mothers, even though most women are, at some time in their lives, wives and mothers. Since men cannot be portrayed as wives and mothers, no one may fairly be presented in those roles. Although the guidelines note that "all group members should be portrayed as exhibiting a full range of emotions, occupations, activities, and roles," writers are forewarned that certain representations are not acceptable because of their past history as stereotypes.

The Riverside guidelines warn about the following kinds of stereotypes:

Emotional stereotyping, in which men are portrayed as strong and brave, while women are portrayed as weepy and emotional. It is, however, appropriate to show women as strong and brave and men as weepy and emotional. Fairness might allow an equal distribution of these emotions, but the guidelines imply that women must not be shown as weepy and emotional and men must not be shown as brave and strong.

Occupational stereotyping means not showing people in roles that are commonly experienced in reality, because opponents of stereotyping hope to change perceptions of convention by not permitting them to be portrayed. So, for example, it is occupational stereotyping to depict an Irish policeman. The fact is that police officers have many different racial and ethnic identities, and historically in some large eastern cities, many were (and are) Irish. But it is stereotyping to show any of them as Irish. Similarly, it is stereotyping to show Asian Americans working in a laundry, even though some Asian Americans do work in laundries. People who work in commercial laundries may be of any ethnic or national origin, but not Asian American. Similarly, African Americans may not be portrayed as maids; this is occupational stereotyping. Only people who are not African Americans are maids, though given the guidelines' strong abhorrence of social distinctions, it is unlikely that anyone will ever be portrayed as a maid or that any-one can afford to hire a maid. Men may not appear as plumbers and lawyers; women can. Women may not be portrayed as nurses and receptionists; this is stereotyping.

Activities stereotyping refers to portrayals of behavior. It is activities stereotyping to show men playing sports or working with tools. It is stereotypical to show women cooking or caring for children or to have older people engaging in sedentary pastimes, like fishing or bak-ing cookies (older people, as we shall see in other guidelines, are usu-ally found jogging, repairing a roof, or doing something else that is physically strenuous).

Role stereotyping is only slightly different from occupational stereotyp-ing, but it is different enough to get a separate entry in the Riverside guidelines. Asian Americans should not be portrayed as academics; African Americans should not be portrayed as athletes; Caucasians should not be portrayed as businesspeople; men should not be por-trayed as breadwinners; women should not be portrayed as wives and mothers. In the ideal world of education-think, women would be breadwinners; African Americans would be academics; Asian Ameri-cans would be athletes; and no one would be a wife or a mother.

Community setting stereotyping refers to neighborhoods. It is a stereo-type to show Asian Americans living in neighborhoods composed of Asian Americans. It is a stereotype to show African Americans living in an urban environment. It is a stereotype to show Caucasians liv-ing in an affluent suburb. Since these "stereotypes" represent reality for significant numbers of people, writers must either omit any community setting or always write counter to the stereotype, Asian Americans never living in an Asian American neighborhood, African Ameri-cans living in affluent suburbs, and whites living in urban environments. Denying reality is a common feature of writing against stereotype.

Physical attribute or abilities stereotyping refers to assumptions about groups, such as that African Americans are good at sports, that men are strong, that women are overly concerned about their appear-ance, that older people are feeble, and that children are "bundles of energy." Older people may never be portrayed as feeble even though some older people, approaching the end of their life span, actually are feeble. Though accurate, that would be a stereotype.

A person with the job of writing test questions has the thankless task of portraying American society in all its diversity, without at the same time giving any stereotypical attributes to any person who is portrayed. Thus, while the rest of us might imagine that the purpose of a test is to find out whether students have learned what they studied in class, test developers spend as much time balancing social imperatives as they do on the academic and cognitive content of test questions.

What is the logic of the bias and sensitivity reviews? When I read the Riverside guidelines closely, I realized that the people who originally selected the passages for the voluntary national test of reading in the fourth grade had also been subject to these guidelines. They had already been thoroughly briefed about the need for representational fairness, the dangers of stereotyping, and the importance of avoiding controversial topics. Yet, even these carefully trained professionals did not foresee how narrowly, intensely, and exquisitely the guidelines would be interpreted by another round of bias and sensitivity reviewers.

Presumably, the people who first picked the passages didn't realize that the owl was taboo to the Navajo culture. They didn't stop to think that a story about a blind man climbing up an icy mountain peak contained regional bias against children who are unfamiliar with mountain climbing and was biased against blind people by suggesting that they have more difficulty in meeting physical challenges than those who are not blind. Probably they did not know that Mount Rushmore was a forbidden topic to members of the Lakota tribe. Very likely the people assembling the test passages thought that the story about quilting was an interesting insight into women's lives in the nineteenth century, not realizing that it was gender bias to show an association between females and domestic work. Undoubtedly they thought that the story of Mary McLeod Bethune and her school was inspiring, and it didn't occur to them that the name of her school was offensive, her divorce was controversial, and her fund-raising among affluent white business leaders was objectionable.

This entire process is designed to impose censorship. Topics and language are banned from the outset. The definition of bias and sensitivity is so broad and so proscriptive that it guarantees the exclusion from national and state tests of many valued works of literature. Whether classic or contemporary, most recognized authors will almost certainly violate the rules about topic or language usage or stereotyping because such authors did not tailor their writing to meet the guidelines. One looks to literature for expressions of imagination, reality, paradox, and complexity rather than carefully crafted orthodoxies. There are stories that are not appropriate for fourth-grade children because of their language or imagery, but none of those censored by the bias reviewers came anywhere near that threshold.

There is no valid educational reason to exclude such a broad list of topics other than to placate the religious right; children should be able to read a test passage about dinosaurs or literary flights of fancy. Similarly, there is no valid educational reason to regulate language usage so tightly other than to placate the feminist and multicultural left; children should be able to read a passage in which a mother prepares dinner or an African American family lives in a city neighborhood without setting off a furor about stereotyping. Furthermore, banning words like "mankind" is just plain silly. By now, our society has evolved to the point where some people will say "humankind" or "the human race" and others will say "mankind." We should be mature enough to live with diversity of language usage. We have never had a language police or a thought police in this country, and we should not have one now.

What kinds of educational materials can survive this heavily proscriptive review? What's left after the language police and the thought police from the left and the right have done their work? Stories that have no geographical location. Stories that have no regional distinctiveness. Stories in which all conflicts are insignificant. Stories in which men are fearful, and women are brave. Stories in which older people are never ill. Stories in which children are obedient, never disrespectful, never get into dangerous situations, never confront problems that cannot be easily solved. Stories in which blind people and people with physical disabilities need no assistance from anyone because their handicaps are not handicaps. Stories in which fantasy and magic are banned. Stories about the past in which historical accuracy is ignored. Stories about science that leave out any reference to evolution or prehistoric times. Stories in which everyone is happy almost all the time. The result of all this relentless purging is dishonesty, a purposeful shielding of children from anything challenging, controversial, or just plain interesting. It is a process that drains literature of its life and blood, converts it into dreary reading materials, and grinds reading materials into pabulum.

The Riverside bias and sensitivity guidelines are not unique. Indeed, Riverside cites guidelines issued by other test publishers and by the American Psychological Association to show that its recommendations are right in the center of the educational publishing mainstream. Once I understood what the guidelines meant and how they were implemented, I could not shake the feeling that something important and dangerous was happening in American education that few people knew about. The more I thought about the ubiquitous application of censorship at the source, the more it seemed to me to be a major intellectual scandal, the more it looked like political correctness run amok, far from public view.

THREE

Everybody Does It:
The Textbook Publishers

There is more than one way to burn a book. And the
world is full of people running about with lit matches.
                    —Ray Bradbury, Coda to *Fahrenheit 451*

OVER THE THREE decades that I have been working as a historian, I
have learned that a historian works like a detective. If a historical controversy captures your attention and you want to find out "what happened," you have to do a lot of investigation. First, you read what other
historians have written. Then you carefully review their evidence, examine primary sources, and begin to shape your own conclusions—your
own explanation of what happened. One asks, again and again, How
do I know that this is so? Is it logical? What is the evidence? Sometimes your inquiries will confirm the conventional account; in other
cases you may be able to find new ways of interpreting the same well-
known facts. That is the fun of doing history. It requires patience,
some ingenuity, a love of research, and a modicum of irreverence
toward the received wisdom. After all, if you are willing to accept
unquestioningly what "everyone" says, then the story is over before the
investigation begins.

It was in this spirit that I began searching to find out whether the
Riverside bias guidelines were unique or typical, and how widespread
was the practice of bias and sensitivity review in educational publishing. I wrote to publishing houses to request their bias guidelines, I
contacted friends in the industry for help in obtaining guidelines,
and I asked colleagues who work in various state and city agencies to

share whatever bias guidelines they used. Some publishers responded promptly with their guidelines, and others pretended that they didn't exist, but I was usually able to acquire these allegedly nonexistent documents.

Bias guidelines are ubiquitous in the world of kindergarten through twelfth-grade schooling. At one level, this is unsurprising: After all, American society has gone through a long and wrenching period, from the 1960s to the present, in which diligent citizens and public officials have tried to eliminate all vestiges of invidious discrimination against people on grounds of their race, ethnicity, gender, religion, age, or disability.

However, as I read current guidelines, it was clear that they went far beyond the original purpose of eliminating bias and had devolved instead into an elaborate language code that bans many common words and expressions. I am not speaking of epithets, scatological terms, ethnic slurs, or name-calling; their unacceptability is so obvious that they are not even mentioned in the guidelines. The guidelines prohibit controversial topics, even when they are well within the bounds of reasonable political and social discourse. They combine left-wing political correctness and right-wing religious fundamentalism, a strange stew of discordant influences. The guidelines aim to create a new society, one that will be completely inoffensive to all parties; getting there, however, involves a heavy dose of censorship. No one asked the rest of us whether we want to live in a society in which everything objectionable to every contending party has been expunged from our reading materials.

Bias guidelines are promulgated by four different kinds of agencies:

> *Educational publishers* issue them as directions for their editors, authors, and illustrators, as well as for the bias and sensitivity panels that review materials before publication.
>
> *Test development companies* (most of which belong to educational publishers) give them to people who write test questions (items) or select reading passages for tests, as well as to the bias and sensitivity committees that analyze every test item before it appears on a test.
>
> *States* adopt rules and laws that serve as bias guidelines, describing, sometimes in exacting detail, what must be included or excluded in educational materials. The states

that do this exert a powerful effect on publishers and
testing companies.

Scholarly and professional associations, like the American
Psychological Association, publish bias guidelines that
authors for their journals must follow if they want their
work to be accepted.

The overlap among all these educational organizations, whether
public or private, is so extensive that it is difficult to disentangle them.

Because of industry mergers, educational publishing was dominated
in the 1990s by four large corporations: Pearson (a British-based company), Vivendi (a French-based company), Reed Elsevier (a Dutch-
based company), and McGraw-Hill (an American-based company).
The K–12 textbook industry had annual sales in 2001 of more than
$4 billion, according to the Association of American Publishers.

These four conglomerates absorbed many long-established textbook
companies in recent years. Pearson owns Scott Foresman–Addison
Wesley, Scott Foresman, Silver Burdett, Ginn, Prentice Hall, Modern
Curriculum Press, Globe Fearon, NCS, and other imprints. Until
2002 Vivendi owned Houghton Mifflin, McDougal Littell, Riverside
Publishing (developer of the Iowa Test of Basic Skills), and other
companies. Reed Elsevier owns Harcourt, which includes Harcourt
Brace; the Psychological Corporation (which produces the SAT-9
test); Holt, Rinehart and Winston; the GED test; and other companies. McGraw-Hill owns Macmillan, Glencoe, Open Court, SRA,
and testing programs such as CTBS and TerraNova.

I was able to get bias guidelines from most of these companies. As
far as I could determine, every educational publisher conducts bias and
sensitivity reviews; I could not find one that does not subject its material to this procedure. It is a well-established, recognized practice in
educational publishing. It is not questioned; it is not controversial.
Everybody does it. Most company guidelines are similar to those used
by Riverside for the proposed voluntary national test. Some are even
more restrictive about the words and phrases that may and may not be
published. My guess is that companies are happy to have bias guidelines to shield them against vociferous advocacy groups. The publishers use their guidelines as a form of preemptive capitulation. With
these documents, they broadcast to all likely protesters, "Leave us
alone; we gave in to your demands long ago."

After reading guidelines from several companies, I concluded that the desire to control writers' language and thought processes has become deeply institutionalized in educational publishing. It is no longer an impulse; it is policy. The guidelines regulate what writers are permitted to say about specific groups in society, including women, the elderly, people with disabilities, and members of racial and ethnic minorities. Anything that is published in textbooks must be satisfactory to representatives of these groups, who are invited to review (and censor) whatever pertains to them. All of these groups must be presented only in a positive light.

The guidelines do not fret about censorship. Their purpose is to ensure that textbook writers do not inadvertently use politically unacceptable language. Textbooks must be sensitive; they must not offend anyone. The guidelines ensure conformity of language and thought. With the best of intentions, the publishers have consented to a strict code of censorship.

One might imagine that today's textbooks reflect the best research about how children learn and about how to convey important subject matter. One might suppose that the goal of a good textbook is to teach students needed skills and knowledge. One might think that the purpose of a reading textbook is to teach children to read fluently and with comprehension; that a history textbook is supposed to teach students about the past and its influence on the present; that a science or mathematics text should teach science or mathematics. Actually, in today's world, all of this takes a backseat to social and political concerns. The books now are expected to teach self-esteem, to present role models, to raise consciousness about various issues, and to show society as it ought to be. This is a tall order indeed. Usually in a democratic society, one pursues social and political change by becoming a part of the political process, by running for office and voting for candidates, by promoting legislation, or by managing a private enterprise. In the topsy-turvy world of educational publishing, advocates for social change have set their sights on controlling reality by changing the way in which it is presented in textbooks.

Consider the *Multicultural Guidelines* published by Scott Foresman–Addison Wesley.[1] Scott Foresman has long experience in the business of writing bias guidelines. In 1972, it published *Guidelines for Improving the Image of Women in Textbooks*. In 1990, it created a "multicultural steering committee" to ensure that the company's editorial products toed that line.

The Scott Foresman–Addison Wesley (SF-AW) bias guidelines comprise 161 pages, longer than most of their counterparts. They lay out a consistent party line for editors, authors, and illustrators. Combining a tone of idealism and authoritarianism, they impose a strict code of political and social correctness. They call for sweeping social and pedagogical changes.

The SF-AW document envisions the creation of a new society composed of "multicultural persons." These are people who look at others and see not an individual but a person who represents a group; the multicultural person understands that people from each group have distinctive ways of thinking, acting, and believing. Ordinarily, in the world of bias guidelines, the identification of the individual with the characteristics of a group is considered stereotyping. Scott Foresman–Addison Wesley overlooks this inconsistency.

The document is an extended celebration of multiculturalism. It is not about so limited a goal as reducing prejudice and promoting understanding among children from different groups. Multicultural education, it says, is not only about changing the content of textbooks and the attitudes of teachers and students, but about demanding specific pedagogical approaches, such as hands-on projects, self-esteem building, collaborative learning, constructivism, multiple intelligences, and an extensive catalog of other innovations. There is nothing wrong with any of these methods, and no doubt good teachers use some or all of them. But it is inappropriate for a publishing company to tell teachers who prefer other classroom methods that they may be guilty of racial, ethnic, and gender bias.

The SF-AW guidelines require that the company's products must each contain "a fair and balanced representation" of people from various cultural groups, racial groups, ethnic groups, and religious groups; males and females; older people; and people with disabilities. Not only the characters in the books, but those portrayed in illustrations must be balanced by race, ethnicity, and gender. Authors too must be selected by their gender and race.

The guidelines say that text illustrations must include people of all physical types, all ages, a mix of tall and short, heavy and thin, including people with disabilities. Although not all groups must be equally represented in every illustration, each book must have a full balance by race, gender, ethnicity, age, and disability. Illustrations must include all varieties of family units, including a family headed by two parents, by one parent, by grandparents, by aunts/uncles, by older siblings, and by other adults. Illustrators must pay close attention to such matters as "skin tones, hair colors and textures, eye colors, and facial features." Portrayals of diverse members of a multicultural society must be positive and uplifting so that students get a "sense of pride and self-worth." The guidelines include forty pages of photographs of children from different racial and ethnic groups so that illustrators will know what an African American boy, a Filipino girl, a Latin American boy, or a European American girl of eight to twelve looks like.

The guidelines admonish writers about what they must not say. It is objectionable, writers are warned, to write "Primitive cultures sometimes lack adequate medical care," because there are no "primitive cultures." One must not say, "Most Vietnamese are poor peasants," because such a statement, even if true, is condescending. One must not say, "Mr. Vargas, an agricultural adviser, is part of a life-and-death struggle to bring black Africa into the twentieth century." Such a statement is biased because black Africa was already in the twentieth century, even if the author intended to say that its agricultural practices were not. It is objectionable for an author to refer to anyone's language as a *dialect;* to refer to African *tribes* rather than African *ethnic groups;* or to refer to African *huts* (the dwellings in rural Africa must be described as *little houses*).

The language code tells how to describe the members of various American Indian groups; they must be identified as specific "nations," such as Shoshone, Ojibwa, or Choctaw, rather than by the generic term *American Indian* or *Native American.* Authors must ask the representatives of the group itself what name they prefer, rather than relying on historical accounts (writers should refer to *Kakota, Dakota,* or *Nakota,* not *Sioux;* to *Tohono O'odham,* not *Papago;* to *Diné Nation,* not *Navajo*). Some American Indian groups use the word *nation;* some use the word *tribe.* The members of the groups themselves should decide what identity they favor (the guidelines do not say how a writer is supposed to find out what the members of the group want to be called or whether they agree). Textbooks are expected to show the positive impact of American Indian groups (tribes? nations?) on American history. For example, the guidelines tell authors to acknowledge the highly dubious notion that the Constitution of the United States of America was "patterned partially after the League of Five Nations—a union formed by five Iroquois nations." The fact that this debt is not mentioned in the well-documented constitutional debates is of no concern. Textbook authors are expected to promulgate ideas that appeal to ethnic pride, even at the risk of endorsing spurious history. Authors are told to ask "American Indian experts" for their choice of role models rather than focusing on familiar figures like Sacagawea, who helped European Americans (the point is to exclude her precisely because she is known for helping European American explorers). The word *Eskimo* is out, to be replaced by *native Alaskan groups* or specific names such as *Inupiak* and *Yupik*. Writers must be neutral in describing conflicts between the U.S. government and American Indians; they may not describe a victory for the U.S. cavalry as a *battle* and a victory for American Indians as a *massacre*.

In its section on Asian Americans, the guidelines advise writers not to use that term but to refer to the specific nation of origin (*Chinese American, Vietnamese American,* and so on). In describing Asian Americans, the word *Oriental* is prohibited as "Eurocentric," as are such words as *distrustful, exotic, frugal, inscrutable, mysterious, passive, rigid, sneaky, studious, submissive,* and *unathletic*. Textbook writers must not refer to the academic success of Asian American students because it would imply a stereotype of Asian Americans as "studious" or as a "model minority."

Although the SF-AW document emphasizes the importance of racial and ethnic pride, it suggests that children of European American descent need to have their pride reduced. European Americans, it says, have received too much credit for achievements that really belonged to other cultures. Pasta did not originate in Italy, but in Asia, where Marco Polo learned about it; this is surely a controversy that not many people knew about or worried about. During the Middle Ages, Scott Foresman–Addison Wesley's guidelines say, European medicine was based on superstition, while Muslim physicians practiced real medicine. European Americans, it seems, are the only group that must be taken down a few pegs; their self-esteem is too high.

The SF-AW guidelines on "ageism" tell writers what they may and may not say about people over the age of sixty-five. They must be fully represented in text and illustrations; there must be a larger number of older women than older men, because 55 percent of older persons are women. The activities of older people are divided into "portrayals we limit" and "acceptable portrayals." Those that are limited are older people "baking, knitting, making crafts, whittling, engaging in inactive sports, reminiscing, rocking in chairs." The portrayals that are acceptable include "gardening, shopping, dancing, attending movies and cultural events, engaging in active sports . . ." The following clothing is unacceptable: aprons, canes, rockers, orthopedic shoes, outdated clothing and hats, walkers, and wheelchairs. Terms like *golden ager* and *senior citizen* are banned, as are *biddy, busybody, codger, crone, duffer, geezer, old lady, old maid, old man, past one's prime, senile,* and *spinster.* Older people may not be described as *bent, dowdy, feeble, frail, hobbling, shuffling, white-haired,* or *wrinkled.* Nor is it permitted to refer to an older person as *cute, dear, docile, mild-mannered, sweet,* or *well-meaning,* all of these being stereotypes. Nor can a writer say that an older person is *bitter, cantankerous, crabby, cranky, eccentric, forgetful, grumpy, meek, nagging, selfish, silly,* or *stubborn.* And it is a stereotype to describe a person over sixty-five as *bored, dependent, inactive, isolated, lonely, poor, sick, unhappy, weak,* or *weary.* Any description of older people that suggests that they act old is to be treated as a stereotype. The wise writer, reading these guidelines, will portray older persons only as healthy, happy, and able to run a marathon.

The section on gender, as one might expect, prescribes an elaborate code of language and representation. Women must be portrayed in equal numbers with men in all texts and illustrations. The following are typical female stereotypes: passive, frightened, weak, gentle, illogical, indecisive, neat, short, dependent, follower, emotional, and warm. Typical male stereotypes are: active, brave, strong, rough, competitive, logical, decisive, messy, tall, leader, unemotional, and confident. Any reference to gender-specific pronouns (*he, she, his, her*) must be replaced by a plural subject (the writer should say, "all students must read their books," never "each student must read his book"). Words that include the prefix or suffix *man* or *men* must be excluded; such words as *manpower, chairman, forefathers, freshman, businessmen,* and *mankind* are banned. (The word *humanity* is acceptable even though it has those horrible three letters [*man*] in its midsection.) Banished too are such words as *gal, lady, tomboy, hussy,* and *sissy.* Writers must never say that "women were granted the right to vote in 1920," but must say instead "women won the vote in 1920," because the first statement implies than men had power over women (which, of course, they did, since everyone in the U.S. Congress at the time was male).

The SF-AW document insists that all educational materials have a fair and balanced representation of people with disabilities. They must be shown with devices such as walkers, crutches, canes, wheelchairs, and braces. Writers may not refer to *the disabled,* but must say instead *people with disabilities.* Nor can they say *the blind,* or *the deaf,* or *birth defects;* they must instead refer to *people who are blind, people who are deaf,* and *people with congenital disabilities.* Words such as *abnormal, crazy, creature, defective, deformed, freak, gimp, idiot,* and *retard* are banned. Writers must not use terms such as *lame;* they must say instead *walks with a cane.* They must not write that someone is *confined to a wheelchair;* they must say instead that the person is a *wheelchair user.* They must not refer to someone as a *midget* or *dwarf* or *little person;* they must instead describe a *person of small stature.* Also objectionable are the terms *special, physically challenged,* and *differently abled;* these must be replaced by *person who has a disability.* It is equally unacceptable to refer to someone as *normal* or *able-bodied* or *whole;* such people are instead to be called a *person without disabilities* or a *person who is nondisabled.*

The textbooks, say the guidelines, must treat religion in a nonjudgmental way, as a "natural part of people's lives." Writers must show a broad diversity of religious beliefs and practices, not just one or two religions that are well known to students. Any reference to religion must be reviewed by "representatives from various religious groups," thus assuring that nothing will be published that offends any such group. There must be no "adversarial or unfavorable comparisons among religious beliefs," thus assuring that all references to religion in history and in contemporary society will be positive. In portraying religion, "no religious practice or belief is characterized as strange or peculiar, or as sophisticated or primitive." Presumably even the practice of human sacrifice would not be considered strange or peculiar in the neutral, nonjudgmental eyes of the publisher. Certain words associated with religion are banished, such as *cult, sect, dogma, fanatic, extremist, pagan,* and *heathen.* The term *myth* is to apply only to Greek and Roman traditional stories; religious stories must be called *narratives* rather than *myths.*

Parents might suppose that the most important aspect of schooling is the quality of teaching and learning, that is, its effectiveness in teaching English, mathematics, science, history, and a foreign language. The SF-AW document, however, asserts that the ultimate goal of the academic curriculum is to advance multiculturalism. The literature curriculum, for example, must focus on the racial and ethnic identity of authors. Editors are warned to avoid literature with "an older copyright" because of its racism and sexism; when such selections are included, teachers must emphasize their problematic content, not the author's literary purposes. In mathematics, what matters most is not whether textbooks effectively teach mathematics, but whether they incorporate multicultural themes and biographies into the math curriculum. In science, textbooks must emphasize science in ancient cultures and point out the scientific contributions that Europeans falsely claimed as their own. There is no recognition that scientific principles are the same in every culture, regardless of "who did it first."

Pity the poor textbook writers who must meet all of these mandates and prohibitions. Imagine the challenge as she or he sits down with a list of forbidden words and phrases and tries to explain American history or write a story for fifth-grade students that includes males and females, families with one or two parents or no parents, people with disabilities, older people who are jogging, a broad array of racial and ethnic groups, and people of different heights and different weights.

In the 1980s, other publishers adopted similar requirements for their editors, authors, and illustrators. Contributors to textbooks either complied or found different work. In 1990, the *New York Times* described an author and an illustrator who couldn't take the shifting mandates anymore. The writer explained, "Maybe it was the messenger at the door with another set of guidelines, updating the set she had received from the publisher a few days before. Maybe it was the elaborate recipes for an ethnic and racial mix in the cast of characters." The article quoted an artist who stopped accepting textbook assignments in 1986 after receiving the latest instructions from the publisher for an illustration:

> It's etched in acid in my mind. They sent 10 pages of
> single-spaced specifications. The hero was a Hispanic boy.
> There were black twins, one boy, one girl; an overweight

Oriental boy; and an American Indian girl. That leaves the Caucasian. Since we mustn't forget the physically handicapped, she was born with a congenital malformation and only had three fingers on one hand.

One child had to have an Irish setter, and the setter was to be female. . . . They also had a senior citizen, and I had to show her jogging.

I can't do it anymore.[2]

Probably the most influential bias guidelines, which are widely copied and cited by others in the industry, are those published by McGraw-Hill. This company has been publishing bias guidelines for its textbooks and tests since 1968. Its most recent guidelines, published in 1993, are titled *Reflecting Diversity: Multicultural Guidelines for Educational Publishing Professionals.*[3] Prepared by a staff of twenty-eight, along with sixty-three consultants, the MH guidelines are shorter than the SF-AW document but far more specific in listing the words, phrases, and images to be avoided.

The following words and phrases are deemed sexist and may not be used in materials published by McGraw-Hill:

Girls (when talking about females over the age of sixteen)
Sissy
Tomboy
You're smart as a man, as strong as a man
Bitch (this word may not be used for a female dog)
Girls are sugar and spice and everything nice
That was a manly act of courage
He took it like a man
Man the sailboats
Henpecked husband
She acted like a man
Lady
One-man band
Coed
Fireman (or any other occupation that includes
    the suffix *man*)
Manpower

Forefathers
Brotherhood
Man-made
Fisherman

It now seems that the "Founding Fathers" must become the "Founding Precursors," or simply "the Founders," ignoring the fact that all of them were men. Presumably one cannot sing "America the Beautiful" (written by a woman, Katherine Lee Bates) without changing the line "And crown thy good with brotherhood/from sea to shining sea," to "And crown thy good with community/from sea to shining sea." It is anyone's guess what to do about the sexism in the line "God shed His grace on thee." (God shed Its grace on thee? God shed Her grace on thee? Gods shed Their grace on thee? God shed the grace on thee?)

Those who write for McGraw-Hill publications may no longer refer to mankind, the rise of man, great men in history, man's achievements, or Cro-Magnon man. Such sexist language must be replaced by terms like *human beings, people, humanity, figures, personalities,* and *Cro-Magnon people.* All individual personal pronouns, whether *he* or *she, his* or *her,* must disappear forever. Animals must be referred to as *it,* not *he* or *she,* and writers must no longer describe a country or a boat as *she* (e.g., "England ruled the seas. Her navy was huge" is no longer permitted).

Illustrators for McGraw-Hill must maintain a 50-50 balance between the sexes in their art, with equal distribution of active and significant roles between them. When illustrators show historical events where women were not full participants, they must include a caption that calls attention to this inequity; for example, a picture of men lined up to vote in the nineteenth century would be accompanied by a caption that said: "The right to participate in the electoral process was restricted to men until the success of the women's suffrage movement in 1920." Presumably a portrait of General George Washington crossing the Delaware River would have a caption pointing out that women were excluded from important roles in the military until the late twentieth century.

The guidelines provide illustrators with a list of sex-stereotyped images, along with alternatives:

Women always wearing aprons must be replaced by males and/or females wearing aprons.

Mother sewing while father reads must be replaced by mother working at her desk while father reads or clears the dining room table.

Mother bringing sandwiches to father as he fixes the roof must be replaced by mother fixing the roof.

Mother doing household chores must be replaced by father doing household chores.

Mother seeing father off to work must be replaced by mother leaving for work with her briefcase or tools.

Mother doing the shopping must be replaced by father doing the shopping.

Mother showing shock or fear must be replaced by both father and mother expressing the same facial emotions.

Father looking calm in trying circumstances must be replaced by mother looking calm in trying circumstances.

Females backing away from action fearfully (e.g., "girl recoiling from snake, boy peering down curiously at it") must be replaced by "both sexes close to the snake, with perhaps a girl reaching toward it."

Boys playing ball, girls watching, must be replaced by coed teams, boys watching.

Females acting emotional, flirtatious, and coy must be replaced by both sexes acting the same way.

Girls looking neat and wearing dresses must be replaced by girls wearing jeans or shorts and being active, perhaps sporting "dirt splotches."

Girls preoccupied with their appearance, playing dress-up, and buying clothes must be replaced by both sexes equally vain, equally concerned about their appearance, with both parents using blow-driers and cologne, and with teenage boys cultivating their beards.

Pink for girls and blue for boys is out; both colors must be used together on baby cribs and carriages.

Girls playing with dolls and baby carriages must be replaced by both girls and boys playing with the same objects, tools, books, fishing rods, and dolls.

In preparing art that portrays the role of women in history, illustrators must search for photos and images that show women taking a leading role and must be on the watch for the following stereotyped images:

> Pioneer women doing domestic chores must be replaced by pioneer women chopping wood, using a plow, using firearms, and handling large animals.
>
> Pioneer woman riding in a covered wagon as man walks must be replaced by both man and woman walking or both riding, or woman walking while man rides.
>
> Women as passengers on a sailboat must be replaced by women hoisting the sails on a boat.
>
> Women depicted as nurses, elementary school teachers, clerks, secretaries, tellers, and librarians must be replaced by women as doctors, professors, managers, police officers, sports figures, and construction workers, and by men as nurses, secretaries, and elementary school teachers.

Some of these replacements require writers and artists to tell lies about history. Until the latter decades of the twentieth century, most women who worked were in fact nurses, teachers, and secretaries; not many women were doctors, professors, managers, police officers, sports figures, and construction workers. To pretend otherwise is to falsify the past. It minimizes the barriers that women faced. It pretends that the gender equality of the late twentieth and early twenty-first centuries was a customary condition in the past.

The MH guidelines express barely concealed rage against people of European ancestry. They deride European Americans for exploiting slaves, migrant workers, and factory labor; they excoriate the land rapacity of the pioneers and mock their so-called courage in fighting Native Americans: "Bigots and bigotry," say the guidelines, referring to European Americans, "must be identified and discussed." European Americans, the guidelines suggest, were uniquely responsible for bigotry and exploitation in all human history. Like the SF-AW guidelines, McGraw-Hill's advise writers to recognize that "the very foundation that our country is built upon is modeled in part after tenets of the Iroquois Confederacy," which is intended to raise Native American self-esteem and bring the European Americans down a few notches.

Writers for McGraw-Hill are warned that if they pay too much attention to figures like Dr. Martin Luther King Jr., Harriet Tubman, George Washington Carver, Booker T. Washington, and Jackie Robinson, it is only because they are "acceptable to the European-American establishment." The guidelines recommend in-depth discussion of figures such as Paul Robeson, Carter G. Woodson, Paul Dunbar, Nat Turner, Angela Davis, and Jesse Jackson, "who are considered controversial by some." This may have once seemed like a radical proposal, but all or most of these figures have received respectful notice in the media and even in textbooks. Woodson was a historian of the black experience in America; Dunbar was a poet who is now frequently anthologized; Robeson and Davis were known for their far-left politics; Nat Turner led a slave revolt; and Jesse Jackson is a well-known activist.

The illustrations in McGraw-Hill's publications must be balanced by race, gender, and disability. The illustrator must take care to avoid a long list of racial stereotypes. When portraying African Americans, the following are considered stereotypes: African Americans who have white features or all look alike; African Americans all having the same skin color; African Americans with the same hairstyles; African Americans with exaggerated African American features. In showing the dress of African Americans, illustrators must avoid showing African Americans wearing loud colors, straw hats, white suits, and exaggerated prints, or, conversely, middle-class clothes. When showing the environment in which African Americans live, they must avoid depicting urban African Americans in crowded tenements on chaotic streets, big bright cars, and abandoned buildings with broken windows and wash hanging out, and they must also avoid showing them in "dull, white picket-fence neighborhoods."

When portraying Native Americans, illustrators must avoid the stereotyped image of long hair, braids, and headbands; they must not depict red skin, impassive expressions, "how" gestures, warlike stances, and comic poses. They must also avoid full headdress, feathers, buffalo robes, war paint, and bows and arrows. Native Americans must not be shown living in teepees surrounded by totem poles and pinto horses or living in shacks or on reservations. Males should not appear hunting or in war parties or passing the peace pipe. Females should not be shown sewing buffalo hides, grinding corn, or carrying papooses. Contemporary Native Americans should not be working on ranches or in menial jobs or in skyscraper construction (they should be lawyers, teachers, sports figures, and professionals). Again, the world may not be depicted as it is and as it was, but only as the guideline writers would like it to be.

Other publishing houses have bias guidelines that are not as detailed as those from Scott Foresman–Addison Wesley and McGraw-Hill. Harcourt's are only a few pages; they have not been released for public review. When I first tried to get a copy of the document, I was told that it was confidential; a friend obtained a copy and sent it to me. It is hard to see why the publishing company is so secretive. It echoes the guidelines of Scott Foresman–Addison Wesley and McGraw-Hill regarding nonsexist language, stereotypes, and balanced portrayal of people of all genders and racial and ethnic groups. But there are a few innovations. One is that textbook writers must "beware of geographical chauvinism in the use of the terms America and Americans," since they refer to North, South, and Central America. Be specific, the writer is warned, because "there is no place simply called America." Harcourt also advises writers to be wary of the geographic terms *Orient, Oriental, the Middle East, Eastern, Western, East, West.* The Harcourt guidelines say "some people consider these terms offensive because they are based on a colonial view of the world as being centered in Europe." Writers should use *Southwest Asia* instead of *Middle East* when referring to geography. The words *Orient* and *Oriental* are absolutely banned.[4]

My efforts to obtain guidelines from Houghton Mifflin were at first unavailing. However, I did unearth a current statement from the publisher saying that the contents of its literature textbooks are based on the most recent Census Bureau statistics. For example, a reading book with twenty-two selections would include three pieces by African American writers, three by Latinos, two by Asian Americans, one by a Native American, and one by a writer with a physical disability.

I eventually discovered Houghton Mifflin guidelines from 1981, called *Eliminating Stereotypes.*[5] These turned out to be a "mother lode" of bias guidelines, if one may be permitted a possibly sexist expression. I don't know if Houghton Mifflin still uses them, since no one there would tell me, but they continue to be cited by other publishers (Riverside, for example, used this 1981 document when writing test items for the VNT). Here in forty-two succinct pages is an extensive listing of what writers are allowed to say and what they must not say. Here are

the forbidden words and phrases related to gender bias and stereotyping. Editors are advised to base their selections and illustrations on the
latest census figures for black Americans, Hispanic Americans, Asian
Americans, Native Americans, disabled Americans, and older Americans (and to remember that the ratio of older women to older men is
precisely 100 to 69). Writers are reminded to portray both sexes in the
same professions and the same activities, exhibiting the same emotions. They must depict members of both sexes as "tall/short, plump/
slender, right-handed/left-handed, light-haired/dark-haired/gray-haired,
short-haired/long-haired, brown-eyed/blue-eyed/green-eyed, etc., having freckles/not having freckles, with/without hearing aids or eyeglasses." Nor should they forget to represent men with and without
mustaches and beards, and men who are bald. Writers and illustrators
are told to show minorities "in stories traditionally lacking ethnic
characters," such as "royalty and members of court," and "townspeople
in fairy tales." In writing about "disabled persons," Houghton Mifflin
contributors must not portray them as "sinister characters" such as
pirates, witches, or criminals because it is wrong to associate "evil with
disabilities." (No more Captain Hook!) Like Harcourt, Houghton
Mifflin advises its writers to avoid the words "America" and "American" and to substitute "the United States" and "a citizen of the United
States." (The guidelines themselves repeatedly use the word "American" to refer to people who live in the United States.)

In 2001, Houghton Mifflin added new criteria for selecting multicultural literature (this document is unpublished).[6] When choosing
stories about African Americans, editors must avoid or limit those that
are about slavery or the Underground Railroad; that contain dialect;
that depict African Americans as athletes, musicians, or entertainers;
that are about controversial people like Malcolm X; and that are about
civil rights. When choosing stories about Asian Americans, editors
must avoid those that "perpetuate the 'model minority' myth, i.e.,
musical prodigy, class valedictorian, etc." When choosing stories about
Latinos, they must limit those that feature migrant workers and avoid
those that are about illegal immigration and religious holidays. Editors
are directed to seek out selections by authors who are of the same ethnic group that they are describing.

The 2001 Houghton Mifflin literature guidelines identify certain
children's books that must be avoided, possibly because the author was
not of the same ethnic group as the main characters in the book. Some

of the prohibited books have received prestigious awards, including Mary Hoffman's *Amazing Grace,* Theodore Taylor's *The Cay,* Paula Fox's *Slave Dancer,* and William Armstrong's *Sounder.* Ellen Levine's *I Hate English!,* about an Asian girl learning English, was excluded because the girl required the intervention of her Caucasian teacher to solve her problems, which was apparently offensive to the bias review panel.

So what should one make of all this mandating and prohibiting and avoiding? Is it a good thing that words like *policeman* and *fireman* are not used in our schools? Should schools change Arthur Miller's play *Death of a Saleman* to "Death of a Sales Representative"? Should Willy Loman trade places with his wife and send her out on the road? Should we stop reading *A Man for All Seasons* or should we convert it to "A Person for All Seasons"? Will schoolchildren never again learn about "The Man Without a Country"? What of George Bernard Shaw's "Person and Superperson," formerly known as *Man and Superman*? And what should be done about Claude Brown's *Manchild in the Promised Land*?

The bias guidelines are censorship guidelines. Nothing more, nothing less. This language censorship and thought control should be repugnant to those who care about freedom of expression. Clearly there must be some commonsense limitations on what people—especially schoolchildren—see and hear. We don't introduce graphic images of carnage into our textbooks or into daily newspapers. In the days after the terrorist attacks on the World Trade Center on September 11, 2001, few newspapers published photographs of people leaping to their death from the highest floors of the two buildings. Few publish photographs of mutilated bodies from crime or battle scenes. Most newspapers do not include printed materials or photographs that are obviously pornographic. Journalists and editors acknowledge implicitly the importance of good taste, judgment, and appropriateness when selecting materials, without laws and regulations to define what cannot be published.

Unfortunately, the textbook publishers have surrendered control of their products to the language police. Browbeaten and intimidated by zealous advocates of censorship, they have accepted self-censorship. They have abandoned the idea that their editors and authors might exercise common sense and discretion. The linguistic and ideological conformity that has been imposed on the American educational publishing industry is an outrage. It insults the dignity and integrity of those who work in publishing. It destroys the possibility of freedom of thought and expression. It creates a formula to which every writer must adhere, or risk rejection and failure.

The guidelines, when faithfully applied, guarantee the exclusion of imaginative literature from our textbooks. They actively prohibit the transmission of our national culture, whose imaginative literature was not written in conformity with the publishers' language codes. They assume that everything that was not written in accordance with their mandates must be racist, sexist, ageist, and harmful to any group that has ever known oppression or exclusion. Is it any wonder that students who read such pap do not enjoy reading, and that they see little connection between art and life? The guidelines discredit the educational mission of the school in the eyes of the young.

Writers of children's literature, like writers of literature for any audience, must be able to write without fear of the censor, without fear that noses will be counted and sorted according to their race, gender, disability, age, and ethnicity. Historians, like writers of fiction, must be able to write what they know, based on evidence and scholarship, without fear of the censor and without deference to political, religious, ethnic, or gender sensitivities.

The very existence of guidelines that limit the words and ideas that may be expressed is offensive. Our nation prides itself on the principle of freedom of speech contained in the First Amendment to our Constitution. It is the cornerstone of our Bill of Rights. Yet the practice of censorship, almost unknown to the general public, has been widely accepted for many years within the educational publishing industry as the normal way of doing business.

FOUR

Everybody Does It:
The Testing Companies

And somehow or other, quite anonymous, there were
the directing brains who coordinated the whole effort
and laid down the lines of policy which made it necessary that this fragment of the past should be preserved,
that one falsified, and the other rubbed out of existence.
—George Orwell, *1984*

JUST AS political pressure groups have imposed censorship on textbook publishers, so too have they compelled test publishers to remove
whatever they dislike from standardized tests. A top official at the
Educational Testing Service told me that his company and other testing agencies deleted test items whenever anyone complained about
them; items might be dropped not only on grounds of bias, very
broadly defined, but also if they might make a student feel "uncomfortable." The very fact that someone objects to a topic or a test item
can be sufficient to make it "controversial." As another ETS official
admitted to me, "It is better to be bland than to be controversial." By
institutionalizing this extreme sensitivity to anything that offends
anybody, publishers of both textbooks and tests have been turning
their products into inoffensive pap for the past generation.

Like textbook publishers, every test publisher screens test questions
for possible bias. Our society's commitment to equality of educational
opportunity surely requires that we seek to eliminate every expression
of bigotry and that we teach people of all ages to respect others. But
this does not mean that literature or history should be censored to
remove anything that might make any reader uncomfortable. Good
literature is *supposed* to make readers uncomfortable, and accurate history includes tragic events and horrifying behavior.

The bias guidelines defer to activists across the ideological spectrum. Conservatives have persuaded the testing companies to avoid topics like evolution, abortion, and divorce. Feminists and multiculturalists have convinced them to exclude any language that offends them. As a result, tests of reading, for example, typically contain passages that are bland, homogenized, sanitized, and boring. How could it be otherwise when every controversial subject has been carefully deleted, every political and social issue has been excluded, and the language itself has been scrubbed to make it utterly inoffensive to all potential readers?

The present era of bias and sensitivity reviewing began in the late 1960s and early 1970s, when civil rights activists attacked standardized tests, insisting that cultural bias in the tests caused large disparities in performance between black and white children. The language of the tests, the critics said, was more familiar to middle-class white children than to disadvantaged black children. Testing companies were shocked by the charges of racism; their experts had for years tried to ignore differences in scores among racial and ethnic groups. When the complaints of racism became persistent, the industry began to look for ways to identify and eliminate biased questions. A spokesman for McGraw-Hill admitted that when this work commenced in the 1970s, the publishers "had little to guide them in their efforts to deal with the now loud accusations of bias." The companies developed bias guidelines, trained sensitivity reviewers, and tried out test items with different ethnic groups. If the items were "undesirable for one or more groups," they were deleted. He further observed, "In fact, the evidence about the effectiveness of these procedures is so thin that one might well wonder how we got into this. The answer is more political than scientific, as one might suspect given the short time period during which the matter has drawn serious study: technical innovation usually takes longer to be applied."[1]

At first, the search for bias focused on the test items that subtly disparaged minorities or contained racial stereotypes. The hunt intensified when feminists added their voices to those of civil rights groups, charging that the academic performance of female students was lowered by gender-biased questions. Since girls typically had higher reading test scores than boys, the claims of gender bias focused on mathematics, where there was a test-score gap in favor of boys. Feminist critics maintained that this gap was caused entirely by sexist language or topics in the test questions.

Emboldened by the perceived gains of their ideological opponents, conservative critics and parents complained vocally to publishers about the introduction of topics that were offensive to *them*. They criticized topics such as witchcraft, satanism, fantasy, abortion, animal rights, or anything that carried a political message that they disagreed with or that might make their children uncomfortable. Publishers, including test publishers, made haste to remove material that might arouse their ire.

To mollify critics, the test developers adopted bias guidelines like those of the textbook publishers. The testing companies addressed the concerns of feminists, civil rights groups, and religious fundamentalists in an evenhanded way. They banned all controversial topics from their tests, reasoning that anything that distracted students would prevent them from showing their real ability.

The more that tests were criticized as culturally biased, the more the developers reduced their cultural content. The only safe areas for testing, it seemed, were basic skills, reasoning skills, and problem-solving skills. What was unsafe was anything that required prior knowledge of history and literature, which was culturally bound. Test makers could not assume that students had learned anything other than abstract skills, which were noncontroversial. They could not assume that any student had ever read anything in particular before taking the test. The tests would assess only what students could do, their skills and aptitudes, not what they had learned in class. Tests of English language arts and social studies reproduced reading passages and asked students if they understood what they read. There was no literature or history that anyone was expected to know, no cultural background that students of any age could be expected to share.

This situation had two independent causes: First, there is no standard curriculum in the United States, no agreed-upon course of study that includes certain facts of history and certain works of literature, thus making it impossible to base test questions on what students should have learned. Second, the search for a "culture fair" or "culture free" test created a presumption against tests of achievement and knowledge. It became necessary to replace tests of achievement with tests of aptitude, tests of thinking skills, tests of the student's abstract intelligence. This was ironic, because aptitude tests were similar to intelligence tests, and most critics considered them to be even more culturally biased than tests of achievement.

During the 1970s, panels of trained bias detectors were deployed to review every test item and to expunge any manifestation of bias. However, by the 1980s, experts had developed a statistical process for determining whether a test item was "biased" even though nothing in the actual wording of the question indicated any discernible bias against any group. This statistical process is known as DIF, or "differential item functioning." A test question exhibits DIF if equally proficient individuals from different groups do not have "equal probabilities of answering the item correctly." For example, if white males and black males of equal ability are not able to answer the same question correctly (regardless of its language or content), then something is presumed to be wrong with the question.[2] The difference between the groups may not be caused by bias as most people understand the term, but might be the result of lack of educational opportunity, lack of knowledge, some malfunction in the design of the test question, or some other unknown source. In the test-development industry, DIF analysis is now standard operating procedure; regardless of their content or wording, test items may be discarded if they exhibit an unacceptable level of DIF. Certain topics are routinely avoided because they are associated with high levels of DIF.

The principles that by now have been institutionalized in the test developers' bias and sensitivity reviews suffer from the same defects as the reviews by the textbook publishers. Bias review narrows the language and topics permitted on tests on political grounds, and DIF analysis constricts what students are expected to know by limiting the range of topics that may be included on tests.

Researchers from the Educational Testing Service examined several major standardized tests, including the SAT and the Graduate Record Examination, to find out what kinds of questions produce DIF for female, black, and Hispanic test-takers.[3] DIF analysis showed that women got lower scores than men on items related to science content or to "practical affairs content" (such as money and its uses, tools and their uses, mechanical objects, sports, and historical topics). Women got higher scores than men on questions related to aesthetics or human relationships (how someone feels, thinks, or reacts).

DIF analysis revealed that women got higher scores on questions related to stereotypically female interests such as sewing and embroidery, and blacks and Hispanics did better on items that contained content relevant to minority concerns. Black examinees performed better on questions about human relationships and worse on items about science. Women scored better on algebra, but worse on geometry and word problems in mathematics. Also, DIF analysis showed that black test-takers did worse than equivalent whites on questions that included maps and charts and other visual materials.

These generalizations, based on DIF analysis, identify topics to be minimized or avoided on tests; they have had a large impact on the bias guidelines now used by major testing companies. The problem with DIF analysis, as the psychologist Lloyd Bond of the University of North Carolina pointed out, is that the very concept of differential item functioning relies on group stereotypes. It "implies a homogeneous set of life experiences on the part of the focal group that are qualitatively different from the reference group and that affect verbal and mathematical reasoning."[4] DIF works only if all women, all blacks, all Asians, and all Hispanics have similar thought processes, rather than exhibiting a range of ways of thinking and learning. So, paradoxically, the main statistical process for identifying test bias relies on and reinforces racial, ethnic, and gender stereotyping. Furthermore, testing experts agree that the number and proportion of test questions that actually display extreme or meaningful DIF are few on any particular test, well under 10 percent. Because there are so few items that display DIF, the application of DIF screening has not changed test scores for women or minorities.[5]

Thus, when all is said and done, after ETS has applied DIF analysis to identify and excise questions on which there is extreme DIF, the scores of women and minorities are virtually unchanged. Nonetheless, DIF analysis has become institutionalized. It shows the world (and test critics) that test companies are on their guard to exclude any questions that might be unfair to women and minorities. The use of DIF shields the testing companies from criticism, even though it makes very little difference in test scores. The other major college-admissions testing service, ACT, also employs DIF analysis for its test questions, but its own research demonstrates that the most important determinant of students' test performance is the academic courses they studied in high school and the quality of the high school they attended, not their race or gender.[6]

ETS, which is responsible for the SAT as well as many other tests, has subjected its tests and publications to intensive fairness and sensitivity reviews since at least 1980. Currently, ETS has layers of review and DIF analysis to seek out any whiff of bias or insensitivity. Its bias guidelines warn reviewers and test assemblers to avoid the following subjects: the military, sports, violence, and specialized vocabulary associated with farming, finance, law, politics, science, technology, tools and machinery, transportation, or charts (and maps and graphs), as well as questions assessing spatial skills. DIF analysis has shown that these topics are associated with group differences in performance.

One can only imagine—and gasp at—the diminution of content in nationally administered tests when such a broad array of topics must be scrupulously avoided. Although the ETS guidelines do not acknowledge which groups are likely to suffer adverse consequences when test items refer to these topics, ETS research indicates that males tend to get higher scores than females on most of these topics. If one believes in gender equality, then girls should be expected to know about sports, the military, law, politics, science, and so on, just as boys are. It may not have been true in 1980, but it is certainly true now that girls and women participate actively in sports, the military, the law, finance, and other fields. Excluding these topics as too "male" is itself a gross form of stereotyping. These are not highly specialized topics that are somehow specific to guys; they are topics that everyone should know about.

In addition to the list of forbidden topics that were generated by DIF analysis, the ETS guidelines contain the customary prohibitions about language and stereotypes related to race, gender, disability, and age, echoing the strictures of the textbook guidelines. In addition, ETS bans anything that suggests ethnocentrism, that is, any test material that is written from the point of view of someone who lives in a Western culture. ETS reviewers are instructed to treat as ethnocentric any test material that focuses exclusively on "Judeo-Christian contributions to literature or art." One cannot imagine educational agencies in Japan or Brazil or Nigeria warning against testing students on the literary or aesthetic traditions of their own society.

ETS enforces elaborate rules for gender balance and minority representation on its tests. Males and females must be represented in equal numbers and in equivalent types of roles; every test must have a representation of at least 10 percent minorities, and preferably more than one minority group should be included. In addition, the authors and illustrators whose work appears on the test (whether or not they are identified on the test) must also be balanced by race and gender. Committees of test assemblers and sensitivity reviewers code passages for gender and racial categories and tally the score for each item and for the test as a whole. Even the "distractors," the wrong answers on a multiple-choice question, must be entered into the tally for gender and racial balance (a question about an Asian American female would be tallied twice, once for "Asian American" and once for "female").

In the decade after ETS adopted its bias guidelines, content experts in literature, the social sciences, and history complained internally that the guidelines were making the achievement tests too bland. The content experts wanted "more provocative materials," but their pleas were rejected. The guidelines prevailed. On one occasion, ETS insiders disagreed about the rigid application of rules for gender balance on a literature test for college students. Sensitivity reviewers complained that the test lacked sufficient representation of female authors. The test makers, however, argued that it already included a "reasonable number of passages by women writers given the nature of the curriculum." The purpose of the test, they insisted, "was not to reflect a particular kind of universe or to represent groups of people but to provide passages from a range of literary works that test a student's ability to analyze and interpret prose, poetry, and drama of different historical periods." Otherwise, they pointed out, it would become very difficult, perhaps impossible, to use great literature from Classical, Renaissance or other premodern eras, thus defeating the main purpose of the test, which was to assess knowledge and comprehension of these periods. A struggle ensued between the test assemblers and the reviewers that was eventually resolved by an arbitration committee. The arbitrators ruled in favor of the reviewers. They directed the assemblers to correct the gender imbalance by adding more passages written by and about women to the literature test.[7]

Besides ETS, other independent test-development companies create assessments for states and school districts. All of them have similar bias guidelines. The American Institutes for Research (AIR), which creates customized tests, follows the *AIR Principles for Bias, Sensitivity, and Language Simplification*. In addition to the usual prohibition of words that contain the terrible three letters *m-a-n*, there are also the customary rules about stereotyping of women, racial minorities, older people, and disabled people, as well as gays and lesbians. AIR lists topics that are too inflammatory or controversial to be included in any assessment. These include death, euthanasia, suicide, teen pregnancy, AIDS, drugs and alcohol, gangs, the occult, disease, serious car accidents, injuries, abortion, animal rights, oppression, war, divorce, slavery, poverty, unemployment, pornography, sexuality or sexual activity, child abuse, evolution, race relations, politics, and religion. These topics, unless they are directly relevant to what is being tested, can "easily cause a negative emotional reaction such as anger or embarrassment and thus distract the student from the purpose of the assessment." To avoid "ethnocentrism," AIR does not refer to people who live in the United States as "Americans," because that term should include Canadians, Mexicans, and South Americans.

AIR also bans language that some groups might be more familiar with than others, such as *junk bond, cotillion, coming out party, social register,* and *yachting.* To avoid regional bias, AIR excludes test questions that refer to "certain regional specific features (e.g., mountains, oceans) or weather phenomena (e.g., hurricanes, typhoons, blizzards)." Based on DIF analysis, AIR excludes the following topics from its tests: the military; sports; terminology associated with agriculture, finance, law, politics, science, technology, construction, and machinery; also, charts and maps and questions requiring spatial skills (unless spatial skills are being measured).

At a certain point, all test and textbook bias guidelines start to look alike. There is a good reason for this: They copy one another. Sometimes they acknowledge their debt to another publisher's guidelines. Often they do not. The different sets of guidelines are all boilerplate replicated from one to another in a mutual effort to comply with and enforce the regulatory regime. It is as if all these guidelines were written by the same humorless committee, whose members' noses were eagerly sniffing the text for any signs of deviance from their tightly prescribed language code. Each cites the other in a nearly perfect circle of consensus, a cordon sanitaire erected to prevent authors or editors from using any prohibited word or inflammatory topic. The guideline writers seem to assume that children have never seen a newscast, never seen MTV, never seen anything on television or in the movies that violated the rules of this perfect, if boring, world.

Despite the sometimes deadening similarity of these guidelines, I found it fascinating to read them, if only to see what innovations had been added to the standard group-think formula. The guidelines published in 1991 by National Evaluation Systems, an independent company that creates tests tailored to the standards of several states, were especially intriguing. At first I thought, Nothing new here. Some of the examples of forbidden words were lifted (with credit) right out of the now venerable McGraw-Hill guidelines. We immediately run into our old friends representational fairness, gender and racial stereotypes, the intolerable gender-specific nouns, the grandparents who are never frail or sedate, and so on. What was new, then?

The NES guidelines admit what others leave implicit. Their goal is to create a portrait of an "ideal toward which society is striving." To reach that goal, children will encounter on their tests a world in which equal numbers of women, men, and racial groups participate fully in all activities and all roles. It will be a world in which older persons suffer no constraints because of their age, a world in which persons with a handicap are entirely unaffected by their handicap. It will be a world in which no one lives in neighborhoods that are not fully integrated. In this world, people with disabilities include not only those with crutches and wheelchairs but also those with "behavioral problems, hearing impairments, learning disabilities, mental retardation, multiple handicaps," etc. The guidelines propose that references to minorities extend far beyond tests of history, English, and art; for example, on a math test, instead of asking students to calculate "the number of cars in a parking lot or the number of soup cans produced in a factory, examinees might be asked to interpret a graph showing the increase in the number of Black persons holding political office in the country." How patronizing to students, whatever their race, that even their mathematics tests are used to make political points.

The specific examples of biased items show how political criteria affect test questions. Consider the following example of "bias toward minority groups" on a history test: "Analyze the causes for the preeminence of Western civilization since the Middle Ages." NES says this statement is biased because it "displays a cultural and ethnic bias toward Western civilization" while ignoring other civilizations in Asia, Africa, the Americas, and elsewhere.

Certainly the statement could have been improved by saying "Analyze the causes of the technological, military, and economic preeminence of the West since the seventeenth or eighteenth centuries." The dominance of the West in recent centuries is a historical reality, not just a biased opinion. Historians who have studied the reasons for this reality have analyzed the importance of capitalism, imperialism, colonialism, technological innovation, cultural diversity, literacy, individualism, religion, war, democratic institutions, and other developments, both good and bad. In the NES guidelines, however, this inquiry is forbidden on grounds of ethnocentrism.

An example of a biased objective for a health test is: "Analyze the effects of poor diet on black women." On the face of it, this is a pretty stupid objective, since poor diet would likely have similar effects on people of various racial and ethnic groups. It is probably a test question designed by someone trying to meet the guidelines' mandate to inject questions about race into every test, even when it is irrelevant to the subject.

An example of a biased item on a social science test is:

Which of the following groups has the highest birth rate?
A. African Americans
B. Asian Americans
C. Hispanic Americans
D. Polish Americans

The NES guidelines note that the item is "cognitively accurate," but "affectively negative" because it may be "offensive to various minority groups." Thus it should be excluded. This example sends a message to teachers and professors to avoid any topic that might be "affectively negative" for any group, regardless of its accuracy.

Another example of bias in a social science test: "Identify cultural advantages of urban living." This "displays a cultural bias toward urban life." Isn't this silly? What is wrong with asking students to think about the cultural advantages that are afforded when large enough numbers of people live in close proximity, such as museums and theaters, which are hard to sustain in an environment where the population is dispersed? To admit that there are advantages, after all, hardly precludes one from also being able to describe disadvantages.

A biased objective for a "technological science test" is: "Analyze difficulties inherent in exporting technological progress from advanced nations to less developed societies." This is the kind of "ethnocentric" statement that people who write bias guidelines really hate: they detest loaded words like *progress, advanced,* and *less developed.* NES prefers instead to say "Analyze issues involved in the transfer of technology from nation to nation." But these questions cover two entirely different subjects: The first question is about problems of technology transfer from rich nations to poor and less developed nations; the second might refer to export controls between developed countries. In effect, the first subject, which is of vital importance in helping to improve poor nations, has been ignorantly censored to avoid offending the sensitivities of the adults who write the guidelines.

An example of a biased objective for a physical education test: "Identify techniques of exercise appropriate for maintaining a youthful appearance and attitude." This objective, say the guidelines, shows a "stereotypical outlook on aging by stressing the desirability of youth." This is one of my favorite examples, probably because I am an "older person" and understand that old age involves a certain acceptance of physical decline. I am not happy about it, and I wish I were thirty again. Yes, I think that being young is more desirable than being old, at least physically. And I don't feel that anyone is biased against me if they suggest that exercise will help me maintain a youthful appearance and attitude. Anyone who believes that this objective is biased is fighting nature, not bias.

Pity the poor wordsmith who must pick his or her way through this minefield of prohibitions. Pity the test developer who must analyze every word to see whom it might offend. No, you can't refer to a *heretic.* A *busboy* is a *dining room attendant.* A *fisherman* is a *fisher.* You must not say *third world,* although it is okay to refer to a *WASP.* You can't say this, you can't say that.

There is a saying among educators that what is tested determines what is taught. If that is true, then we can well understand why "what is taught" today lacks depth. Test developers are told to avoid value judgments that favor the society in which we live; to avoid controversial or sensitive topics; to be wary of passages written before 1970; to omit references to any specific region; to keep all questions as neutral and minimalist as possible; and to insert positive material about minorities, the aged, the handicapped, women, and other groups into test questions, regardless of its relevance to the subject being assessed. This overloaded social agenda helps to explain why so many standardized tests today probe little more than basic skills. Depth, complexity, and subtlety have been ruled out.

The question that keeps occurring to me is whether educational testing can meet its primary responsibility to gauge student performance accurately and fairly while attempting at the same time to meet so many diffuse political and social goals.

FIVE

Censorship from the Right

And shall we just carelessly allow children to hear any casual tales which may be devised by casual persons, and to receive into their minds ideas for the most part the very opposite of those which we should wish them to have when they are grown up?
—Plato, *The Republic,* Book II

THE WORD *censorship* refers to the deliberate removal of language, ideas, and books from the classroom or library because they are deemed offensive or controversial. The definition gets fuzzier, however, when making a distinction between censorship and selection. Selection is not censorship. Teachers have a responsibility to choose readings for their students, based on their professional judgment of what students are likely to understand and what they need to learn. Librarians, however, unlike teachers, are bound by a professional code that requires them to exclude no publication because of its content or point of view. It is also important to remember that people have a First Amendment right to complain about textbooks and library books that they don't like.

Censorship occurs when school officials or publishers (acting in anticipation of the legal requirements of certain states) delete words, ideas, and topics from textbooks and tests for no reason other than their fear of controversy. Censorship may take place before publication, as it does when publishers utilize guidelines that mandate the exclusion of certain language and topics, and it may happen after publication, as when parents and community members pressure school officials to remove certain books from school libraries or classrooms. Some people believe that censorship occurs only when government officials impose it, but publishers censor their products in order to secure government contracts. So the result is the same.

Censors on the right aim to restore an idealized vision of the past, an Arcadia of happy family life, in which the family was intact, comprising a father, a mother, and two or more children, and went to church every Sunday. Father was in charge, and Mother took care of the children. Father worked; Mother shopped and prepared the meals. Everyone sat around the dinner table at night. It was a happy, untroubled setting into which social problems seldom intruded. Pressure groups on the right believe that what children read in school should present this vision of the past to children and that showing it might make it so. They believe strongly in the power of the word, and they believe that children will model their behavior on whatever they read. If they read stories about disobedient children, they will be disobedient; if they read stories that conflict with their parents' religious values, they might abandon their religion. Critics on the right urge that whatever children read should model appropriate moral behavior.

Censors from the left believe in an idealized vision of the future, a utopia in which egalitarianism prevails in all social relations. In this vision, there is no dominant group, no dominant father, no dominant race, and no dominant gender. In this world, youth is not an advantage, and disability is not a disadvantage. There is no hierarchy of better or worse; all nations and all cultures are of equal accomplishment and value. All individuals and groups share equally in the roles, rewards, and activities of society. In this world to be, everyone has high self-esteem, eats healthful foods, exercises, and enjoys being different. Pressure groups on the left feel as strongly about the power of the word as those on the right. They expect that children will be shaped by what they read and will model their behavior on what they read. They want children to read only descriptions of the world as they think it should be in order to help bring this new world into being.

For censors on both the right and the left, reading is a means of role modeling and behavior modification. Neither wants children and adolescents to encounter books, textbooks, or videos that challenge their vision of what was or what might be, or that depict a reality contrary to that vision.

· · ·

As a student in the Houston public schools, I had firsthand experience with the political pressures exerted by extreme right-wing forces. When I was a senior at San Jacinto High School in 1955–56, I worked one class period each day in the library. One day I discovered a pile of books stashed under the main circulation desk, all of which were about Russia and the Soviet Union. When I tried to replace them on the shelves, the librarian stopped me and said that they had been removed from circulation. My curiosity piqued, as soon as I had free time, I went straight for the banned books under the counter and read them. Anything that is forbidden is almost by definition attractive to adolescents who want to know what the big deal is. I learned a lot about Russia, more than anyone else in my school, since no one else had access to any books about it. The only book I still remember is Walter Duranty's *I Write As I Please;* I didn't know it at the time, but Duranty was very controversial. As the *New York Times's* correspondent in Moscow in the 1930s, he consistently rationalized and covered up Stalin's terror tactics. Historians and biographers now recognize that he failed to report Stalin's most egregious crimes.[1] His book would probably have been way over the heads of most students at San Jacinto High School, and if they were told to read it, they would not have been interested anyway. But it seemed to me that suppressing it made it more alluring. Because I read it clandestinely, I knew nothing about its context. It would have been better to read it critically and discuss it, along with other books about Russian and Soviet history; as it was, all that we heard in our classes was crude anticommunist propaganda.

While I was in junior high school and high school, a right-wing group called the Minute Women of the USA wreaked havoc on the school system with a campaign of intimidation and name-calling. The Minute Women were a potent political force in school politics in those years; they waged letter-writing campaigns, heckled speakers, harassed political opponents, and ran candidates for public office. For several years, they actually dominated the school board and used their control to toss out textbooks and humiliate teachers and administrators whose views offended them. I don't think it is an overstatement to say that the Minute Women unleashed a reign of terror during their brief ascendancy.

Minute Women appeared unannounced in classrooms to monitor what teachers were saying. A survey by the National Education Association found that 37 percent of the city's teachers thought there was a spy system in the schools, and 60 percent had personally experienced "unwarranted pressures" by outsiders. Teachers knew that they were being watched, that their every word was noted; the fear among them was palpable. School board members pored over textbooks in search of words, phrases, and ideas that were "socialistic" and "communistic."[2]

The great battle for the soul of the Houston schools began in 1951, when the local chapter of the Minute Women was organized. About two hundred men and women formed the organization, which determined to combat what they perceived as creeping socialism in the public schools. The Minute Women devoted themselves to fighting communism, socialism, socialized medicine, and racial integration, as well as any textbooks that appeared to further these causes. They were fiercely opposed to the New Deal and to any expansion of the federal government, which they believed was synonymous with socialism; socialism, in their eyes, was a stage on the way to Soviet-style communism. Houston was a politically conservative city, and the chapter grew rapidly. In November 1952, the Minute Women succeeded in electing some of its members to the city's school board.

In 1951, I was a seventh-grade student at Albert Sidney Johnston Junior High School. What I learned in school was at odds with what I learned at home. My parents were yellow-dog Democrats (a yellow-dog Democrat, it was said, would vote for a yellow dog before he would vote for a Republican). At the dinner table, my parents told me that Franklin Delano Roosevelt was a great president, but at school I heard that FDR's New Deal was the beginning of creeping socialism. My parents loved Harry S Truman, but at school I was informed that he had undermined the military by firing General Douglas MacArthur. The general, we learned in school, was a heroic personification of American individualism. In the spring of 1951, all the loudspeakers in our junior high school broadcast MacArthur's "farewell speech" to a joint session of Congress ("Old soldiers never die, they just fade away," he said), and we students were expected to listen. Knowing how my parents felt and being somewhat rebellious by nature, I defiantly read a book while the general spoke, and I was given a "U" conduct rating for the semester because of my insubordination. And this was before the Minute Women got organized.

In 1952, the school system announced an essay contest on the subject of the United Nations. Apparently some administrator had made a terrible mistake, because the topic was hastily withdrawn (the subject, said an assistant superintendent, was "too controversial") and replaced by a new topic, "eternal vigilance is the price of liberty," a slogan that happened to be the credo of the Minute Women.

In junior high school, our classes were regularly assembled in the auditorium to hear anticommunist speakers or watch propaganda movies about the dangers of socialism and communism (the words were used interchangeably). One especially frightening film depicted life under socialism, in which a bewildered American family confronted a totalitarian state. A sepulchral voice told the family where to live and commanded the father to work at a job not of his choosing. Again and again the Godlike voice boomed out at the terrified family, telling them what to do. These stridently anticommunist films replaced the movies that taught racial and religious tolerance, like Frank Sinatra's *The House I Live In,* which I had seen as a seventh grader. That was the kind of "socialist" thinking that the Minute Women had organized to fight.

The school board scrutinized textbooks, especially those that dealt with political issues, and rejected anything that offended the right-wing majority. The leading textbook critic on the board was Mrs. Earl Maughmer, who objected strenuously to any positive mention of the United Nations or any "one world" philosophy. (She was always referred to as Mrs. Earl Maughmer; her own first name was never mentioned in newspaper articles.) Led by Mrs. Maughmer, the Houston school board rejected geography and economics textbooks that had already been approved by the state of Texas; Mrs. Maughmer said that they contained "UN propaganda" and advocated federal control of public services. The school system dropped a proposed high school geography course because the board had barred the textbooks needed to teach the course. In a cartoon in the *Houston Post,* a comic character said, "Texas is bounded on the north by the Red River," and another character replied, "There goes *that* geography book."[3]

I had two history instructors who represented opposite political extremes. My eleventh-grade American history teacher, Anastasia Doyle, believed that Senator Joseph McCarthy was the greatest living American. My ninth-grade world history teacher, Nelda Davis, stood up to the right-wing zealots who ran the school board and achieved heroic status in the eyes of many fellow teachers. Not long after I was a student in her class, Davis became the school district's supervisor of social studies. She was appointed during a two-year period when the right-wingers were briefly out of power. When Davis applied for funding to attend the annual meeting of the National Council for the Social Studies in Cleveland, the school board rejected her request. Mrs. Frank Dyer, a leader of the right-wing bloc, warned that there were two speakers at the Cleveland meeting who were associated with "communist-front groups." Mrs. Dyer said that she would not allow any school employee to go to any meeting at public expense unless she had personally reviewed the list of speakers and the content of their speeches. Colleagues of Davis, members of the public, and even the so-called liberal group on the school board contributed the necessary funds, and Davis, a thirty-year veteran of the Houston schools, went to the meeting despite the board majority's wrath.

Davis then ran afoul of the board again when it rejected geography and economics textbooks that a panel of teachers recommended. Davis was in charge of social sciences, and Mrs. Maughmer blamed her when the selection committee kept recommending the rejected books. Mrs. Maughmer charged that Davis had a conflict of interest in the textbook battle because she was under contract to write a world geography textbook for Macmillan, which had published one of the rejected books.

My former world history teacher was in the front-page headlines day after day as a target of Mrs. Maughmer and the other extremists on the board. She wasn't confrontational, but she didn't back down. Actually the school board made itself a laughingstock, because of the majority's wacky ideas and bullying tactics.

Davis stuck it out as supervisor of social studies until 1958, when she resigned to take an administrative position in Prince George's County in Maryland. About the same time, Macmillan and the Houston school board reached an agreement about the company's disputed geography textbook. Macmillan agreed to delete any words and sentences that were offensive to Mrs. Maughmer. The revised book no longer contained suggestions that the nations of the world needed to find common solutions to common problems and that the United Nations might help to secure international peace.

The publisher's surrender to the censors on the Houston school board was the high point of the right-wingers' reign. As McCarthyism waned in the rest of the country, it also waned in Houston. After years of contention, the school board changed hands, and the Minute Women never again controlled the schools. Over the next decade, black Houstonians were elected to the board, the schools were desegregated, and the right-wingers' irrational fears of subversion, the federal government, and the United Nations became historical curiosities rather than live causes. It was a source of joy to me that the Houston Independent School District, half a century later, won national recognition for its school reforms under the leadership of an African American superintendent, Rod Paige, who became U.S. secretary of education.

Battles over the political orientation of textbooks are nothing new in American educational history. Over the years, publishers have revised their textbooks or written new ones in response to political protest. For more than half a century after the Civil War, textbook publishers could not sell the same school histories in both the North and the South. When southern states demanded textbooks that presented the Confederacy sympathetically, and northern states insisted on textbooks that taught children about the southerners' treason, compliant publishers produced northern and southern editions of their histories. In the late nineteenth century, southern states initiated statewide textbook adoptions to make sure that no "partisan" (i.e., anti-Confederate) schoolbooks got into their children's hands. After World War I, during a period of superpatriotic fervor and xenophobia, American history textbooks were criticized by patriotic societies and ethnic organizations. The Veterans of Foreign Wars and the American Legion complained that "un-American" textbooks failed to instill a love of country. Ethnic organizations representing Irish Americans, German Americans, Jewish Americans, and African Americans demanded inclusion of their heroes in the textbooks. The Hearst newspapers launched a textbook investigation, as did elected officials in various cities and states. The most outspoken textbook critic was "Big Bill" Thompson, the mayor of Chicago, who accused the leading American history textbooks of being "pro-British," a charge that resonated with his Irish and German supporters. The textbooks' allegedly slavish devotion to all things British, he claimed, undermined children's respect for our Founding Fathers and their achievements. One of the targets was David Saville Muzzey's history of America, the most widely used high school textbook in the nation. Three state legislatures passed bills banning the adoption of any textbook that slighted the founders of the Republic or the preservers of the Union. Textbook authors and publishers responded to the critics by deleting allegedly pro-British passages and judgments from their books (such as the observation that some colonists did not want to separate from Britain) and increasing their patriotic references.[4]

At the same time, textbooks were attacked by other groups, such as antievolutionists, extremist xenophobes (like the Ku Klux Klan), the Daughters of the American Revolution, organized labor, the public utilities industry, and the Women's Christian Temperance Union. If the outcry was loud enough, the textbook publishers did some more trimming and revising. Some deleted any reference to evolution from their biology textbooks, in response to the agitation against Darwinism and the well-publicized trial of teacher John Scopes in Tennessee. Some strived to present organized labor in a favorable light, in cooperation with the American Federation of Labor's textbook review. At the same time, the public utility industry invested in a campaign to persuade publishers to remove material that it did not like and to write new interpretations that showed it in a favorable light.

In the late 1930s, with the political atmosphere overheated by omens of war in Europe and Asia, superpatriotic groups became concerned about radicalism in the schools and universities. The DAR and the American Legion were worried; so too was the Hearst press, which wrote scare stories about the influence of leftist professors on campus. Anticommunist crusaders issued lists that "named names" of individuals and organizations that had "knowingly or unknowingly" contributed to the growth of communist sentiment in the United States; these lists were used in many communities by right-wing textbook critics, who scrutinized references and bibliographies in textbooks to determine whether the books were relying on "subversive," "communist front" sources. A score of state legislatures enacted loyalty oaths for public school teachers. In 1938, the House of Representatives approved funding for its Un-American Activities Committee to investigate subversive activities by both fascists and communists. A number of states set up investigating committees to look for subversion in their public schools and colleges.

The series that caught the brunt of this wave of antiradicalism was Harold Rugg's social science textbooks. Rugg was a professor at

Teachers College, Columbia University, who had developed his series over many years while working at the experimental Lincoln School. His textbooks were read by millions of students in some five thousand schools across the country. Rugg was a leftist reformer who was part of a Teachers College group of professors who called themselves "frontier thinkers" and saw themselves as advocates of a new age of collectivism. In 1940, articles in two journals—*Nation's Business* and the *American Legion* magazine—accused Rugg of fomenting treason in his textbooks. Both articles were lurid exaggerations, but they found a ready audience. The Rugg books were burned in Ohio and banned in many other districts. Within a few years, the sales of the Rugg textbooks had fallen to a trickle.[5]

After World War II, as Cold War tensions grew, so too did the hunt for subversives and subversive textbooks in the schools. A variety of Red-hunting groups took up the cause, including the Minute Women, the Sons of the American Revolution, and various ad hoc organizations (such as the Guardians of American Education). As in the 1930s, they circulated names of writers and public figures whom they believed were communists or communist sympathizers, and the censors cited the appearance of these names in textbooks as evidence of a subversive political slant. If it gave too much attention to civil rights issues (or in some cases, any attention at all), a textbook might be branded as "pro-Red," especially in the South. In 1949, a new quarterly publication called *Educational Reviewer*, written by Lucille Cardin Crain, began to criticize textbooks for subversive leanings. One of her targets was a widely adopted high school civics book, Frank Magruder's *American Government*. Radio commentators and newspapers repeated her charges, and the book was dropped by some school districts. After the publisher agreed to revisions and deletions, the controversy subsided and the book was once again widely adopted. In 1958, E. Merrill Root's *Brainwashing in the High Schools* charged that eleven American history textbooks paralleled the Communist Party line; a year later the DAR published its own list of 170 subversive textbooks. These lists fueled many state and local textbook censorship battles. The well-worn themes were revived in the 1960s by the John Birch Society, which warned that communist-inspired ideologues were promoting sex education and promiscuity in the schools.

The anticommunist campaign against subversive textbooks was replaced in the 1980s by an equally impassioned crusade against immoral books and textbooks. Right-wing groups shifted their focus from the communist threat to religious and moral issues. Groups such as the Reverend Jerry Falwell's Moral Majority, Phyllis Schlafly's Eagle Forum, the Reverend Donald Wildmon's American Family Association, Dr. James Dobson's Focus on the Family, the Reverend Pat Robertson's National Legal Foundation, and Beverly LaHaye's Concerned Women for America, along with Mel and Norma Gabler's Educational Research Analysts in Texas, pressured local school districts and state boards of education to remove books that they considered objectionable. The New Right attacked textbooks for teaching secular humanism, which they defined as a New-Age religion that ignored biblical teachings and shunned moral absolutes. If it was right to exclude the Christian religion from the public schools, they argued, then secular humanism should be excluded too. If it was acceptable to teach secular humanism, they said, then Christian teaching should have equal time. The textbooks, said the critics, failed to distinguish between right and wrong, and thus taught the "situation ethics" of "secular humanism." They disapproved of portrayals of abortion, out-of-wedlock pregnancy, homosexuality, suicide, drug use, foul language, or other behavior that conflicted with their religious values. The right-wing critics also opposed stories that showed dissension within the family; such stories, they believed, would teach children to be disobedient and would damage families. They also insisted that textbooks must be patriotic and teach a positive view of the nation and its history.

Textbook publishers were in an impossible situation. On the one hand, they were pressed on all sides to be studiously neutral by removing every point of view and every potential controversy from their books; on the other, fundamentalist parents complained that the textbooks' neutrality was a failure to take a stand on behalf of correct morality. The harder the textbook editors tried to make their products inclusive of all points of view without endorsing any, the more impossible it was to satisfy both the Christian New Right and those who did not share its fundamentalist theology.

The teaching of evolution was extensively litigated in the 1980s. The scientific community weighed in strongly on the side of evolution as the only scientifically grounded theory for teaching about biological origins. Fundamentalist Christians, however, insisted that public schools should give equal time to teaching the biblical version of creation. Several southern legislatures passed laws requiring "balanced treatment" of evolution and creationism, but such laws were consistently found to be unconstitutional by federal courts, which held that evolution is science, and creationism is religion. In 1987, the United States Supreme Court ruled 7–2 against Louisiana's "balanced treatment" law. Yet fundamentalist insistence on "creation science" or "intelligent design" continued unabated. When states debated the adoption of science textbooks or science standards, critics demanded that competing theories should get equal time. In 2000, Republican primary voters in Kansas defeated two state school board members who had voted to remove evolution from the state's science standards.

The religious right mounted numerous challenges to textbooks in the 1980s. The most important was the case of *Mozert* v. *Hawkins County Board of Education* in Tennessee. In 1983, fundamentalist Christian parents in Hawkins County objected to the elementary school textbooks that were required reading in their schools. The readers were published by Holt, Rinehart and Winston (now owned by Harcourt). The parents complained that the textbooks promoted secular humanism, satanism, witchcraft, fantasy, magic, the occult, disobedience, dishonesty, feminism, evolution, telepathy, one-world government, and New Age religion. They also asserted that some of the stories in the readers belittled the government, the military, free enterprise, and Christianity. At first the parents wanted the textbooks removed from the local public schools. Eventually, however, they sought only that their own children be allowed to read alternate books that did not demean their religious views.

The parents received legal support from the Concerned Women for America. The school board was backed by the liberal People for the American Way. The battle turned into an epic left-right political showdown: one side claimed that the case was about censorship, and the other side argued that it was about freedom of religion.

For five years the case garnered national headlines as it wound its way up and down the federal court system. In 1987, the parents lost in federal appeals court, and in 1988, the United States Supreme Court decided not to review the appellate court decision. The judges decided that "mere exposure" to ideas different from those of the parents' religious faith did not violate the First Amendment's guarantee of free exercise of religion.

Defenders of the Holt Basic Readers celebrated their legal victory, but it was a hollow one. In a comprehensive account of the case, Stephen Bates noted that the Holt readers were "once the most popular reading series in the nation," but were brought to "the verge of extinction" by the controversy associated with the court case.[6] If publishers learned a lesson from the saga of the Holt reading series, it was the importance of avoiding controversy by censoring themselves in advance and including nothing that might attract bad publicity or litigation. The 1986 revision of the series, designed to replace the 1983 edition that was on trial in Tennessee, omitted some of the passages that fundamentalist parents objected to. The Holt readers won the legal battle but were commercially ruined. This was not a price that any textbook publisher would willingly pay.

A third major area for litigation in the 1980s involved efforts to ban books, both those that were assigned in class and those that were available in the school library. The first major test came not in the South but in the Island Trees Union Free School District in New York. There the local board directed school officials to remove ten books from their libraries because of their profanity and explicit sexual content, including Bernard Malamud's *The Fixer,* Richard Wright's *Black Boy,* Kurt Vonnegut's *Slaughterhouse-Five,* and Eldridge Cleaver's *Soul on Ice.* The courts traditionally deferred to school officials when it came to curriculum and other policy making, but in this instance the students who objected to the school officials' decision won by a narrow one-vote margin. In 1982, the United States Supreme Court ruled that the students had a "right to receive information." The decision was far from conclusive, however, as the justices wrote seven opinions, none of which had majority support.

Many book-banning incidents were never challenged in the courts. In the 1970s and 1980s, school officials in different sections of the country removed certain books from school libraries or from classroom use, including J. D. Salinger's *Catcher in the Rye,* John Steinbeck's *Grapes of Wrath,* Aldous Huxley's *Brave New World,* George Orwell's *1984,* MacKinley Kantor's *Andersonville,* and Gordon Parks's *Learning Tree.* In most cases, parents criticized the books' treatment of profanity, sex, religion, race, or violence.

The battle of the books shifted to Florida in the late 1980s. In Columbia County, a parent (who was a fundamentalist minister) complained to the local school board about a state-approved textbook used in an elective course for high school students. The parent objected to the book because it included Chaucer's "The Miller's Tale" and Aristophanes' *Lysistrata*. The school board banned the book, and its decision was upheld in federal district court and in an appellate court. In Bay County, a parent complained about Robert Cormier's *I Am the Cheese,* a work of adolescent fiction that contains some mild profanity and not especially explicit sexual scenes. The school superintendent suppressed not only that book but required teachers to write a rationale for every book they intended to assign unless it was on the state-approved list. The superintendent then proscribed a long list of literary classics that he deemed controversial, including several of Shakespeare's plays, Charles Dickens's *Great Expectations,* F. Scott Fitzgerald's *Great Gatsby,* and Ernest Hemingway's *A Farewell to Arms.* Parents, teachers, and students sued the local school board and the superintendent to prevent the book-banning, and a federal district judge ruled that it was acceptable to remove books because of vulgar language but not because of disagreement with the ideas in them. The litigation soon became moot, however, when the superintendent retired, and all of the books were restored in that particular district.

During the 1980s and 1990s, and after, there were numerous challenges to books by parents and organized groups. Many were directed against adolescent fiction, as authors of this genre became increasingly explicit about sexuality and more likely to utilize language and imagery that some adults considered inappropriate for children. The thirty "most frequently attacked" books from 1965 to the early 1980s included some that offended adults from different ends of the political spectrum. Some were assigned in class; others were in the school library. The list included:

> *The Adventures of Huckleberry Finn* by Mark Twain
> *The Diary of a Young Girl* by Anne Frank
> *Black Like Me* by John Howard Griffin
> *Brave New World* by Aldous Huxley
> *The Catcher in the Rye* by J. D. Salinger
> *Deliverance* by James Dickey
> *The Electric Kool-Aid Acid Test* by Tom Wolfe
> *A Farewell to Arms* by Ernest Hemingway
> *Go Ask Alice* by Anonymous

The Good Earth by Pearl Buck

The Grapes of Wrath by John Steinbeck

A Hero Ain't Nothin' but a Sandwich by Alice Childress

If Beale Street Could Talk by James Baldwin

I Know Why the Caged Bird Sings by Maya Angelou

Johnny Got His Gun by Dalton Trumbo

The Learning Tree by Gordon Parks

Lord of the Flies by William Golding

Love Story by Erich Segal

Manchild in the Promised Land by Claude Brown

My Darling, My Hamburger by Paul Zindel

1984 by George Orwell

Of Mice and Men by John Steinbeck

One Day in the Life of Ivan Denisovich by Alexander
   Solzhenitsyn

One Flew Over the Cuckoo's Nest by Ken Kesey

Ordinary People by Judith Guest

Our Bodies, Ourselves by the Boston Women's Health Book
   Collective

The Scarlet Letter by Nathaniel Hawthorne

A Separate Peace by John Knowles

Slaughterhouse-Five by Kurt Vonnegut

To Kill a Mockingbird by Harper Lee[7]

By 2000, the American Library Association's list of the "most attacked" books had changed considerably. Most of the classics had fallen away. At the beginning of the new millennium, the most challenged books were of the Harry Potter series, assailed because of their references to the occult, satanism, violence, and religion, as well as Potter's dysfunctional family. Most of the other works that drew fire were written specifically for adolescents. Some of these books were taught in classes; others were available in libraries.[8]

The most heated controversy over textbooks in the early 1990s involved a K-6 reading series called Impressions, which was published by Holt, Rinehart and Winston. The Impressions series consisted of grade-by-grade anthologies with a cumulative total of more than eight hundred reading selections from authors such as C. S. Lewis, Lewis Carroll, the Brothers Grimm, Rudyard Kipling, Martin Luther King Jr., and Laura Ingalls Wilder. Its purpose was to replace the old-fashioned "Dick and Jane"–style reader with literary anthologies of high interest for children.

The texts may have been altogether too interesting, because they captured the avid attention of conservative family groups across the country. Before they became infamous among right-wing groups, the books were purchased by more than 1,500 elementary schools in thirty-four states. A small proportion of the series' literary selections, some of them drawn from classic fairy tales, described magic, fantasy, goblins, monsters, and witches.

Right-wing Christian groups, including Focus on the Family, Citizens for Excellence in Education, and the Traditional Values Coalition, organized against the Impressions series. The controversy became especially fierce in the early 1990s in California. The state-approved textbooks came under fire in half of California's school districts. Large numbers of parents turned out for school board meetings to demand the removal of the readers, which they claimed were terrifying their children. One district glued together some pages in the books to satisfy critics. Some districts dropped the series. Critics objected to stories about death, violence, and the supernatural. They charged that the series was promoting a New Age religion of paganism, the occult, and witchcraft. In one district, angry parents initiated a recall campaign against two local school board members who supported the books (the board members narrowly survived the recall vote). In another district, an evangelical Christian family filed a lawsuit charging that the district—by using the Impressions textbooks—violated the Constitution by promoting a religion of "neo-paganism," which relied on magic, trances, a veneration for nature and animal life, and a belief in the supernatural. In 1994, a federal appeals court ruled that the textbook series did not violate the Constitution.

Public ridicule helped to squelch some of the ardor of those who wanted to censor books. Editorial writers across California uniformly opposed efforts to remove the Impressions series from the public schools, providing important encouragement for public officials who were defending the books. The editorial writers read the books and saw that they contained good literature. Most reckoned that children do not live in a hermetically sealed environment. Children, they recognized, see plenty of conflict and violence on television and in real life as well. They confront, sooner or later, the reality of death and loss.

Most know the experience of losing a family member, a pet, a friend. Over the generations, fairy tales have served as a vehicle for children to deal with difficult situations and emotions. Even the Bible, the most revered of sacred documents in Western culture, is replete with stories of violence, betrayal, family dissension, and despicable behavior.

One cannot blame parents for wanting to protect their children's innocence from the excesses of popular culture. However, book censorship far exceeds reasonableness; usually, censors seek not just freedom from someone else's views, but the power to impose their views on others. Parents whose religious beliefs cause them to shun fantasy, magic, fairy tales, and ghost stories will have obvious difficulties adjusting to parts of the literature curriculum in public schools today. They would have had equal difficulty adjusting to the literary anthologies in American public schools one hundred years ago, which customarily included myths and legends, stories about disobedient children, even tales of magical transformation. It may be impossible for a fundamentalist Christian (or Orthodox Jew or fundamentalist Muslim) to feel comfortable in a public institution that is committed to tolerance and respect among all creeds and promotion of none. This conflict cannot be avoided. Much of what is most imaginative in our culture draws upon themes that will prove objectionable to fundamentalist parents of every religion. Schools may offer alternative readings to children of fundamentalist parents, but they cannot provide readings of a sectarian nature, nor should the schools censor or ban books at the insistence of any religious or political group.

Even though the religious right has consistently lost court battles, its criticisms have not been wasted on educational publishers. The Impressions series, for all its literary excellence, was not republished, and quietly vanished.

Fear of the pressures that sank the Impressions series has made publishers gun-shy about any stories that might anger fundamentalists. Textbook publishers are understandably wary about doing anything that would unleash hostile charges and countercharges and cause a public blowup over their product.

Publishers of educational materials do not want controversy (general publishers, of course, love controversy because it sells books in a competitive marketplace). Even if a publisher wins in court, its books are stigmatized as "controversial." Even if a textbook is adopted by a district or state over protests, it will lose in other districts that want to avoid similar battles. It is a far, far better thing to have no protests at all. Publishers know that a full-fledged attack, like the one waged against Impressions, means death to their product. And the best recipe for survival in a marketplace dominated by the political decisions of a handful of state boards is to delete whatever might offend anyone.

SIX

Censorship from the Left

Any writer who follows anyone else's guidelines ought
to be in advertising.

—Nat Hentoff

THE PRESSURE groups of left and right have important points of
convergence. Both right-wingers and left-wingers demand that publishers shield children from words and ideas that contain what they
deem the "wrong" models for living. Both assume that by limiting
what children read, they can change society to reflect their worldview.

Neither side, however, acknowledges that its efforts at censorship
are doomed to fail since schools compete for children's attention with
far more powerful media. Does it really matter if a child never reads
a textbook story with strong males or disobedient children, never
encounters the word *mankind* or images of the occult, if that same
child also watches television or sees movies where such images prevail?

The left-wing groups that have been most active in campaigns to
change textbooks are militantly feminist and militantly liberal. These
groups hope to bring about an equitable society by purging certain
language and images from textbooks.

Lee Burress, a leader of anticensorship activities for many years in
the National Council of Teachers of English, describes in *The Battle of
the Books* how feminists and liberals became censors as they sought to
"raise consciousness" and to eliminate "offensive" stories and books.
Joan DelFattore, in *What Johnny Shouldn't Read*, writes that political
correctness, taken to its extreme, "denotes a form of intellectual terror-

ism in which people who express ideas that are offensive to any group other than white males of European heritage may be punished, *regardless of the accuracy or relevance of what they say*" (italics in the original). The censors from the left and right, she says, compel writers, editors, and public officials to suppress honest questions and to alter facts "solely to shape opinion." Once a society begins limiting freedom of expression to some points of view, then "all that remains is a trial of strength" to see whose sensibilities will prevail.[1]

While the censors on the right have concentrated most of their ire on general books, the censors on the left have been most successful in criticizing textbooks. Although left-wing censors have occasionally targeted books too, they have achieved their greatest influence by shaping the bias guidelines of the educational publishing industry. Educational publishers have willingly acquiesced even to the most far-fetched demands for language censorship, so long as the campaign's stated goal is "fairness." Only a George Orwell could fully appreciate how honorable words like *fairness* and *diversity* have been deployed to impose censorship and uniformity on everyday language.

Since the 1950s, the leading target of left-wing censors has been Mark Twain's *The Adventures of Huckleberry Finn*. This book has unsettled people ever since it was published in 1885. The only thing that has changed over the years has been various groups' reasons for banning it. As soon as it was published, libraries began excluding it because of Twain's use of dialect and Huck Finn's rude behavior. Since the 1950s, black civil rights activists have sought to remove it from the classroom because of its repeated use of the word *nigger* and Twain's portrayal of the runaway slave Jim. The New York City Board of Education dropped the book in 1957 because it was "racially offensive." In 1982, in one of the ironic moments in the history of censorship, the principal of the Mark Twain Intermediate School in Fairfax County, Virginia, attempted to remove the book, calling it "racist trash." Black parents have complained about the book in many different school districts across the nation, trying to get it banned. Sometimes they succeeded, sometimes they didn't, but in every case their complaint was the same: The book's language is insensitive and offensive.

There are many reasons not to censor *Huckleberry Finn*. The book's centrality in American literature is chief among them; Ernest Hemingway famously wrote in *The Green Hills of Africa* that "all modern literature comes from one book by Mark Twain called *Huckleberry Finn*."

Twain was not racist; on the contrary, he was one of the most powerful voices of his age against racism and social injustice. Teachers and students alike must learn to grapple with this novel, which they cannot do unless they read it.

Twain's use of the word *nigger* will ensure that *Huckleberry Finn* remains controversial long into the future. Some publishers have replaced the word with substitutes, like *slave* or *servant* or *hand.* The literary critic Lionel Trilling insisted that the book should be read as Twain wrote it, including that word: "This is the only word for a Negro that a boy like Huck would know in his place and time—that is, an ignorant boy in the South before the Civil War."[2] Even if offensive words were blotted from our language, he wrote, "the fact that they were once freely used ought not be suppressed. For it is a fact that forms part of our national history, and a national history is not made up of pleasant and creditable things only. And it is a part of the consciousness of themselves of each of the ethnic groups who have had to endure one or another degree of social disadvantage; it is something to be confronted and dealt with, not evaded or forgotten."

Perhaps the best single treatment of the controversy surrounding the book is Jocelyn Chadwick-Joshua's *The Jim Dilemma: Reading Race in Huckleberry Finn.*[3] The slave Jim, she points out, is a man of great dignity, integrity, and humanity in a world of scoundrels and hypocrites; as a black man (and as an escaped slave), he knows when to wear a mask and when to disguise his voice. Chadwick-Joshua, an African American scholar, has defended the book to local school boards and argued for its importance in understanding our nation's history and literature. *The Jim Dilemma* explains why black and white students should read *Huckleberry Finn* without bowdlerization.

The organization that led the left-wing censorship campaign was the Council on Interracial Books for Children (CIBC). Founded in 1966 in New York City, CIBC was active over the next quarter-century as the best-known critic of racism and sexism in children's books and textbooks. Directing its critiques not as much to the general public as to the publishing industry and educators, CIBC issued publications and conducted seminars for librarians and teachers to raise their consciousness about racism and sexism.

CIBC ceased its organizational life in 1990; its most enduring legacy proved to be its guidelines, which explained how to identify racism, sexism, and ageism, as well as a variety of other -isms. They were the original template for the detailed bias guidelines that are now pervasive in the education publishing industry and that ban specific words, phrases, roles, activities, and images in textbooks and on tests. The CIBC guidelines are still cited; they circulate on many Web sites, and they continue to serve as training materials for bias and sensitivity reviewers.[4]

CIBC's initial goal was to encourage publishers to include more realistic stories and more accurate historical treatments about blacks, Hispanics, Native Americans, and women. It awarded annual prizes for the best new children's books by minority writers. However, soon after it was founded in the mid-1960s, the political and cultural climate changed dramatically. In the wake of riots and civil disorders in major American cities, including New York, the racial integration movement was swept away by movements for racial separatism and black power. CIBC was caught up in the radicalism of the times. Its goals shifted from inclusion to racial assertiveness, from the pursuit of racial harmony to angry rhetoric about colonialism and the "educational slaughter" of minority children. As its militancy grew, CIBC insisted that only those who were themselves members of a minority group were qualified to write about their own group's experience. It demanded that publishers subsidize minority-owned bookstores, printers, and publishers. It urged teachers and librarians to watch for and exclude those books that violated its bias guidelines.

CIBC's critiques of racial and gender stereotyping undoubtedly raised the consciousness of textbook publishers about the white-only world of their products and prompted necessary revisions. However, in the early 1970s, CIBC demanded elimination of books that it deemed "anti-human," racist, and sexist. Insisting that children's books "mold minds," CIBC urged librarians to take action against racist and sexist books. To help librarians and teachers identify books that were racist and sexist, CIBC evaluated current titles. Its representatives lobbied the American Library Association to change its policies on intellectual freedom and to encourage librarians to exclude "biased" books. CIBC spokesmen argued that the First Amendment rights of textbook writers and publishers were superseded by the Fourteenth Amendment rights of students to be protected from books that "inflicted injury that required remedial action." Arguing that current educational materials were so biased that they harmed students who were not white males, CIBC urged the federal government to regulate the publishing and communications industries.[5]

Under pressure from CIBC, the American Library Association debated whether librarians should take a stand against reprehensible expression. In 1973, the ALA passed a resolution called "Sexism, Racism, and Other -Isms in Library Materials," which reaffirmed the organization's opposition to any efforts to remove, restrict, or attach stigmatizing labels to books that were "allegedly derogatory to specific minorities or which supposedly perpetuate stereotypes and false images of minorities." The statement ended with a ringing affirmation that "intellectual freedom, in its purest sense, promotes no causes, furthers no movements, and favors no viewpoints. It only provides for free access to all ideas through which any and all sides of causes and movements may be expressed, discussed, and argued. The librarian cannot let his own preferences limit his degree of tolerance, for freedom is indivisible. Toleration is meaningless without toleration for the detestable."[6]

This eloquent statement did not end the debate, however. CIBC pressed on, demanding that the ALA abandon its neutrality and firmly oppose racism and sexism in library collections. In 1979, CIBC won a surprise victory at the annual meeting of the ALA. Although it was not scheduled to participate in the conference, it lobbied for a resolution against racism and sexism and in favor of sensitivity training for librarians and library users. During a two-and-a-half-hour debate on the conference floor, some librarians expressed fears of censorship but the resolution swept through to approval. CIBC scoffed at those who worried about censorship and hailed the resolution as a far-reaching plan to combat racism and sexism in American libraries.[7]

The ALA did initiate workshops to raise consciousness about racism and sexism, but over the next few years it maneuvered back into its traditional defense of intellectual freedom. In 1982, it rescinded its earlier policy on "Sexism, Racism, and Other -Isms" and replaced it with a policy called "Diversity in Collection Development." This statement decried censorship and said that "removing or not selecting materials because they are considered by some as racist or sexist" was an example of censorship. It also affirmed the librarians' responsibility to give all library users equal protection in their "liberty to read, view, or listen to materials and resources protected by the First Amendment, no matter what the viewpoint of the author, creator, or selector." It dropped the rather elegant argument that intellectual freedom "promotes no causes, furthers no movements, and favors no viewpoints," but reiterated that "intellectual freedom, the essence of equitable library services, provides for free access to all expressions of ideas through which any and all sides of a question, cause, or movement may be explored."[8]

Even as it was battling to persuade the nation's librarians that they must label or isolate racist and sexist texts, CIBC attacked numerous literary classics as racist, including Hugh Lofting's Dr. Dolittle books, Pamela Travers's *Mary Poppins*, Harriet Beecher Stowe's *Uncle Tom's Cabin*, Theodore Taylor's *The Cay*, Ezra Jack Keats's books (*Snowy Day* and *Whistle for Willie*), Roald Dahl's *Charlie and the Chocolate Factory*, and William H. Armstrong's *Sounder*.[9] The American publisher of Dr. Dolittle, agreeing that the series contained stereotypical images of Africans, expurgated the books to remove offensive illustrations and text. The original version of the books has now disappeared from library shelves and bookstores.

CIBC attacked fairy tales as sexist, asserting that they promote "stereotypes, distortions, and anti-humanism." It charged that such traditional tales as "Little Red Riding Hood," "Cinderella," "Jack and the Beanstalk," "Snow-White," "Beauty and the Beast," "The Princess and the Pea," "Rumpelstiltskin," and "Hansel and Gretel" were irredeemably sexist because they portrayed females as "princesses or poor girls on their way to becoming princesses, fairy godmothers or good fairies, wicked and evil witches, jealous and spiteful sisters, proud, vain and hateful stepmothers, or shrewish wives." The "good" females were depicted as beautiful, the "bad" ones as evil witches. The males were powerful and courageous, while the females were assigned to "traditional" roles as helpers. Typically, the characters in fairy tales rose from poverty to great wealth, CIBC complained, but no one ever asked about "the socioeconomic causes of their condition"; no one ever talked about the need for "collective action" to overcome injustice. In the eyes of CIBC, fairy tales were not only rife with sexist stereotypes, but with materialism, elitism, ethnocentrism, and racism too.[10]

CIBC's *Human (and Anti-Human) Values in Children's Books* listed 235 children's books published in 1975. Each was evaluated against a checklist that measured whether it was racist, sexist, elitist, materialist, ageist, conformist, escapist, or individualist; or whether it was opposed to those values or indifferent to them; whether it "builds a positive image of females/minorities" or "builds a negative image of females/minorities"; whether it "inspires action vs. oppression"; and whether it is "culturally authentic." Only members of a specific group reviewed books about their own group: Blacks reviewed books about blacks, Chicanos reviewed books about Chicanos, and so on. Few of the books reviewed had any lasting significance, and few of them are still in print a quarter-century later. One that is still read is John D. Fitzgerald's *The Great Brain Does It Again,* which CIBC rated as racist, sexist, materialist, individualist, conformist, and escapist.

The author Nat Hentoff reacted angrily to what he called CIBC's "righteous vigilanteism." Although he agreed with the council's egalitarian goals, he warned that its bias checklists and its demands for political correctness would stifle free expression. He interviewed other writers who complained about the CIBC checklist but were fearful of being identified. CIBC's efforts to eliminate offensive books and to rate books for their political content, he argued, were creating a climate in which "creative imagination, the writer's and the child's, must hide to survive." Its drive against "individualism," he said, was antithetical to literature and the literary imagination: "Collectivism is for politics," he said, not for writers.[11]

In retrospect, CIBC appears to have had minimal impact on general books. Despite having been denounced as racist, *The Cay* and *Sounder* remain commercially successful. Fairy tales continue to enchant children (although they are seldom found in textbooks and are usually bowdlerized). The public was only dimly aware, if at all, of CIBC's lists of stereotypes, its reviews, and its ratings. Publishers kept printing and selling children's books that defied CIBC's strictures.

Where CIBC did make a difference, however, was with publishers of K–12 textbooks. Textbook houses could not risk ignoring CIBC or its labeling system. No publisher could afford to enter a statewide adoption process with a textbook whose contents had been branded racist or sexist or ageist or handicapist or biased against any other group. The publishers' fear of stigma gave CIBC enormous leverage. When publishers began writing their own bias guidelines in the late 1960s and early 1970s, they consulted with CIBC or hired members of its editorial advisory board to counsel them about identifying bias. James Banks, a member of the CIBC advisory board, wrote the bias guidelines for McGraw-Hill; his wife, Cherry A. McGee Banks, was one of the main writers of the Scott Foresman–Addison Wesley guidelines.

CIBC multiplied its effectiveness when it worked in tandem with the National Organization for Women (NOW), which was also founded in 1966. Unlike CIBC, which operated from New York City, NOW had chapters in every state. CIBC and NOW frequently collaborated to fight sexism and to promote language censorship in the publishing industry and in textbooks. Feminist groups, some associated with NOW, others operating independently, testified at state hearings against unacceptable textbooks, pressured state and local school boards to exclude such books, and lobbied publishers to expunge sexist language from their books. Feminists demanded a 50–50 ratio of girls and boys, women and men, in every book. They counted illustrations to see how many female characters were represented. They noted whether girls and women were in passive or active roles as compared to boys and men. They made lists of the occupations represented, insisted that women have equal representation in professional roles, and objected if illustrations showed women as housewives, baking cookies, or sewing. They hectored publishers, textbook committees, and school boards with their complaints. And they made a difference.

In 1972, a group called Women on Words and Images published a pamphlet titled *Dick and Jane as Victims: Sex Stereotyping in Children's Readers,* which documented the imbalanced representation of boys and girls in reading textbooks. In the most widely used readers of the mid-1960s, boys were more likely to be lead characters and to play an active role as compared to girls, who were portrayed as dependent, passive, and interested only in shopping and dressing up. At textbook hearings around the country, feminist groups brandished the book and demanded changes. Within a year of the pamphlet's appearance, the authors reported that they had drawn national attention to the problem. Publishers consulted with them for advice about how to revise their materials.[12] By the mid-1970s, every major publishing company had adopted guidelines that banned sexist language and stereotypes from their textbooks.

By adopting bias guidelines, the publishers agreed to police their products and perform the censorship demanded by the politically correct left and the religious right. Publishers found it easier to exclude anything that offended anybody, be they feminists, religious groups, racial and ethnic groups, the disabled, or the elderly, rather than to get into a public controversy and see their product stigmatized. It was not all that difficult to delete a story or a paragraph or a test item, and most of the time no one noticed anyway.

The publishers reacted differently to pressure groups from the left and right. Companies did not share the Christian fundamentalist values of right-wing groups; they sometimes fought them in court, as Holt did when its elementary readers were challenged in Tennessee in the mid-1980s. By contrast, editors at the big publishing companies often agreed quietly with the feminists and civil rights groups that attacked their textbooks; by and large, the editors and the left-wing critics came from the same cosmopolitan worlds and held similar political views. The publishers and editors did not mind if anyone thought them unsympathetic to the religious right, but they did not want to be considered racist by their friends, family, and professional peers. Nor did they oppose feminist demands for textbook changes, which had the tacit or open support of their own female editors. In retrospect, this dynamic helps to explain why the major publishing companies swiftly accepted the sweeping linguistic claims of feminist critics and willingly yielded to a code of censorship.

Publishing companies zealously protect the confidentiality of their internal discussions. However, in the mid-1980s, when fundamentalist parents in Hawkins County, Tennessee, sued Holt, Rinehart and Winston in *Mozert v. Hawkins County Board of Education*, 2,261 pages of correspondence among editors and executives at the company were subpoenaed and entered into the court records. Stephen Bates, the author of *Battleground*, a study of that controversy, first reported on the content of these documents, and he made them available to me for this book. These files reveal in clear detail the political warfare waged against Holt's reading series by partisans of both right and left, as well as the private exchanges among editors about how to react to the latest salvo from a left-wing or right-wing group.

The Holt reading series reached the market in 1973, just as the great wave of feminist criticism broke over the publishing industry, and it was in trouble with feminists from the beginning. The Holt Basic Readers contained a good deal of excellent literature, but by today's standards, the 1973 edition was undeniably sexist: Women and girls played subordinate roles, while men and boys were frequently shown in active and dominant occupations. The first-grade book declared that dolls and dresses were for girls, and that trains and planes were for boys. Stories and illustrations contained more male characters than female characters. All of this material had passed through the hands of female authors, female editors, and female text designers, with no one noticing the disparate treatment of boys and girls. But as feminist criticism intensified, Holt, Rinehart and Winston issued its guidelines on "the treatment of sex roles and minorities" in 1975, and revised its popular readers in 1977 to expand the representation of females and minorities in the text and art and to eliminate any sexist language.

As soon as the Holt series was published, the complaints began to pour in from conservative parents as well. The Indianapolis school board said that it would not adopt the series unless certain words, phrases, paragraphs, and stories that offended conservative parents were deleted. These parents objected to stories that included the word *hate* or that seemed to condone lying or bad behavior or anger or family disunity; they positively despised a story called "How to Keep the Cousin You Hate from Spending the Whole Weekend at Your House and Maybe Even Longer" because it used the word *hate* and showed two boys sharing the same bed, which might foster "homosexualism."[13]

No sooner had the editors begun changing offensive words, cutting paragraphs, eliminating problematic stories, and pasting in new material in response to conservative complaints than the feminist tide rose up and crashed over them. In 1973, feminists in California attacked every reading textbook considered for statewide adoption, including the Holt Basic Reading series. NOW lodged a formal complaint with the state's curriculum commission, and a group called the Task Force on Sexism urged the California State Board of Education to reject dozens of reading and literature textbooks because of their sexism. Feminists lined up to testify against the textbooks at public hearings and gathered signatures and testimony from large numbers of sympathetic academics. Letters started arriving at the Holt offices with precise counts of the number of females and males represented in the text and artwork. Holt's California representative cautioned the home office that "the movement is gaining momentum like you have never seen in this state and I am sure that it is going to spread to every other state in the same manner."

Even in Texas, known for its conservatism, the state board of education reacted to complaints from feminists. It ruled in 1973 that textbooks henceforth would have to present both men and women in a variety of roles and activities, including "women in leadership and other positive roles with which they are not traditionally identified." This directive coexisted with the Texas board's existing mandate that textbooks promote citizenship, patriotism, and "respect for recognized authority," while excluding any selections "which contribute to civil disorder, social strife, or flagrant disregard of the law." In the fall of 1974, feminists in Oregon and Arizona joined the protests against reading textbooks, and Holt internally decided to issue a special revised "California edition" for California, Oregon, and Arizona.

As feminists raised the heat on textbook publishers, other critics objected to the depiction of race and ethnicity in literature books. In 1974, a group in California called the Standing Committee to Review Textbooks from a Multicultural Perspective identified racism in such phrases as "the deputy's face darkened," "the afternoon turned black," and "it's going to be a black winter." This committee also complained that the reading textbooks were unacceptably biased toward Judeo-Christian teaching, ignoring other religious traditions.

As they began revising the reading books to meet feminist and multicultural demands, the Holt editors quickly concluded that the next edition would have to contain a precise ratio of at least 50 percent females and a representation of minority groups based on their percentage of the population. The editors began fumbling their way toward a consensus about portraying women and ethnic minorities. They agreed they would show American Indians in business suits, not in traditional "hides and headdress." Girls would be pictured fixing a bicycle tire, not looking for a boy to do it, and a "Caucasian boy or man would be shown unashamedly crying if the situation were appropriate." Girls would be seen working with electricity, studying insects, and solving math problems, while boys would read poetry, chase butterflies, and pay attention to their personal appearance. Older people would not be depicted as living in nursing homes, wearing glasses, and using canes or wheelchairs. Almost overnight, the editors became absorbed in images, stereotypes, males cooking, and females driving tractor trailers.

Even the editors of Holt's high school literature series (*Concepts in Literature*) joined the effort to expunge older literary works that reflected outmoded views about women and minorities and to increase the representation of authors from these groups. Literary quality became secondary to representational issues. The female editor in charge of the high school series lamented that many of "the best modern works by and about members of these groups" were unacceptable for textbooks because of their language and "candid subject matter." Worse, from Holt's point of view, "attempts to have authors modify such works have rarely met with success." Recognized authors of "the best modern works" by and about women and minorities refused to permit the bowdlerization (or "adaptation," as the editors put it) of their writings to meet the publisher's need for stories that had no offensive language and the right head count of females and minorities.

During 1975, as the textbooks were being revised, the Holt editors worked with a numerical quota system, imposed by their own internal guidelines. These guidelines directed them to "familiarize yourself with the latest U.S. population figures so that our materials reflect current statistics. . . . Counting and chart-keeping should not be regarded as a useless editorial exercise. Careful tallies and analysis of how people are represented will reduce the need for costly reprint corrections and may prevent the loss of an adoption."

Trying to comply with these directives, the editors began searching, almost frantically, for new stories to increase the representation of females and minorities. In the internal exchange of memos, Bernard J. Weiss, the editor of the reading series, frequently admitted that a proposed story lacked literary quality but at least it had the right gender and ethnic representation. He said about one story: "I like the ethnic aspect. I like the use of a girl as the lead. I don't like the story. The urban setting is a plus." Another story was added that the editors agreed was "not great literature," but "We gain two points—a female leading character and characters with Spanish-American names." Weiss observed of another selection: "I agree that this story has very little literary merit. . . . However, it does help us to achieve some ethnic balance in a very *unbalanced* book." Stories were freely rewritten to change a character's job or role or ethnicity, even their gender. The editors changed the gender of the main character in Judy Blume's story "Freddie in the Middle," which became "Maggie in the Middle," with the author's consent (in the same story, Mrs. Jay became Mrs. Chang, to increase ethnic representation). In another story, a grandmother was added to increase the count of elderly persons in the book. Some stories were added to the revised edition even though Weiss thought they were of poor quality, in order to boost the number of female characters. After extensive revisions, an editor reported numerical success for one volume in the series: "The in-house count shows 146 female and 146 male characters, or a ratio of 1:1. Animal characters were not included in this count."

Despite Holt's valiant efforts to balance its characters by gender and ethnicity, the 1977 revised edition came under fire from feminists and multiculturalists anyway. Seattle's Ethnic Bias Review Committee found the new edition "unacceptable" because "while blacks are emphasized, it is a narrow representation of those in athletics and music," and besides, one of the books contained intolerable ethnic stereotypes: a black waiter and an Asian cook. A textbook adoption committee in New Mexico was not satisfied with Holt's statistics showing the proportion of characters by gender and minority status; it demanded to know the ethnic balance of both characters and authors. (Holt promptly responded with a list identifying their authors as Black, Puerto Rican, Oriental, American Indian, Hispanic, Jewish, Dutch, Polish, Greek, German, Italian, Scandinavian, Japanese, French, or Indian, as well as a breakdown of all main characters by gender and race.)

In 1980, the education task force of Texas NOW battered the Holt readers yet again at state textbook hearings. Holt's editors thought they had achieved a perfect 1:1 balance of male and female characters, but the Texas feminists said that when they added in animals, males actually outnumbered females by 2:1. A feminist critic pointed out "Children of this age are influenced by a story about Mr. Rabbit just as much as they are by a story about Mr. Jones." Reeling from the latest criticism, the Holt editors invited a feminist critic from Texas, members of the California committee that evaluated textbooks for sexism and racism, and the director of CIBC to review the company's bias guidelines.

Editors at Holt learned to look at every potential story through a political lens: What might anger the religious right? What might anger feminists and representatives of racial minorities? Does the story have a strong female character or a positive portrayal of an ethnic minority? Every entry, every chapter, every volume was measured against a detailed checklist to ensure that there was the right proportion of males, females, and minorities; even workbooks, drill sheets, and spelling exercises were carefully scrutinized, because California officials would reject the entire series if there was a gender imbalance in any part of it, including workbooks and drill sheets. At the same time that Holt editors were balancing these political demands, they were also simplifying the vocabulary of their readers, in response to complaints that they were too hard.

Occasionally Holt editors reminded themselves that the purpose of the reading series was to teach children to read, but their internal notes show that discussion of literary quality, pedagogical effectiveness, and interest level steadily diminished.

Ultimately, however, it proved impossible to please everyone. Holt did a better job of reaching out to left-wing pressure groups than to those on the right. The supervising editor of reading books at Holt described right-wingers as the kind of "censors" that one finds in "totalitarian societies," but characterized left-wing critics as "positive pressure groups," with whom the editors were prepared to collaborate. The more that Holt pleased "positive pressure groups" by increasing their feminist and multicultural content, the more the books offended conservatives. In the mid-1980s, conservative Christians in Tennessee sued their children's school district to stop them from mandating the Holt readers. Eventually the school district won, but afterward the publishing company let the Holt Basic Reading series go out of print. There were no more revisions. The Holt textbooks were destroyed by the censors of left and right. The textbooks became victims in a political Ping-Pong game that doomed them.

In my role as historian-detective, I searched for additional evidence of the influence of political pressures on textbooks. I asked several major publishers for access to their files related to these issues and, unsurprisingly, got polite turndowns. However, I did get a positive response from Blouke Carus, the founder of Open Court, which had been sold to McGraw-Hill in the mid-1990s. Since he no longer owned the business, Carus agreed to share letters and documents about its experiences in dealing with political pressures.

Open Court began publishing its reading books for elementary school in the mid-1960s. Unlike most other readers, which were a mélange of reading lessons and miscellaneous stories, the Open Court books were purposefully based on a traditionalist philosophy. As Carus wrote in an internal memo in the early days of the company, "We believe a solid dose of good literature in the tradition of the humanities, well taught, will do more than any other single thing to help children develop taste and judgment in the written and spoken word."[14] The reading lessons were grounded in phonics (at a time when phonics was out of favor among pedagogues), and the stories were carefully selected examples of high-quality classic children's literature (myths, fairy tales, legends, *Alice in Wonderland, Peter Rabbit,* "Horatius at the Bridge," etc.), along with biographies of famous people and hero tales. Open Court's primary goal was to teach children to read, which it apparently did with great success, but the publisher also aimed to convey a rich and positive immersion in the Anglo-American cultural heritage.

Almost as soon as the readers were published, the political complaints began to arrive. Some came from the right wing, which objected to stories about evolution; some came from African Americans, who wanted more attention to black heroes; eventually, most came from feminists criticizing the books' gender imbalance. The publisher at first tried to defend the books by reminding critics that they were a reading and literature program, not a social studies curriculum, but that got him nowhere. He told right-wing critics that if he excluded entries because he didn't agree with the author's political views, then he would have to eliminate everything by writers like Mark Twain and Benjamin Franklin, as well as Greek mythology; that too got him nowhere. As the books were revised, stories that offended the right and the left were quietly dropped, and new ones were added to plump up the number of ethnic and female characters.

It wasn't enough. In 1974, California rejected the Open Court readers because the books did not give appropriate representation to females and ethnic groups. The head of the State Curriculum Framework section of the state education department said that the books were unacceptable because they "contained old fashioned material and reflected against girls and ethnic groups." The state considered the books derogatory toward these groups because they did not have equal numbers of males and females and did not portray them in roles of equal status, especially in myths and fairy tales; the same went for ethnic groups, who were seldom included in European fairy tales and Greek myths. Losing the adoption meant that the state would not pay for the books if districts wanted to buy them. This was a huge disappointment for Open Court. A district superintendent in Fort Bragg, California, complained to the state education department that "the same rationale could place The Bible, Rubyiatt of Omar Khayan [sic],

Grimm's Fairy Tales, and Tales from the Decameron on the undesirable list."

After Open Court lost the California adoption, feminist organizations continued to criticize its books as sexist. Although the books contained references to women such as Mary McLeod Bethune, Pocahontas, Helen Keller, Joan of Arc, Anne Frank, Shirley Chisholm, Edith Cavell, and Mahalia Jackson, there were far more male heroes in the classic tales.

Eager to gain acceptance in California, the publisher invited representatives from NOW and other feminist organizations to collaborate on the revision. These groups identified stories about female heroes, including Elizabeth Blackwell, Marian Anderson, Susan B. Anthony, Harriet Tubman, Jane Addams, Mary Cassatt, Elizabeth I, and Amelia Earhart, which were incorporated into the new edition of the readers.

While Open Court was revising, its reading series came under attack in Teaneck, New Jersey, where one group of parents charged that the books were racist and sexist, while other parents praised them, saying that their children were learning to read well. When the readers came up for approval, the Teaneck Board of Education only narrowly approved them by a 5–4 margin, despite the fact that both white and black children who used the Open Court books were performing better than their peers in other reading programs.

In the fall of 1975, Open Court resubmitted its readers for adoption in California. Once again, they were rejected, because they still failed the state's demand for strict gender equality, both in numbers and roles. Open Court appealed the decision, complaining that the state unfairly objected to any portrayal of women in any household role, and, "further, one of these objections pertains to a quick reference to Mother Hubbard. . . . It is our belief that California law does not proscribe representation of traditional folk tales. . . . We therefore are not sure that Mother Hubbard can be accurately described as a stereotyped figure." The state also rejected Open Court's whimsical illustrations, which it called "simplistic and dehumanizing." Again, Open Court appealed, saying that the state guidelines did not require realistic art. The state also complained that the Open Court readers contained too many stories about animals; the publisher objected that nothing in the law banned anthropomorphic folktales. Even *The Little Engine That Could* was criticized by the state evaluators as gender imbalanced because the engine was portrayed as male (in future revisions, the engine was identified as female).

After this rejection, the publisher and his staff engaged in frank internal discussions about the propriety of "improving" classic folktales by changing the gender or ethnicity of its characters. The editors agreed that the readers would have to be balanced by race, gender, and culture, which was a commercial necessity. They were insistent that the books would "remain securely anchored in Western culture, particularly Anglo-Western culture," and that their content would distinguish them from other mass-market readers, which they called "the same old mush."

Open Court's efforts to win a spot on the California adoption list landed them in hot water with the right-wing textbook critics Mel and Norma Gabler. In 1979, the Gablers' "Recommended Textbook List for Private Schools" praised Open Court's phonetic reading methods but criticized the content: "During the 1960s the content was very good. However, we understand that the content was changed somewhat for the worse (evolution, integration, etc.) beginning with the 1970 edition. The greatest change came with the 1976 edition which added 'realistic' content (negative and depressing) and changed many of the pictures to gaudy 'contemporary' illustrations." Blouke Carus continued to receive letters from angry right-wing parents, complaining about the use of terms like *spelling demon* and *ghost*, which was offensive to their religious views. A parent in Michigan wrote Carus to express her outrage toward a story about a disobedient child, which she was certain had taught her own child to be disobedient. If the story was not promptly deleted, she threatened, she and her husband would "go to any lengths to have this book banned from our school system."

In various districts and states, Open Court continued to be whipsawed between pressure groups. Consistently, however, teachers defended them because their students were reading well. Blouke Carus discovered how difficult it was to create reading textbooks that consisted of strong literature: "What really does present an obstacle to better readers," he wrote to a friend, "are the racial/ethnic/gender 'balance' requirements of the state and district legal compliance commissions. The classics of the culture just simply were not 'fair' in our modern sense." Holding on to them while meeting legal requirements was a tough balancing act, and few other publishers even attempted to do so. They found it easier to hire freelance writers to write new stories that met all requirements and offended no one rather than to risk losing an adoption.

By the end of the 1980s, every publisher had complied with the demands of the critics, both from left and right. Publishers had imposed self-censorship to head off the outside censors, as well as to satisfy state adoption reviews. Achieving demographic balance and excluding sensitive topics had become more important to their success than teaching children to read or to appreciate good literature. Stories written before 1970 had to be carefully screened for compliance with the bias guidelines; those written after 1970 were unlikely to be in compliance unless written for a textbook publisher. So long as books and stories continue to be strained through a sieve of political correctness, fashioned by partisans of both left and right, all that is left for students to read will be thin gruel.

SEVEN

The Mad, Mad, Mad World
of Textbook Adoptions

> For it is a mad world and it will get madder if we allow
> the minorities, be they dwarf or giant, orangutan or
> dolphin, nuclear-head or water-conversationalist, pro-
> computerologist or Neo-Luddite, simpleton or sage, to
> interfere with aesthetics.
> —Ray Bradbury, Coda to *Fahrenheit 451*

WHY HAVE publishers of school textbooks willingly and enthusiastically imposed upon themselves the language codes that control what
their authors are allowed to write? Why do they bowdlerize text whenever a parent or pressure group complains? The short answer is that
they want to sell textbooks, and that they must respond to the
demands of their marketplace. To succeed in this highly regulated and
politicized environment, it is essential for educational publishers not
to become embroiled in controversy.

Unlike general trade books, which are sold to millions of consumers, or college textbooks, which are sold to thousands of individual
professors, textbooks prepared for the schools are not sold in an open
competitive marketplace. Publishers must invest millions of dollars to
"develop" a new textbook series, and their eventual success or failure
depends on decisions made by a few large states. The buying and selling of textbooks is more akin to a government procurement process
than it is to a real marketplace with consumer choices. The best insurance policy for stability in this highly political environment, these
publishers have found, is to live within the confines of a prescriptive
set of guidelines to protect them from trouble.

A small number of pressure groups that care passionately how their
interests are represented in the textbooks have a large influence on

adoption decisions. Most members of the public don't know and don't care what is contained in textbooks. Ordinary people tend to assume that the textbooks in public schools are up-to-date, accurate, and useful. Unlike general books, textbooks are almost never reviewed in public by expert scholars. With the exception of two small organizations (the Textbook League in California and the American Textbook Council in New York), there is no regular independent scrutiny of textbooks other than the pressure groups that have made textbooks their business. Because the decision about whether to buy a textbook is limited to a relatively few state and local education officials, instead of being made individually across a large population of consumers, the number of those who might be interested in obtaining independent reviews of textbooks is too small to be economically viable.

Certain states, particularly Texas and California, magnify the political power of textbook lobbyist groups because of the way that these states make their selections. They are the largest of the nearly two dozen states that approve textbooks for the entire state; the books that win adoption in either or both states win a huge prize (California alone has 11 percent of the national textbook market). Publishers whose textbooks do not get adopted in one of these states sustain an economic blow and must struggle to sell their books to smaller states and individual districts. The state adoption process gives enormous leverage to the departments of education in Texas and California and to activist pressure groups there.

In each of the big adoption states, the education department evaluates textbooks for each subject area. It invites public comment and holds public hearings. Critics use the adoption process to agitate against textbooks they oppose. Even a small group can make a lot of noise and block an adoption. Texas for years was known as the state where publishers got ambushed by right-wing conservatives; California is the state where publishers must jump the hurdles of very prescriptive social content guidelines.

I participated in the early stages of one of the more sensational textbook adoption battles in California. What I learned may shed light on what publishers must deal with, especially in the contentious field of history. (Similarly disputatious stories could be told about battles over evolution in science, where conservatives who espouse creationism or "intelligent design" have pressured school boards to give equal time to evolution and creationism.)

In 1985, I was invited by Bill Honig, the state superintendent of instruction in California, to join a committee of educators to help revise the state's history–social science framework. In California, the framework summarizes the curriculum and testing standards for each subject. It is a content guide for the state's textbooks. This particular framework was unusually important because it would establish standards for the next generation of history textbooks in California. Over the months that the committee met, we had many internal debates about the curriculum. Some thought it was best to make only minimal changes, so that there would be continuity with existing textbooks. Eventually, however, we decided to write a new framework, centered on history, with the hope that it would generate better textbooks and a coherent history curriculum. We agreed that elementary grades should introduce historical stories and biographies, in place of the long-standing banal curriculum of "me, my neighborhood, my community." We were aware of recent studies documenting the absence of any mention of religion in history textbooks, so we urged that texts acknowledge the influence of religion in history. The toughest challenge, however, was finding the right balance between the demands of ethnic groups for recognition and the need to teach the fundamentals of American citizenship. We proposed that American history courses acknowledge the contributions of the nation's diverse groups; we also recommended that world history study increase from one required year to three.

After numerous revisions and consultations, our committee approved a new framework (Charlotte Crabtree of the University of California at Los Angeles and I were the primary writers). The framework tried to strike a balance between the nation's *pluribus* and its *unum,* between our common American democratic heritage and the newly awakened forces of ethnic heritage. It spoke about a common culture that is multicultural, hoping thereby to paint a new portrait of American community. After many public hearings, the State Board of Education approved the new framework in 1987.

As news about the framework filtered out to the larger public, people who represent ethnic groups demanded changes. Armenian activists complained that there was no mention of the Turkish genocide of Armenians. Because there is a significant population of persons of Armenian descent in California (including, at that time, Governor George Deukmejian), the state legislature directed the Department of Education to produce a model curriculum on human rights and genocide. That curriculum included an overview of human rights and genocide in history, as well as a lengthy appendix about the genocide suffered by Armenians.

Polish activists objected to the framework's reference to the Holocaust, claiming that it gave too much attention to Jewish victims instead of Polish Christian victims. A paragraph about Poland was added to the tenth-grade world history course, which became an opportunity to teach about the dangers of totalitarianism and the importance of free, democratic institutions.

Arab American activists asked that the framework give more sympathetic attention to Arab cultures. Some reviewers complained that the framework was "too Jewish," because of its references to the Inquisition, the Holocaust, and Israel. Feminist activists decried the lack of gender balance in the framework (this was true, because there was not equal opportunity in other times and civilizations). Some professors of social studies complained that there was too much history and not enough social studies. A member of the State Board of Education wanted to insert language defining a family as headed by a father and a mother; failure to do so, he said, would be a sop to the gay community in San Francisco. Even after the trimming and compromising, the framework came out as strong content guidelines for the study of U.S. and world history, centered on the importance of democratic institutions. It eventually received high praise from external reviewers.

The education department invited representatives of the leading publishing companies to California to learn about the new framework. Members of the committee described the introduction of myths, legends, and history into the early grades, the two additional years of world history (including a full year of ancient history in the sixth grade), the increased attention to the experiences of many different groups in our common democratic culture, and so on. The publishers were not happy. One after another, their representatives got up to explain that their company would not develop history textbooks for California because the framework was too different from what was taught elsewhere. We cited research to show that large proportions of students thought that their textbooks were boring, and that American students were not learning much history, but they insisted that their books were based on market research. In short, they said, buy what is already on the shelf and forget about trying to change our products.

True to their word, few publishers submitted books to meet the specifications of the new framework, and in that first round, the state adopted only one series for K–8, published by Houghton Mifflin. The primary author of the Houghton Mifflin texts was Gary B. Nash of the University of California at Los Angeles. Nash was a prominent historian who prided himself on being a man of the left; his historical works were highly critical of racism and other injustices in American history. He was a proponent of the new social history, which emphasized race, class, and gender and scorned heroes and so-called great men in history. Nash was second in command at the National Center for History in the Schools, which was directed by Charlotte Crabtree. Crabtree was not only cowriter (with me) of the history framework but also chair of the state curriculum commission that selected Nash's textbooks. More than any history textbooks ever written to that date, Nash's books were characterized by multicultural content and scathing criticism of traditional historical accounts.

The ethnic antagonism directed at the framework was piffle compared to the deluge of criticism that greeted the Houghton Mifflin textbooks at public hearings. Despite Nash's credentials, his books were accused of being anti-black, anti-Semitic, anti-Muslim, anti–American Indian, anti-gay, and anti-Christian. There was scarcely an associational group in the state that did not take offense.

No group liked the way it was portrayed. Critics denounced the books as Eurocentric. A spokeswoman for the Hoopa, Yurok, and Karok tribes of Northern California complained that the books misinterpreted Indian religions. Muslim groups claimed that the books misrepresented their religion and that only a Muslim could write an accurate account of Muslim history. Chinese Americans said that the books marginalized Chinese people. Japanese Americans said that the books should have referred to World War II internment camps for Japanese Americans as "concentration camps." Gays claimed that the books failed to name homosexual public figures who might serve as role models. The anti-gay Traditional Values Coalition insisted that the books were anti-Christian. An African American member of the state curriculum commission charged that the books were written from the perspective of slave masters, immigrants, and pilgrims; some black educators demanded the adoption of Afrocentric textbooks to show that ancient Egypt was a black African nation and the source of all civilization's greatest advances. Latinos carped about underrepresentation. Jewish groups said that the books expressed a Christian point of view, showing Judaism as a way station toward Christianity. Atheists objected that there was too much text devoted to religion in history.

In October 1990, after numerous revisions of the Houghton Mifflin texts to placate ethnic, religious, and gender activists, the State Board of Education voted unanimously to approve them. There were all sorts of ironies in this decision. The books were the most multicultural histories ever written, yet faced a barrage of criticism for being insufficiently multicultural. Despite the books' lavish attention to cultural diversity, the critics asserted that they were full of stereotypes, distortions, omissions, and lies. The main author had made his reputation as a champion of ethnic history and a critic of American society, yet his books were scorned as Eurocentric by people representing the state's many ethnic groups. Nonetheless, Houghton Mifflin, which had invested $15 million in the Nash series, won a big prize: near-exclusive ownership of the state's history market for grades K-8, which guaranteed large rewards for their investment.

Not many people, unless they are professionals in education, know how children's textbooks are written and what kinds of political pressures shape them. Most parents, if they thought about it at all, would expect that their children's textbooks were selected by their teachers. They might imagine that teachers carefully examine the leading textbooks in their field, then select the one from which they thought their pupils would learn the most. They might even think that publishers compete in a wide-open marketplace to get their products into the hands of teachers, and that they make their case by gathering data showing how their textbooks motivate students and stimulate higher achievement than other textbooks.

If parents think about it, they probably believe that their children's textbooks were written by an author who worked for many years to compose the great, heavy tomes that children bring home from school. Perhaps they imagine an experienced scholar reviewing the latest research in the field, consulting with other scholars, and crafting and polishing the words until the text has been perfected.

None of these assumptions is correct. The reality is that publishers do not compete in a wide-open marketplace; they do not sell their books to the ultimate consumers, the teachers who will eventually use them and the students who will read them. The publishers operate in a procurement system, where they must win the approval of state education agencies. In nearly two dozen states and in many districts, the teachers who use the textbook as a daily teaching tool have little to say about which ones the state buys, unless they happen to be one of the few who serve on a textbook evaluation committee.

Textbooks today are rarely written by a single author. Almost every title represents a massive corporate effort. With few exceptions, textbooks have multiple authors, multiple editors, and multiple consultants. Some carry the names of authors who have been dead for many years. Some carry the names of distinguished historians who supplied "overall direction" but did not write the text. Some are actually written or compiled by specialized firms ("chop shops") that cater to the specific editorial needs of big publishing houses. These firms make sure that each text is aligned with the curriculum standards of the states where the publisher is hoping to win adoption or make a sale. Textbook editors study state curriculum standards, create a unified checklist, and make sure that every state's list of facts, names, topics, and concepts is mentioned in the textbook. With plenty of these brief "mentions," the textbook will meet the specifications of every state. The editors also take care that the textbook conforms to whatever "readability formula" the states want, that is, making sure that the reading level is just right, with not too many difficult words or long sentences. The publisher hires a team of consultants to create activities, questions, and study aids. Another team assembles an elaborate package of graphics, maps, charts, and so on. The editors make sure that their textbooks do not violate any state's bias guidelines, which will cause them to be "out of compliance" and ineligible for adoption.

When all of these processes are put together, the resultant textbook is beautiful to look at, glossy, dazzling, but, more often than not, boring to read because of its lack of authorial voice. When textbooks are written and edited by successive committees, they get a certain dull and distant tone. The very nature of the review process guarantees that the resultant books will be bland and inoffensive.

In the peculiar world of textbook publishing, it is commonplace for states to require that their textbooks have a current date, so that parents can be assured that their children are reading up-to-the-minute information. No one, it seems, wants a history textbook that is five years old, even though the revised edition has nothing more than a tacked-on chapter about the events of the past few years and fleeting references to the most recent president. The demand for a recent publication date compels publishers to revise their history textbooks, even if only superficially, every few years. This makes textbooks very expensive to produce and minimizes competition by raising the cost of doing business.

Since textbooks are evaluated by committees whose members seldom have the time or expertise to read them carefully, publishers load them up with impressive, expensive graphics. They become even more expensive because states and school districts expect publishers to include CD-ROMs, videos, teachers' guides, posters, teaching aids, workbooks, Spanish-language editions, and other add-ons, all of which increase the cost of the ultimate product.

The states that have a centralized adoption process for approving and buying textbooks are located mainly in the South and in the West. California buys textbooks for grades K–8. Texas buys textbooks for all grades, which makes its high school textbook adoptions especially important. Few districts can afford to buy textbooks that are not on the state list. Besides, district officials presume that the state must have had a very good reason to choose the books that it did, and good reasons to pass over the others. Publishers spend millions of dollars merely to prepare for the textbook adoption process. A rejection in the big states may be the death knell not only for a series but for the publisher as well, unless it happens to be a deep-pockets corporation.

The rigors of the adoption process have accelerated the consolidation of the industry and its domination in the 1990s by four megacorporations: McGraw-Hill, Reed Elsevier, Vivendi, and Pearson. (Vivendi sold its American publishing interests in 2002.) Small textbook companies, no matter how excellent their products, find it difficult to underwrite the high up-front cost of product development, particularly when they may be excluded from the marketplace by decisions in two states and get no return on their investment. Given the constrained nature of the competition, many small publishers have folded or been purchased by larger companies. As smaller publishers disappear, competition shrinks, as do the choices available to school districts in states other than California and Texas.

The nature of the adoption process has given extraordinary power to political pressure groups in the two key states. By making enough noise, pressure groups can make a textbook controversial, block its adoption by state officials, or compel revisions. Each state has its own guidelines for the textbooks it will adopt. These may include not only specifications for the books' manufacture (even their typeface), but specifications as to content. In the mid-1980s in Texas, for example, textbooks were required to emphasize patriotism, the "positive aspects of the United States," and the benefits of the free-enterprise economic system; they were deemed unacceptable if they included "material which serves to undermine authority," if they contained "blatantly offensive language," or if they encouraged "life styles deviating from generally accepted standards of society." In 1995, Texas revised its laws so that textbooks were required only to be factually accurate and to comply with the state's curriculum standards in each subject area. Pressure groups, however, continue to scour textbooks for views that they don't like and to lobby against them when the state board of education holds public hearings.

In Texas, Mel and Norma Gabler have scrutinized textbooks for decades, watching for any hint of leftist, anti-family, anti-Christian, or anti-American views. Since the 1960s, any publisher that expected to win adoption of their textbooks in Texas had to anticipate that the Gablers would review the contents and values in their books and teachers' guides on a line-by-line basis. Knowing this, publishers engaged in self-censorship to head off possible confrontations with such conservative critics. The Gablers knew that their influence in the adoption process would reverberate among like-minded conservatives nationally, and they maximized their opportunities to demand and win revisions.

The Gablers composed their own bias guidelines for textbooks submitted to the Texas State Board of Education. These were a reverse image of the guidelines used by the major publishing companies. They opposed stories that encouraged permissive child rearing or portrayed rules and laws as unimportant or criticized the nation or traditional values. They did not like selections that showed blackmail, bribery, cheating, indecency, and profanity, especially when bad behavior went unpunished. And they objected to an overemphasis on alienation, death, discontent, problems, skepticism, and depressing thoughts. They also complained when a book contained violence, civil strife, vandalism, or gory content. The Gablers disapproved of behavioral techniques like "questions with no firm answers," role-playing, and sensitivity training; nor did they favor books that taught "humanism," sex education, "one-worldism," "women's lib," or the occult.

When Holt, Rinehart and Winston offered the Holt Basic Reading series for adoption in Texas in 1980, the Gablers submitted seventy-six pages of objections to the books. They criticized the readers for promoting a religion of secular humanism, in violation of the Constitution. They objected to pedagogical activities in the teachers' guides. Role-playing, the Gablers said, was "affective education," which took valuable time away from teaching academic skills. The teachers' guides recommended that teachers ask students about their feelings or their home life, which the Gablers considered an invasion of student privacy.

The Gablers interpreted every story literally as a model for children's behavior. If characters lied and got away with it, then the story taught children to do the same. The Gablers sometimes recognized that they were using the same weapons of analysis as feminists, whom they disdained. At one point, while criticizing a children's poem that was written without punctuation, they wrote, "In recent years we've heard much from women libbers [sic] about the importance of role models. If true, this poem is uneducating children by teaching them to use ungrammatical language—no capitalization or punctuation."

The Gablers and the feminists agreed on one crucial point: Children's minds would be shaped, perhaps forever, by the content and images in their textbooks. When Texas turned down the Holt readers, the decision sent a negative signal to such states as North Carolina, Oklahoma, and Louisiana, where the readers also failed to win state adoption.

Holt editors learned their lesson: as they started making revisions for the 1983 edition, they wrote new guidelines to ensure that gender roles would be exactly balanced in the future, while at the same time trying to delete everything that offended the Gablers. "With the ultra-conservative movement now prevailing in our country," the editors wrote, "here are a few pointers to keep in mind as a selection is evaluated for possible inclusion:

> Does the story support a positive value such as respect for parent, teacher, or other authority figure?
> Does any part of the selection (even one word or sentence) imply a support for the theory of evolution?
> Violence, lying, cheating, stealing, and other negative

behaviors are often a part of some good literature, contemporary and traditional. It is important that these behaviors be *clearly* resolved within the framework of the selection.

Invasion of privacy is an issue that becomes evident in questions about a story. An effort must be made to avoid this type of question . . . in the Pupil Texts, Workbooks, and Teacher's Editions.

Although they were sworn enemies, the feminists and the Gablers both won.

In California, the adoption process presents another set of hurdles for publishers, but from a different direction as compared to Texas. Since the early 1970s, the policies of the California Department of Education have required textbooks to pass a "social content review" or "legal compliance review" (both terms refer to the same process). Committees appointed by the department of education review instructional materials for kindergarten through eighth grade to determine whether they meet the state's requirements.

California's social content standards have evolved over the years. Their purpose, however, has been consistent, and that is to ensure that instructional materials adopted by the state reflect positively on all groups in society. This message, the state believes, will encourage children to have positive attitudes and help them have a positive school experience. Since all children are members of one or more groups in society, if all groups are portrayed positively, then children will have positive feelings about themselves and about everyone else. They will have high self-esteem and they will appreciate others as well.

California's standards send a clear signal to publishers about what is and is not acceptable in textbooks (and other instructional materials) adopted by the state. They are very similar to the publishers' bias guidelines. This is hardly surprising, because publishers carefully scrutinize every nuance of the California guidelines when writing their own, to make sure that their products are in full compliance with the requirements of the state with the biggest school enrollments in the nation.

The California guidelines are imposed not only by the state department of education; the most important of them are written into state law. The guidelines require that instructional materials "accurately and equitably" portray the cultural and racial diversity of American society and "the contributions of minority groups and males and females to the development of California and the United States." Nobody in the state of California or the United States is left out. For every group—male and female, ethnic and cultural minorities, older persons, and people with disabilities—the state requires not only proportional representation, but no adverse reflection. "No adverse reflection" means that "descriptions, depictions, labels, or rejoinders that tend to demean, stereotype, or patronize" any of the aforementioned groups are prohibited.

Regarding gender roles, instructional materials must portray equal numbers of males and females in texts, illustrations, roles, emotions, types of activities in which they engage, and achievements. All language must be gender neutral. There must be no adverse reflection on anyone because of his or her gender. Similar standards regulate the representation of minority groups, older persons, and persons with disabilities and similarly prohibit adverse reflection on them.

The state makes a few important exceptions to its otherwise absolute requirement of gender equality and proportional representation of groups. It recognizes that in the case of "literary, historical, and cultural perspectives . . . complete compliance with the guidelines may be inappropriate." Classic literature, for example, is supposed to be exempt from social content review, which means that Emma, Jane Eyre, Captain Ahab, Richard III, Macbeth, Madame Bovary, and other famous literary characters can go ahead and be stereotypically male or female (literature textbooks, on the other hand, are scrutinized for the gender, ethnicity, disability, and age of every character and illustration). Math problems do not have to include references to human beings, and therefore need not submit to a representation count for gender, ethnicity, disability, and age. Furthermore, if a story has a small number of characters and they are all in the same family, the author is relieved of the obligation to present a balanced array of ethnic groups and roles and contributions. It is not necessary to revise literary classics to make them conform to the social content guidelines, or to show equal numbers of women, African Americans, Latinos, older persons, and persons with disabilities participating in historical events like the framing of the Constitution when they were actually absent. Historical accuracy supposedly counts. But the message of proportionality is powerful, and most history textbooks today stretch the bounds of accuracy to meet the presumption of gender and ethnic representation.

California also has standards for the representation of entrepreneurs, managers, and labor, which dictate that there is to be no adverse reflection on people in any particular occupation. Additional standards require fair treatment of religion; developing "a sense of responsibility" for the environment; discouraging the use of alcohol, drugs, and tobacco; instilling basic values such as thrift, fire prevention, and humane treatment of "animals and people." The state also prohibits any reference to brand names and corporate logos. (Publishers grumble that they are compelled to screen their books to remove references to Coca-Cola, Big Macs, or M&M's.) Publishers are expected to include representations of "nutritious foods" and regular exercise; illustrations of food are supposed to emphasize those that are low in fat, salt, and sugar, and high in fiber. One publisher was told to remove an illustration of a birthday party, because the children were gathered around a cake, which the state does not consider nutritious.

In 1982, when the social content guidelines were still fairly new and not yet formalized, some members of the state board of education wondered if they had gone too far. The vice president of the board noted that the department had issued more than six hundred citations to publishers for violations based on "minutiae and trivia," and he said, "There are so many requirements, it's amazing to me that a book can be published at all." The president of the state board said that the guidelines had succeeded in eliminating "negative portrayals," but she nonetheless observed that in "trying to create a positive picture" of women, minorities, and other groups, "we're demanding the textbook writers create books that are not realistic."[1]

By the 1990s, publishers had stopped complaining about the adoption process. Their own bias guidelines reflected what California required, and they had become accustomed to its legal compliance review. Every publisher knew the checklist and the criteria, and they came to appreciate the stability of the state's guidelines. In time, textbooks in every subject area incorporated what California and Texas demanded. Even textbooks in science and mathematics grew fatter as publishers added biographies of mathematicians and scientists who were women, African Americans, Hispanic Americans, Asian Americans, and people with disabilities. Students became used to seeing sidebars about social issues in their textbooks, even when they were irrelevant to the lessons.

But teachers and students never knew about the words and phrases that were revised or deleted before publication. Here are some examples of language that was revised or cut by various publishers before submission to the state adoption process in Texas in 2002:

A headline in a literature textbook originally read: "Chatting with the Devil, Dining with Prophets: Seer, bard and oddball, artist-poet William Blake poured his passions into uniquely visionary images." This was revised by editors as follows: "Chatting with Angels, Dining with Prophets: Artist-poet William Blake poured his passions into uniquely visionary images."

A headline in the same literature book read: "Going to Hell? Tickets Please: An exhibition in Scotland looks at the various ways people celebrate death and the afterlife." This headline was replaced by: "Portraits of an afterlife."

A headline in an eleventh-grade American history textbook read: "An Awful Human Trade: In West Africa, an alleged slave-ship snafu reflects the trauma of an ongoing business of marketing children as forced labor." The editor deleted it with the comment: "Too depressing and portrays Africans negatively."

A headline in a twelfth-grade history textbook read: "Death Stalks a Continent: In the dry timber of African societies, AIDS was a spark. The conflagration it set off continues to kill millions." The editor deleted it with the comment: "Too full of inappropriate issues; too negative, we don't want to portray Africa as AIDS-ridden."

An article written for a twelfth-grade textbook had this headline: "To Be Young and Gay in Wyoming: Despite its dangers, Matthew Shepard loved his home state. Now he is part of its legacy." The editor wrote: "Even though the article focuses on tolerance and acceptance, Shepard's homosexuality can't be mentioned. Can you redo the article so that Shepard's sexuality is ignored." (Shepard was murdered because he was gay.)

In the same textbook, another article was titled: "Preaching Chastity in the Classroom: More sex-education classes are teaching kids only about abstinence. Will they listen?" The editor replied: "Though we think this story is wonderful and would resonate with 12th graders, we can't mention sex—or teen drinking—in any way, shape, or form."

In a science textbook, editors rejected this statement: "A scientific panel says fossil fuels are the main culprit in Earth's heating up." The comment: "We'd never be adopted in Texas."

In a textbook about Texas, a pie chart showed the racial profile of the state, with slices for White, Black/African American, American Indian, Asian, Native Hawaiian/Pacific Islander, and Other Races. The chart also included a slice for "2 Plus Races," that is, people of mixed race. The editors proposed deleting this last category to avoid offending people who object to mixed-race families. Ultimately, the pie chart was deleted, because eliminating one of its categories made it inaccurate.[2]

Once textbooks are carefully sanitized, they are guaranteed to be blander and less realistic than a daily newspaper, a weekly news-magazine, or a television newscast, and far less interesting than any of them.

At the beginning of the twenty-first century, a new status quo emerged in which the textbook industry and the major adoption states became comfortable with one another. They shared the same bias guidelines, which quieted the critics, left and right. Feminists were happy, because the publishers had accepted a nonsexist language code. Ethnic and cultural minorities, people with disabilities, and the older population had no grounds for complaint, because they had won rep-resentation. Right-wingers were generally satisfied, because the topics that angered them were excluded.

The only problem was that all this activism had made the textbooks dull. Studies showed that they also had a simpler vocabulary, that they had been dumbed down at the same time that they were being "puri-fied." With everything that might offend anyone removed, the text-books lacked the capacity to inspire, sadden, or intrigue their readers. Such are the wages of censorship.

EIGHT

Literature: Forgetting the Tradition

> Ours is the first age in history which has asked the child
> what he would tolerate learning, but that is a part of the
> problem with which I am not equipped to deal. The
> devil of Educationism that possesses us is the kind that
> can be "cast out only by prayer and fasting." No one has
> yet come along strong enough to do it.
> —Flannery O'Connor,
> "Total Effect and the Eighth Grade"

CENSORSHIP HAS a long history in textbook publishing. As long as there have been textbooks, publishers have tried to avoid violating the taboos of regional, religious, racial, ethnic, or economic groups. Until the 1960s, publishers did not include photographs of racially integrated groups in their textbooks, for fear of losing the southern market. In 1962, Texas officials told publishers that they would not buy any textbooks that mentioned Vera Micheles Dean, Pete Seeger, or Langston Hughes, because of their "connections with groups cited by the House Un-American Activities Committee" or other investigators. An official at Macmillan said that authors and publishers of textbooks had learned "to restrain themselves here and tiptoe there. It is surprising that so much controversial material remains."[1]

Over the years, publishers have cut selections in literary anthologies for a variety of reasons. Sometimes they cut to make them shorter, which is known as *abridgement*. Sometimes they rewrite selections to make them easier, which relieves children from the bother of learning new words or figuring out the meaning of an unfamiliar passage. Sometimes they alter selections to eliminate sexual or religious references, which might upset sensitive parents or teachers. The best-known practitioners of expurgation for the sake of moral purity were

Dr. Thomas Bowdler and his sister Henrietta Maria Bowdler. Their edition of the *Family Shakespeare,* published in 1807, removed lines and sections from the Bard's plays that contained sexual language, profanity, or irreverent references to God or Jesus. Before long, the Bowdler name became a verb to describe expurgation of a literary work for reasons of sex, politics, or religion.[2] Shakespeare, more than any other writer, has been bowdlerized by editors hoping to clean up his language for the school market or the home. Shakespeare's *Romeo and Juliet* has frequently been sanitized, especially in high school anthologies, where as many as four hundred lines may be quietly deleted.

Bowdlerization is not easily detectable. Unless someone has taken the time to sit down and make a comparison between the original and the version that appears in a textbook, the expurgations go unnoticed. Certainly publishers do not attach notices to warn readers that the text has been "purified," as the Bowdlers did in the early nineteenth century. Unfortunately, they seldom insert ellipses to show that some text has been deleted or altered.

Sometimes publishers make revisions to forestall problems, knowing that states like California and Texas won't tolerate certain words. For example, a story titled "A Perfect Day for Ice Cream" by Patricia Zettner was selected by two textbook publishers for inclusion in junior high school literature anthologies after it had appeared in *Seventeen* magazine. To comply with California's ban on junk foods, the publishers removed references to chili burgers, pizza, and ice cream and changed the title of the story to "A Perfect Day." The story's allusions to "kamikaze ball" and Gloria Steinem were edited out to avoid likely complaints in California about ethnic stereotyping and likely objections in Texas to feminist references.[3]

In 1985, Barbara Cohen, author of a children's book called *Molly's Pilgrim,* was thrilled to learn that a textbook publisher wanted to reprint a condensation of her story about a Russian Jewish immigrant girl's first Thanksgiving in America. However, when she got the page proofs, she realized that the story was not merely cut; it had been "maimed. All mention of Jews, Sukkos, God, and the Bible had been excised." When she protested, the editor said, "Try to understand. We have a lot of problems. If we mention God, some atheist will object. If we mention the Bible, someone will want to know why we don't give equal time to the Koran. Every time that happens, we lose sales." The editor insisted that the textbook would not sell if it contained anything objectionable. After much negotiation, the editor agreed to include Jews and Sukkos, but was adamant that there could be no references to God or the Bible. In the revised story, Molly's family came to America, like the Pilgrims, to worship in their own way, but the text story did not say that they were worshiping God; the story said that the Pilgrims knew about the Jewish harvest festival, but did not say that they had learned about it from the Bible. Cohen sadly concluded, "Censorship in this country is widespread, subtle, and surprising. It is not inflicted on us by the government. It doesn't need to be. We inflict it on ourselves."[4]

I have been able to discover only two sustained efforts that document bowdlerization of literary texts. One is a doctoral dissertation that examined censorship in textbooks in Tennessee in 1975; the other is a review in 2002 of literary passages in the New York State Regents examinations.

Dorothy Thompson Weathersby studied censorship in twenty-two high school literary anthologies adopted by Tennessee. She found that the publishers had practiced "silent editing" to placate state education officials and avoid potential controversy. The publishers omitted and revised objectionable material. None of the omissions was marked by an ellipsis or note. The words most likely to be altered or omitted were references to God or Christ, such as "by God," or "for God's sake," or "God A'mighty," or "God!" or "for Christ's sake." Sometimes the publishers deleted some oaths and left a few in, apparently assuming that their infrequent appearance would be less offensive. In Stephen Vincent Benét's "The Devil and Daniel Webster," the original line read: "Help me! For God's sake, help me!" It was changed to: "Help me! I beg of you, help me!"[5]

One textbook included the novel *The Ox-Bow Incident* by Walter Van Tilburg Clark. Weathersby found seventy-nine alterations in this one novel, including the following examples of "silent editing":

"By the Lord God, men" was changed to "By heaven, men"
"A Goddamned rustler's bullet" was changed to "a blasted
    rustler's bullet"
"By God" was changed to "By gum"
"No, by God" was changed to "No, by heaven"
"My God" was changed to "Hey!"

"My God" was changed to "You don't mean it"
"God" was changed to "Well"

A few textbooks deleted language about Jews, and several made changes in entries about blacks. There were alterations in Mark Twain's works, not only *The Adventures of Huckleberry Finn*, but also Twain's autobiography and short stories. Some texts changed the word *nigger* to *slave* or *Negro* or *folks;* others just deleted the entire sentence to resolve the problem. Carson McCullers's *Member of the Wedding* was extensively bowdlerized to expunge her frequent use of the word *nigger,* curses, and a description of a homosexual. Scott Foresman dropped a paragraph from an excerpt of Herman Melville's *Redburn* that described brutal conditions on a slave ship.

Weathersby discovered that chunks of material were removed from Chaucer's *Canterbury Tales* (on account of bawdiness), Jonathan Swift's "Modest Proposal" (including a passage that suggested abortions), Swift's *Gulliver's Travels* (an allusion to genitals), and John Bunyan's *Pilgrim's Progress* (an offensive allusion to Catholics). Even Benjamin Franklin's *Autobiography* was expurgated to remove evidence of his irreligious views.

In 2002, a diligent parent in New York discovered that state education officials had expurgated literary passages on the Regents English examinations for high school students. Unlike Tennessee, New York does not have a significant population of fundamentalist Christians. The New York State Education Department had bowdlerized the readings on its examinations to comply with its own bias and sensitivity guidelines.

The parent, Jeanne Heifetz, compared literary passages from ten different English Language Arts tests over a three-year period to the original publications. She found that the majority of passages had been altered to remove references to race, religion, alcohol, profanity, and sex as well as other purportedly controversial subjects. Her purpose, as an anti-testing activist, was to embarrass the state education department and to discredit its examinations. She certainly achieved her first goal; Richard Mills, the New York State commissioner of education, promptly pledged to put a halt to the practice in order to salvage the reputation of the examinations (however, the very next round of Regents English examinations contained bowdlerized literary passages).

The Heifetz study garnered national and even international attention after it was reported on the front page of the *New York Times;* "The Elderly Man and the Sea? Test Sanitizes Literary Texts," said the headline.[6] (A bias review would have rejected the *New York Times* headline as age-biased and regionally biased, replacing it with "A Person Who Is Older Catches a Fish.") Heifetz demonstrated that the state had deleted and revised words and phrases in literary passages without getting permission from the authors or indicating changes with ellipses or brackets. She discovered that state officials removed any language that mentioned cultural differences, even when those differences were key to understanding the text. In one case, where John Holt's *Learning All the Time* described the Suzuki method for violin instruction, the state deleted his comment that Japanese women spend more time at home with their children than American women. In a selection from Ernesto Galarza's *Barrio Boy,* the state revised his ethnic descriptions. He wrote about "a gringo lady," but the state changed her to "an American lady." He wrote that "we were sure to be marched up to the principal's office for calling someone a wop, a chink, a dago, or a greaser," but the state converted that to "we were sure to be marched up to the principal's office for calling someone a bad name." The state changed "a skinny Italian boy" to "a thin Italian boy"; "a fat Portuguese" to "a heavy Portuguese"; and "small Japanese Ito, squinty-eyed and shy" became "Japanese Ito, small and shy."

Another expurgated work was Annie Dillard's *An American Childhood.* She described herself as one of the few white people in a library in "the Negro section of town," but the state cut out references to the race of the other people who used the library, thus distorting her insights into the realities of race in America as she was growing up. In a passage from Isaac Bashevis Singer's *In My Father's Court,* a memoir about life in his native Poland, the state excised references to Jews and Gentiles, as well as contrasts between the lives of Jews and Poles, completely obliterating the cultural context of Singer's story.

Any language that referred to God, religion, or the soul was removed. The state deleted an exclamation of "Oh, God" from one passage, as well as talk about confessing to a priest in a Chekhov story. Elie Wiesel wrote, "Man, who was created in God's image, wants to be free as God is free: free to choose between good and evil, love and vengeance, life and death"; after bowdlerization, the sentence read:

"Man wants to be free: free to choose between good and evil, love and vengeance, life and death." In a Frank Conroy story, the state changed the word "hell" to "heck" and deleted a description of two boys killing a snake.

Heifetz was shocked that the authorities had censored well-known writers, and her astonishment was shared by the national press. What she and the members of the media did not realize was that the New York State Education Department was punctiliously following its bias and sensitivity guidelines. The reviewers who bowdlerized literary passages had been trained and certified by the state as "New York State Education Department Sensitivity Reviewers."[7]

The department had adopted new procedures in 2000 to screen all test questions for bias and sensitivity. These procedures were based on "industry standards" as well as the guidelines used in other states. The state's bias review relied on DIF analysis, the statistical procedure that I described in chapter 4. Reviewers were trained to eliminate material that seemed to favor or stereotype one group or religion; that portrayed a racial or ethnic group in a pejorative or stereotypic manner; that presented gratuitous violence or speech; that presented "controversial" themes such as war; that assumed values not shared by all test-takers; that presented sexual innuendoes, and so on. The sensitivity reviewers did what they were trained to do, which was to eliminate, delete, remove, replace, revise—that is, *censor*—offensive material. The mistake of New York education officials was to think that no one would know or care that they did it; other state and national testing agencies either had not been found out yet or had the good sense to select only those passages that could pass a sensitivity review without needing expurgation.

As a result of this episode, the public became aware of sensitivity censorship. The press ridiculed the practice. One editorialist imagined the Gettysburg Address revised to comply with the New York sensitivity guidelines. First, he said, change the name, because it evokes images of gratuitous violence. Don't use the word *score* (as in "four score and seven years ago") because it suggests winners and losers, and all of our students are winners. Don't say "our fathers brought forth" because it is sexist. Drop "conceived in liberty" because it suggests birth and death. Out goes "dedicated to the proposition that all men are created equal"; it is sexist. Too much talk about battles and war, too militaristic. The religious stuff about dedicating, consecrating, and hallowing has to go too. On and on he went, carving out one line after another, until all that was left was: "The Biglerville Address, by Abraham Lincoln: We have a really cool country, and we should keep it that way."[8]

Behind the public uproar about censorship and sanitizing literary texts were important questions: What had happened to the teaching of literature? Had the pressures for censorship from both the politically correct left and the morally correct right changed what was taught in school? Were students still reading the works of recognized authors or had they been quietly shelved for political reasons?

To answer these questions, I looked to several different kinds of evidence. One was the national standards written by the National Council of Teachers of English and the International Reading Association (NCTE-IRA), which would indicate what these authoritative organizations say about the teaching of literature today. Then there were the English language arts standards promulgated by forty-nine states (all but Iowa, which does not set state standards). And last, there were the literature textbooks, which supply the curriculum in many—perhaps most—English classes.

I began this quest with a strong belief that schools are supposed to lay a foundation for love of literature by exposing children incrementally, based on age appropriateness, to the best writings of our common language and, to the extent possible, to the best writings from other cultures. There are so many superb novels, short stories, poems, plays, and essays to choose from that it is impossible for any student to read them all. But this fact makes it all the more important that teachers make the effort to identify the writers and works that will broaden their students' horizons beyond their own immediate circumstances and reveal to them a world of meanings far beyond their own experiences. Great literature is "relevant" not because it echoes the students' race, gender, or social circumstances, but because it speaks directly to the reader across time and across cultures. A child who is suffering because of a death in the family is likely to gain more comfort from reading a poem by John Donne or Ben Jonson or Gerard Manley Hopkins than from reading banal teen fiction about a death in the family.

In 1996, the NCTE-IRA published its national standards for the teaching of English language arts. These standards do not identify any authors or literary works that are essential for American students to read. They are concerned with literacy but not literary appreciation. They give equal weight to every sort of text, in any format. They acknowledge the value of reading classic and contemporary texts, but also commend the reading of textbooks, lab manuals, reference materials, student-produced texts, computer software, CD-ROMs, laser discs, films, television broadcasts, magazines, newspapers, editorials, advertisements, letters, bulletin board notices, signs, and memos.

One searches in vain through the proposed national standards of the NCTE-IRA for any suggestions about what students should read. They do not identify the authors whose works are foundational in American or British literature. They offer two pieces of advice: Student reading should be relevant to their interests and their "roles in society," as if students cannot acquire new interests and cannot profit by reading about people who do not share their "roles in society"; and the works that students read should reflect the United States' population in terms of gender, age, social class, religion, and ethnicity.

The NCTE-IRA national standards contain vignettes of classrooms where students are reading specific texts. These are miscellaneous, such as Katherine Paterson's *Lyddie*, Dr. Seuss's *Lorax*, Mark Twain's *Adventures of Huckleberry Finn*, Shakespeare's *Romeo and Juliet*, S. E. Hinton's *Outsiders*, Margaret Wise Brown's *Goodnight Moon*, and Robert Cormier's *I Am the Cheese*. The NCTE and IRA offer no help to teachers about how to select literature for their classroom. The two organizations adopt the same laissez-faire approach to the teaching of English; they endorse bilingual education and refrain from endorsing such conventions as spelling, syntax, grammar, or the other usages associated with standard English. One finishes reading their document convinced that they believe that there are no standards for teaching the English language or for teaching literature.

When they were first published, the NCTE-IRA standards were widely derided in the press for their pedagogical jargon and indifference to anything recognizable as standards; in 1994, before they were released, the Clinton administration suspended funding for them because of their lack of content. Nonetheless they have had a great influence on the standards written and adopted by the states. With only a handful of exceptions, the standards promulgated in many different states look much like the national standards. In almost every state, the English language arts standards are about skills. What they are not about is literature, otherwise known as "content," which was once the heart and soul of the field called English. The standards are mind-numbingly detailed about the varied strategies that students will use to analyze, predict, interpret, criticize, synthesize, and summarize what they have read, but completely blank about what students should read. Most of the state standards seem to have been written by the same group of pedagogues, all steeped in the same jargon.

For this book, I gathered the states' English language arts (ELA) standards. I wanted to determine whether any state expects students to read any particular literary work or author. In the typical state ELA document, children learn to read in order to interact with a variety of texts for a variety of purposes, mainly of their own choosing, not in order to encounter great literature. This is what I found.

Which states identify specific works of literature or specific authors that all children should read? None.

No state requires students to read a specific work of literature or specific author. In no state will all students complete high school having at some time read Ernest Hemingway or Henry David Thoreau or Emily Dickinson or Ralph Ellison or Walt Whitman or John Steinbeck or Charles Dickens or Shakespeare or Abraham Lincoln. No state requires all students to read the Gettysburg Address or Martin Luther King Jr.'s "I Have a Dream" speech or Franklin Delano Roosevelt's "Four Freedoms" speech. Some students with literature-loving teachers may actually read these authors and more, but no state sets forth the expectation that they will do so.

How many states have a recommended reading list that is part of their ELA standards? Four: California, Massachusetts, Indiana, and New York. Each of these states has compiled a lengthy recommended reading list that includes hundreds of classic and contemporary writings; some of the entries on these lists are evanescent, to say the least. The guiding principle of the compilers seems to be that the list should be so extensive that no one can complain about not being included (the California list, for example, has nearly three thousand entries). Teachers may use the list in deciding what to teach, but they are not required to do so.

Massachusetts has the most discerning lists of recommended readings; its ELA standards include two appendices with names of recognized literary works and authors. The first appendix is a list of classic works and authors; the second is a list of contemporary works and authors. Appendix A contains "Suggested Authors, Illustrators, and Works Reflecting Our Common Literary and Cultural Heritage." Appendix B is "Suggested Authors and Illustrators of Contemporary American and World Literature." In what must be considered a direct rebuke to the leaders of the National Council of Teachers of English and the International Reading Association, which did not recommend a single work or author, and which abhor lists on principle, the Massachusetts standards say: "All American students should acquire knowledge of a range of literary works reflecting a common literary heritage that goes back thousands of years to the ancient world. In addition, all students should become familiar with some of the outstanding works in the rich body of literature that is their particular heritage in the English-speaking world."

When Massachusetts first published its two lists of recommended authors, classic and contemporary, there was an outcry from educators who complained about the dangers of giving too much attention to dead white men, Eurocentrism, and old-fashioned stuff, but the state stuck to its guns. Its lists are superb compilations of the authors and writings that American students and adults should read at some time in their lives, including their time in school. For example, it identifies the important American writers of the eighteenth and nineteenth centuries: James Fenimore Cooper, Stephen Crane, Emily Dickinson, Frederick Douglass, Ralph Waldo Emerson, Benjamin Franklin, Nathaniel Hawthorne, Henry James, Thomas Jefferson, Herman Melville, Edgar Allan Poe, Henry David Thoreau, Mark Twain, Phillis Wheatley, and Walt Whitman (Lincoln is referenced elsewhere). One may quibble about whether other writers should be added, but it is hard to deny the significance of these writers. Their work represents an invaluable cultural heritage, yet most states do not even mention them, and few students will ever read them. The contemporary list contains more names of women and people of color than the list of classics, which reflects the reality of the times (women and people of color had greater opportunities to write in the twentieth century than in the nineteenth).

How many states mention any specific work of literature or writer in their state standards? Only eight: Massachusetts, Connecticut, Mississippi, Alabama, California, Delaware, Arkansas, and Utah.

Four of these states (Arkansas, Utah, Delaware, and Alabama) mention specific works of literature or writers only in passing.

In Arkansas, the standards include a brief reference to Alan Paton's *Cry, the Beloved Country.* This is suggested as an example of the sort of reading students might do; it is not a required reading. There is no other literature mentioned in the Arkansas standards.

In Utah, the ninth-grade course description mentions *The Adventures of Huckleberry Finn, The Old Man and the Sea,* and *A Wrinkle in Time,* without requiring anyone to read them.

Delaware's ELA standards include "vignettes" of good teaching, in which teachers are using works such as Aldous Huxley's *Brave New World,* John Steinbeck's *Of Mice and Men,* and Harper Lee's *To Kill a Mockingbird.* None of these books is required.

In Alabama, the standards do not require students to read any specific literary work or writer, but they do at least mention Phillis Wheatley, Alice Walker, Amy Tan, Langston Hughes, William Cullen Bryant, and William Bradford.

Four states give significant attention to literature in their English standards, implying that students are expected to undertake serious reading in their English classes. As one would expect, given its excellent literature appendices, Massachusetts offers numerous examples of outstanding literature in every grade. It suggests *The Red Badge of Courage, The Scarlet Letter, The Cricket in Times Square,* Jonathan Edwards's sermon "Sinners in the Hands of an Angry God," T. S. Eliot's *Old Possum's Book of Practical Cats,* Toni Morrison's *The Bluest Eye,* and Amy Tan's *The Joy Luck Club,* among numerous other classic and contemporary works. Massachusetts's standards for English are exemplary.

California's ELA standards refer readers to its voluminous recommended reading list. In addition, the standards specifically mention Shakespeare's *Macbeth,* Lincoln's Gettysburg Address, Martin Luther King Jr.'s "I Have a Dream" speech, and Shakespeare's *Henry V* as the kind of work that students should be reading at a specific grade level (but none is required reading).

Mississippi recommends an extraordinary amount of literature. In kindergarten, children will hear *Peter's Chair;* Ezra Jack Keats's *The*

Snowy Day (and it doesn't snow in Mississippi; it is just a terrific children's book); *Three Bears; Three Little Pigs; The Little Red Hen;* Mem Fox's *Koala Lou;* Judith Viorst's *Alexander and the Terrible, Horrible, No Good, Very Bad Day;* and Bernard Waber's *Ira Sleeps Over.* In sixth grade, there is a reference to Mildred Taylor's *Roll of Thunder, Hear My Cry,* though it is not required.

In Mississippi's high schools, the literature teachers must have won their battles with the anti-literature forces. In ninth grade, students read a sonnet by Elizabeth Barrett Browning, "The Gift of the Magi," *Romeo and Juliet, Antigone,* selections from *The Odyssey,* George Orwell's *Animal Farm,* and Charles Dickens's *Great Expectations.* The word *required* is never used, but it is clear that students will be expected to read good literature. Eleventh graders read William Faulkner's "Barn Burning," Edgar Allan Poe's "Cask of Amontillado," Henry David Thoreau's *Walden,* and selections from Puritan or colonial writers. In twelfth grade, there is another strong course of literature, with Elizabeth Barrett Browning's *Sonnets from the Portuguese,* William Golding's *Lord of the Flies,* Septima Clark's *Ready from Within* (a biography about a civil rights pioneer), *Beowulf, Macbeth, Oedipus Rex, Of Mice and Men,* Chaucer, and Maya Angelou. Do they actually read all of this? I don't know, but certainly some teachers in Mississippi have made conscious decisions about how to introduce students to the world of literate culture.

The fourth state that names works of literature is Connecticut. The excellence of the examples suggests that students will read outstanding literature. In K–4, the standards refer to *The Velveteen Rabbit,* "The Tortoise and the Hare," *Encyclopedia Brown,* "Rikki-Tikki-Tavi," *Charlotte's Web,* and other children's books. In the middle school years, the examples are Langston Hughes, James Lincoln Collier's *My Brother Sam Is Dead,* Howard Fast's *April Morning,* Robert Frost, Jack London's *Call of the Wild,* Gary Soto, Nikki Giovanni, Laura Ingalls Wilder's *Little House on the Prairie* series, and Anne Frank's *Diary of a Young Girl.* In the high school years, the standards cite such works as Jane Austen's *Pride and Prejudice, Macbeth, Hamlet, Romeo and Juliet,* T. S. Eliot's "The Waste Land," Amy Tan's *Joy Luck Club,* Chinua Achebe's *Things Fall Apart,* Crane's *Red Badge of Courage,* Steinbeck's *Of Mice and Men,* and Margaret Mitchell's *Gone with the Wind.*

It is rare that a state cites specific works and authors. Forty-one states and the District of Columbia do not mention even a single work or author, not even as an example or a recommendation. Considering that some states have English standards that are as long as fifty pages, it must have taken an act of will not to find even a single writer or literary work that was worthy of mention.

What then are these English language arts standards, and what do they recommend instead of literature? Recall that the English language arts include reading, writing, listening, speaking, viewing, and visually representing. The study of literature is only a small part of the reading strand, and almost any text seems to serve the purpose.

Virtually every state says that students should read a variety of genres for a variety of purposes. Most suggest that students should "self-select books and stories" by setting their own purposes and drawing on their own personal interests. What matters most in ELA is how students feel and respond to the text. The student, not the work of literature, is at the center of the reading experience. Whatever literature has to say to readers seems to be unimportant, as compared to how readers feel about it.

Most state standards say that literature is to be read by students for a social or political message, as though every poem or novel is meant to be a social or political commentary rather than an expression of the writer's emotional, spiritual, or aesthetic concerns. Other than Massachusetts, none encourages the reading of any core group of literary works that every educated person should absorb in order to understand the ideas of our civilization and its literary tradition. Nowhere in the state or national standards did I find any discussion of the intrinsic joy and aesthetic understanding that one might gain by reading a stirring poem, nothing about how a beautiful novel can make you cry or laugh or reflect. The study of literature as knowledge and as art is either missing from the standards or has been supplanted by utilitarian concerns.

In the forty-plus states that adhere to the NCTE-IRA standards and forsake literature, reading has become a technical process of "interacting with text." To take examples from different states, students who interact with text will be able to "apply word analysis and vocabulary skills to comprehend selections"; they will "relate reading to prior knowledge and experience and make connections to related information"; they will use "language processes" as "meaning-making processes"; they will use language for "communication through symbolic forms"; they will have "a positive attitude about self as a reader, writer, speaker," because of their "engagement in meaningful literacy activities"; they will develop "social and cultural understandings"; they will "construct, examine, and extend the meaning of literary, informative, and technical texts through listening, reading, and viewing"; they will "use literary knowledge accessed through print and visual media to connect self to society and culture"; they will "self-monitor comprehension"; they will "make and revise predictions as needed"; they will "distinguish between the reader's response and the author's purpose"; they will "relate the content of the text to real-life situations"; they will "analyze and evaluate critically"; they will "offer a personal response to texts"; they will "use a variety of comprehension strategies, including prediction, sequencing, cause/effect, fact/opinion, main idea, compare/contrast, vocabulary development, summarizing, drawing conclusions, and making inferences"; they will "use effective reading strategies to achieve their purposes in reading"; they will "make text-to-text, text-to-self, and text-to-world connections"; they will "use cueing systems to establish the meaning of unfamiliar words or phrases," including a "semantic cueing system," a "syntactic cueing system," and a "graphophonic cueing system."

All of this is quite clinical. This is the cold analytical language of the reading process. This is pedagoguese striving to sound technical and expert. The reading process has become an end in itself, without regard to literary or aesthetic values. If all texts are of equal value, it hardly matters if some are neglected or bowdlerized.

Why don't states identify the content that students are expected to master? Like textbook publishers, they prefer to avoid controversy. It is much easier to say that "students should read a variety of texts for a variety of purposes" than to identify the giants of American and world literature whom students should read to become literate. Suppose the state's list does not have the right gender balance? Suppose it has too many white males? What if the works selected include some that contain offensive language or topics? What if someone complains that the work contains too many authors from one region, or not enough from another? These are the problems that are certain to arise if a state begins to compile a reading list. There will be protests from feminists and ethnic minorities because they don't like this book or that play. There will be protests from the religious right because a novel has themes that anger them. The inclusion of *The Adventures of Huckle-berry Finn* or a specific fairy tale might cause trouble. It is far easier for the state to steer clear of controversy.

When literature is missing from the states' list of goals for students, it is likely that many will graduate from high school without having any acquaintance with our nation's cultural heritage (the words *cultural heritage* do not appear in the ELA standards of any state except Massachusetts). It seems that many education officials are no longer willing to take responsibility for teaching the American cultural heritage or the cultural heritage of English-speaking people. They appear to be embarrassed to admit that our culture—like other cultures—has a heritage. By their timidity, they disconnect American youngsters from the great works of literature that inspired earlier generations of students.

I am not calling for a canonization of a particular list of books, not even the list that appears at the end of this book. But a conscious effort must be made to expose young minds to the writers whose words and ideas have had an enduring influence on American culture. By refusing to name those writers and their key works, the education system abdicates its responsibility for transmitting our cultural heritage and improving the taste and judgment of the younger generation. This reluctance to take a stand comes not from the teachers, but from university faculties infected by postmodernism, relativism, and other fashionable -isms, as well as from professors of education who disparage content. This unwillingness to teach the poems, plays, novels, essays, and short stories that have long been recognized for their excellence and significance abandons young people to be shaped by others. Untouched by enduring and inspiring literature, the students are left to be molded by the commercial popular culture. The popular culture—making machine cares not a whit for taste and judgment but reaches insistently for the lowest common denominator, the point at which its purveyors can maximize their profit. As a result, we are systematically failing to introduce the younger generation to the writers who might enlarge their imaginations, enrich their emotional lives, and challenge their settled ways of thinking.

One purpose of state standards is to identify what students will be held responsible for on the state assessments. To compensate for the fact that most students have not read anything in common, the tests ask students about literature that they have presumably never seen before the test. The tests present students with a literary passage, a poem, or an excerpt that is new to them, and the students are expected to demonstrate their skills of analysis by responding to questions about these items. Students are tested on their ability to analyze, rather than their knowledge of something that they have previously read and studied and thought about. Some educators object to testing students on what they have studied, claiming that these are tests of "recall." But to ask students to reflect on what they have learned and thought about over time is a test of their knowledge and judgment, not a test of their recall. Such questions cannot be asked anymore because students do not have any shared base of knowledge about literature.

Today's literature textbooks reflect the state of the field of English language arts: large, beautifully packaged, and incoherent. They are incoherent in the sense that they lack any unity of principle; they are not logically or aesthetically organized. They are a potpourri of fiction, nonfiction, social commentary, graphics, special features, and pedagogical aids. Even when the selections are good, the texts are almost painful to read because of their visual clutter and sensory overload. They make no attempt to teach children about the time-honored tradition of literature shared by English-speaking peoples, nor do they recognize and honor the great writers of the American literary tradition. To the contrary, today's textbooks strain to obscure any sense of literary tradition; they pretend that there is no such tradition. Nor do they attempt to teach students how to make judgments among literary works. They instead indiscriminately mix pieces by writers who are great, ordinary, and undistinguished.

The literature textbooks for middle school and high school from the major publishers are compilations of odds and ends. They have no overarching ends. The books are littered with nonliterary features, such as an essay about homelessness or air pollution. One teaches students how to read a weather map, a time line, and a telephone book. Another contains features about careers. All include some excellent literature, some mediocre selections, and lots of advice about how to think, to read, to write, to summarize, to take tests, to find the main idea, or to read a classified ad. Some include social studies articles, science articles, and other miscellany.

None of the textbooks is designed to build a foundation of cultural knowledge; none encourages students to discern why some pieces of writing are considered classic. Writing is writing; text is text. Everything is treated as literature, just because it happens to be printed. No effort is expended to teach students the differences among writing that is banal, good, better, or best. The stories of Edgar Allan Poe, Mark Twain, and O. Henry are mixed haphazardly with student essays, study skills, and never-heard-of, soon-to-be-forgotten pieces by little-known writers. One book, published by Prentice Hall (with the subtitle "Timeless Voices, Timeless Themes") has an excerpt from a script of the once-popular television program *Xena: Warrior Princess*. This script would not qualify as "literature" by any standard other than one in which absolutely everything in print is "literature."

The literature textbooks for these grades (5–10) contain from 650 to 1,200 pages. Often the selections are accompanied by photographs and biographies of authors so that students are made aware of their gender and ethnic background. Every textbook has a representation of well-known authors, but they are mainly seasoning in a very big and varied stew. The textbooks include selections by recognized writers, such as O. Henry, Edgar Allan Poe, Robert W. Service, Henry Wadsworth Longfellow, John Greenleaf Whittier, Ray Bradbury, Walt Whitman, Emily Dickinson, John Ciardi, Lewis Carroll, Christina Rossetti, Robert Frost, Jack London, Robert Louis Stevenson, Isaac Bashevis Singer, Arthur Miller, Sara Teasdale, E. B. White, Shakespeare, Carl Sandburg, Doris Lessing, and Mark Twain. But one will not find too many of them in any single volume. Nor will one find many traditional American tall tales or legends in the reading books. The student is more likely to encounter folktales from Japan, China, Africa, or India than to read one from the American past.

There is a new canon in today's literature textbooks. Certain writers appear again and again. They are Sandra Cisneros, Nikki Giovanni, Toni Cade Bambara, Jane Yolen, Gary Soto, Lawrence Yep, Pat Mora, Julia Alvarez, Walter Dean Myers, Naomi Shihab Nye, and Rudolfo A. Anaya. Most of them are not well known to the general public, but their stories, essays, and poems are omnipresent in the textbook world. Students may never encounter Herman Melville, Ralph Waldo Emerson, Joseph Conrad, or Nathaniel Hawthorne, but they will certainly know the work of Cisneros; there is hardly a literary textbook at any grade level, regardless of publisher, that does not include her writing.

Even McDougal Littell's senior high school textbook, ostensibly devoted to a chronological treatment of major American literature, cannot resist the temptation to trivialize that tradition by randomly adding to it without regard to chronology. In a section allegedly devoted to American works written from "2000 B.C. to A.D. 1620," the editors insert a short story written in 1969 by a Native American writer, a 1982 travelogue by another Native American writer, and an excerpt from Maya Angelou's autobiography. The section covering the era from 1620 to 1800 offers such writers as Jonathan Edwards, Benjamin Franklin, and Thomas Jefferson, but also includes Martin Luther King Jr., Malcolm X, and a Chicano poet.

Today's literature textbooks are motivated by a spirit of miscellany. None of them consists only of text and pictures, like a real book; that would be way too simple. Even when the entries are well chosen and enjoyable, the textbook pokes the reader in the eye with pedagogical strategies. The reason that the books are so large is that they are puffed up with instructions and activities that belong in the teachers' edition. The people who prepare these textbooks don't seem to have much faith in teachers. The books strive to be "teacher-proof." They leave nothing to the teacher's initiative or ingenuity. They lay out in minute detail precisely what the teacher should ask and do, which is incredibly distracting to the reader. Despite the fact that the NCTE-IRA national standards say that teachers and administrators should make their own selections of literature, many of the professional leaders of the NCTE and IRA edited the textbooks that make the selections for teachers and tell them exactly what to say when they are teaching.

The National Council of Teachers of English was not always opposed to reading lists. In 1935, for example, the NCTE's curriculum commission compiled an extensive list of readings that began with traditional nursery tales and fairy tales in kindergarten (such as *Peter Rabbit* and "Jack and the Beanstalk"), and advanced in complexity through high school, with selections from Whitman, Riis, Tennyson, Dickens, Eliot, Twain, Cooper, Thackeray, the Brontës, Hawthorne, Longfellow, Alcott, Defoe, Ferber, and Shakespeare. The commission said, "Like the fight for health, the struggle for culture must be systematic and persistent."[9]

We have come a long way since then, and so has the NCTE. It opposes any list of recommended readings for fear that it will become a dreaded canon. In 1997, the NCTE elected a new president, Sheridan Blau of the University of California at Santa Barbara, who suggested that the organization might consider constructing a reading list, because "in a nation as diverse as ours we must count on schools to provide the materials for building a common culture beyond that created by commercial TV and popular music." He noted that there were already many lists in circulation and that the profession should take control of decisions about what to teach away from the textbook publishers. Some NCTE members reacted with horror, fearful that a list would represent only the politically powerful, that it would exclude the voices of the powerless, that the people of the United States do not have a common culture, that they should not have a common culture, and that only middle-class whites would be part of a national culture. Faced with overwhelmingly negative responses from professors of education in the NCTE (not the teachers!), Blau's proposal was tabled by the organization's executive committee. The NCTE chose to leave control of what to teach in the hands of the textbook industry by default.[10]

The NCTE's opposition to a reading list has many sources, but some deserve special attention.

One is the rise of young adult fiction since the late 1960s, popular novels written for adolescents by an author who writes in the voice of an adolescent. Such novels, like those of Robert Cormier, S. E. Hinton, and Judy Blume, deal with adolescent problems about self-esteem and issues like drugs, alcohol, sexuality, peer pressure, and relationships with parents. Some of these books are engaging, and some are utterly banal. Defenders of this genre fear that it would be excluded from any list of great American literature. It might be. Some teachers are not sure that teen fiction deserves class time. Carol Jago, a California teacher who is a leader in the NCTE, maintains that students read two kinds of books, what she calls "mirror books" and "window books." The mirror books reflect their experiences with peers, parents, school, drugs, and sex; the window books offer "access to other worlds, other times, other cultures." Teenagers, she says, don't need help reading mirror books, but they need teachers to guide them through the unfamiliar language and references of window books. "If students can read a book on their own," she writes, "it probably isn't the best choice for classroom study. Classroom texts should pose intellectual challenges to young readers."[11]

A second, and related, reason for rejecting a reading list is the conviction, supported by the NCTE-IRA standards, that whatever is taught in school must be relevant to today's teens. The story must "include" them. It must be about them, not about adults in another era and culture. It must connect to their personal life experience, and it must be interpreted through the lens of their personal response. If students can't "relate" personally to *Lord Jim* or *Madame Bovary* or *Emma*, there is no point expecting them to read the book. This assumption encourages the narcissism of adolescence. Students are taught to look for themselves in the stories they read, rather than activate their imagination to enter other lives and other worlds.

A third, and related, source of opposition to a reading list is the assumption that students can comprehend only the literature written by and about people who share their racial, ethnic, or gender identity (embedded in this assumption is the belief that people have a single identity rather than multiple, intertwined identities). Girls must read stories about girls, which will then boost their self-esteem, and African American students must read stories by and about people who are also African American, for the same reason. Forgotten is W. E. B. Du Bois's statement about how his reading of classic literature liberated him and allowed him to break through "the veil" that white racists used to keep black people subjugated. He wrote: "I sit with Shakespeare, and he winces not. Across the color line I move arm in arm with Balzac and Dumas, where smiling men and welcoming women glide in gilded halls. From out the caves of evening that swing between the strong-limbed earth and the tracery of the stars, I summon Aristotle and Aurelius and what soul I will, and they come all graciously with no scorn nor condescension. So, wed with Truth, I dwell above the Veil." Certainly American schools must teach the nation's rich heritage of African American literature, which is a vital part of the American literary tradition, but it is wrong to exile the classic literature that inspired writers such as Du Bois, Ralph Ellison, Langston Hughes, Zora Neale Hurston, and Richard Wright.

Is reading a tool for social change? Those who are familiar with the sensational impact of Harriet Beecher Stowe's *Uncle Tom's Cabin* or James Baldwin's *The Fire Next Time* or Rachel Carson's *Silent Spring* would insist that it is. Is reading a tool for personal transformation? Those who have fallen in love with a poem and learned it "by heart"

NINE

History: The Endless Battle

Historians in free countries have a moral and professional obligation not to shirk the difficult issues and subjects that some people would place under a sort of taboo; not to submit to voluntary censorship, but to deal with these matters fairly, honestly, without apologetics, without polemic, and of course, competently. Those who enjoy freedom have a moral obligation to use that freedom for those who do not possess it.
—Bernard Lewis, "Other People's History"

IN HER BOOK *America Revised*, Frances FitzGerald wrote about the frenzied cutting and pasting of American history textbooks during the 1970s. The social upheavals of the previous decade, she observed, prompted "the most dramatic rewriting of history ever to take place in American schoolbooks." Responding to the demands of racial minorities and women, publishers dropped old heroes and added new ones. But the changes went well beyond the addition of new heroes. After years of civil disorder and antiwar protests, the upbeat, patriotic tone of American history textbooks written in the 1950s looked hopelessly naïve. The post-Vietnam textbooks rearranged not only surface details about American history, FitzGerald said, but also "the character of the United States." In place of the traditional coherent narrative about a nation that was constantly strengthening and expanding its democratic institutions, the textbooks presented what she called a "bewildering" litany of problems, crises, and conflicts.[1]

FitzGerald recognized that revision of history textbooks was both inevitable and necessary, but she concluded that the attempts over the years by both fundamentalists and progressives to impose on the books an idealized version of the past had resulted in ubiquitous censorship. This censorship occurred not in local communities, but at the source, in the publishing offices where the books were written and edited.[2]

Before the 1970s, American history textbooks had told a story of steady progress and (as one popular high school textbook was titled) "the triumph of the American nation." That triumphant march forward, however, left out important events and participants in American history. Until the civil rights movement, African Americans were scarcely noticed, except for their role as slaves, then forgotten. The transatlantic slave trade was mentioned in passing, rather than as one of history's most heinous crimes against humanity. The older texts ignored the wanton brutality of European explorers toward indigenous peoples in the New World. Women were offstage characters, as were immigrants and other ethnic minorities. The revisions of the early 1970s aimed to rectify these omissions.

As we have seen in earlier chapters, the political orientation of textbooks has long been contested. As publishers reached for a national market, they sought to avoid the controversies that might sink their books. Authors and editors cultivated an omniscient tone, radiating objectivity and authority. Unfortunately, the very format of the history textbook compels distortions; it presumes that a single book can render objective and decisive judgment on hundreds or thousands of controversial issues. In fact, the only sure truths in the books are dates and names (and sometimes the textbooks get those wrong). Beyond that, there is seldom, if ever, a single interpretation of events on which all reputable historians agree. The soul of historical research is debate, but that sense of uncertainty and contingency seldom finds its way into textbooks. By its nature, the textbook must pretend that its condensation of events and its presentation of their meaning are correct. In reality, every textbook has a point of view, despite a facade of neutrality; the authors and editors select some interpretations and reject others, choose certain events as important and ignore others as unimportant. Even when they insert sidebars with point and counterpoint on a few issues, they give the false impression that all other issues are settled when they are not. The pretense of objectivity and authority is, at bottom, just that: a pretense.

To the facade of pretend authority and pretend objectivity is added the necessity of simplification, the need to cram hundreds or even thousands of years of human history into a single volume, along with huge amounts of pedagogical aids and dazzling graphics. To produce history textbooks, teams of writers and editors have mastered the art of compression, reducing complex controversies to a few lines or a page, smoothing out the rough edges of reality, eliminating the confusion and rancor that invariably accompanied major crises. Historical debates disappear or shrink to a few leaden sentences. Historical conflicts lose their drama, and the ideas of passionate individuals shrivel to simple platitudes. When history is compacted as severely as space requires, with the life squeezed out of it, the predigested pap that is left is not memorable, does not establish a foundation for future learning, and is guaranteed not to inspire in young people a sense of excitement about the past.

Since the revisions of the 1970s, the field of history has undergone some wrenching changes, and a new generation of textbooks has appeared. The books published in the late 1990s reflect the political debates that roiled education in their time. None of them celebrates the evolution and triumph of American democratic institutions; that was the narrative of the 1950s. Nor do they reveal the confusion and incoherence that FitzGerald found in the books of the 1970s. The history books of the late 1990s resonate with the themes that dominated academic and political discourse in the last fifteen or twenty years of the twentieth century: race, gender, ethnicity, and in some, class conflict.

Most of those who wrote and edited the current crop of history textbooks came of age during the Vietnam War. This was the generation that experienced sharp divisions in American society. They were witnesses to or participants in the student rebellion, the antiwar movement, the counterculture, the civil rights movement, the feminist movement, the environmentalist movement, and other protests against the status quo. The protest movements of the 1960s and 1970s deeply influenced the academic world. During this era, radical ideologies took root in the academic disciplines, especially in the humanities departments. It became commonplace to read articles in academic journals asserting that American history was an ongoing struggle between oppressive white male elites and victim groups, that it exhibited a mere illusion of democracy but certainly not the real thing.

The political and social climate inevitably affected K–12 schooling. In the 1980s, American public schools became embroiled in emotionally charged debates about multiculturalism and, at the extremes, Afrocentrism. Curriculum experts asserted that traditional accounts of American history were not only racist and sexist but Eurocentric as well. Extreme advocates of multiculturalism insisted that history should teach ethnic pride, not the capacity to think analytically and dispassionately about events, and they disparaged accounts of world history or American history that paid too much attention to the influence of Europe. The more extreme multiculturalists wanted to revise the history curriculum to boost the self-esteem of non-European children, and they ignored concerns about the dangers of turning history into a tool for group therapy or political action.

With racial and ethnic diversity increasing across the nation as a result of increased immigration, educational leaders were keen to embrace multiculturalism. As they did, they shunned civic assimilation and Americanization, once considered the primary responsibility of the public schools. Patriotic exercises were discouraged for fear that they were insensitive to newcomers, who were taught instead to retain their allegiance to their ancestral cultures. After the end of the Cold War, there seemed to be no more external threats, no exigency to promote a common civic culture, no need to induct newcomers into a shared national identity. The greatest challenge for the future, it appeared, was to prepare children to live harmoniously in an interdependent global society, liberated from archaic nationalism and alert to global environmental issues.

The moment was right to tell a new story about the American past. In 1987, two states—California and New York—revised their curriculums in history to emphasize the participation of different groups in America's development. Their intention was to advance a generous, pluralistic interpretation of the American past, one that acknowledged the contributions of women, African Americans, Hispanics, Asian Americans, and others to the familiar American story and that added new heroes to the national pantheon. They sought not to replace the democratic narrative, but to enhance it by broadening its cast of characters. Two years later, Afrocentric critics denounced the New York curriculum for failing to recognize the primacy of Africa in world history. The California framework, however, became a national model for advocates of history instruction and survived intact for the next fifteen years, which was remarkable in that famously fractious state. Teachers responded positively to its call for myths and biographies in the elementary grades, and three years of world history in the upper grades.

As the states attempted to update the nation's story, the federal government entered the picture. In 1992, the Department of Education in the first Bush administration gave funding to various organizations to create voluntary national standards in academic subjects, one of which was history (I was assistant secretary for the Office of Educational Research and Improvement, which awarded grants for national standards). The group that won federal funding (from both the Department of Education and the National Endowment for the Humanities) was the National Center for History in the Schools at the University of California at Los Angeles, which was directed by Charlotte Crabtree, an education professor, and historian Gary B. Nash. The American history standards produced by the UCLA center reflected Nash's views about multiculturalism and his disdain for the "great man" approach to history. Ironically, it was Nash's textbooks for Houghton Mifflin that had won statewide adoption in California in 1990 after a political fracas over whether they were sufficiently multicultural.

When the center released its proposed standards for U.S. history and world history in 1994, Lynne V. Cheney attacked them. As chairman of the National Endowment for the Humanities in the first Bush administration, Cheney had provided the money to create the UCLA center and had subsidized the history standards as well. Cheney charged that the U.S. standards were leftist and politically correct, and that they stressed multiculturalism and the nation's sins while ignoring its achievements and heroes. Her complaints set off a media firestorm. Editorialists, talk-show hosts, and columnists battled over the political slant of the standards, and in early 1995 the United States Senate passed a resolution censuring them by a vote of 99–1. To quell the storm, the UCLA center revised the standards, cutting out the most politically charged language.

Although the UCLA center's standards promoted rigorous history, they set off a major culture war because of their relentless emphasis on identity politics. The controversy that they ignited doomed national academic standards by convincing both political parties that the issue was radioactive. After the collapse of the Bush administration's effort to launch national standards, the Clinton administration funded the development of state standards and tests with its Goals 2000 program.

The controversy over the history standards subsided, but their influence persisted. The defining mark of the UCLA standards was their claim that American history began as the meeting of three worlds: African, Amerindian, and European. This was a rejection of the traditional interpretation, which had traced the origins of the American nation to the English influence on American language, law, government, religion, culture, and institutions. The UCLA standards asserted that the nation began with cultural blending, in which no culture took precedence over any other. This formula, which perfectly fitted the political moment, was quickly adopted in many state standards, textbooks, and even the framework of the federally administered test, the National Assessment of Educational Progress (the UCLA project's director, Charlotte Crabtree, was a member of the NAEP governing board).

To write this book, I reviewed history standards from forty-nine states and the District of Columbia. I was pleasantly surprised to discover that history is making a comeback. When Goals 2000 was passed in 1994, only a few states—California, Virginia, Massachusetts, and Texas—had adopted history standards. As of 2002, in my judgment, there were fourteen states with strong U.S. history standards. Another ten had reasonably good U.S. history standards.

Which states have strong U.S. history standards? Alabama, Arizona, California, Delaware, Indiana, Kansas, Massachusetts, Nebraska, Nevada, New Mexico, Oklahoma, Pennsylvania, Texas, and Virginia. The best are California and Massachusetts. The standards in these states clearly identify the ideas, events, and individuals that students should learn about, without prescribing interpretations. This builds a solid body of knowledge about history and provides guidance to teachers, students, assessment developers, and textbook writers.

Which states have good but not great U.S. history standards? Colorado, Connecticut, Hawaii, Maryland, New Hampshire, New Jersey, New York, North Carolina, South Carolina, and Vermont. These states acknowledge the importance of history, but fail to identify any significant individuals in American or world history. (When criticized for leaving them out, New Jersey inserted the names of Washington, Jefferson, and Lincoln into its state standards.)

The remaining states have standards that consist of concepts and skills with minimal or no historical content. The standards in these states are so vague that it would be hard to assess what students have learned and hard for students to know when they have achieved proficiency.

Here are some examples of standards so vague that they cannot inform teaching or assessment:

> Account for and define the shift from the industrial society at the beginning of the twentieth century to the technological society at the end of the twentieth century. (Idaho)
>
> Analyze how United States political history has been influenced by the nation's economic, social, and environmental history. (Illinois)
>
> A student shall illustrate the influence of diverse ideals or beliefs on a theme or an event in the historical development of the United States. (Minnesota)
>
> The student will understand the way people in the United States and throughout the world perceive themselves over time. (Mississippi)

The states that ignore content are very prescriptive about the skills that students must learn. They call on students to do research, use technology, evaluate information, discover relationships, solve problems, work in teams, communicate, and exercise minutely specified "critical thinking skills" or "applied learning skills." But they leave blank the historical knowledge to which these skills should be applied.

The states without history standards presumably prefer to avoid the contentiousness associated with writing a state curriculum. Better, they apparently conclude, to let sleeping dogs lie and let teachers rely on their textbooks.

For this book I reviewed textbooks in American history and world history that are reputed to be widely used in junior high school and high school. I wanted to find out the narratives that currently prevail in the texts. What stories do they tell about American and world history? Do they prepare students to understand the major issues of our time? Have they been influenced by the consensual censorship that has afflicted literature textbooks and standardized tests?

Scholarly sources were of little help in this undertaking. While there are excellent histories of textbook controversies, such as Frances FitzGerald's *America Revised* and Jonathan Zimmerman's *Whose*

America? Culture Wars in the Public Schools, they do not evaluate current schoolbooks. Scholarly journals do not review history textbooks for the schools. The American Textbook Council in New York issues an excellent annual report about history textbooks, and the Textbook League in California reviews textbooks in many fields, including history, but these small organizations are not the American Historical Association or the Organization of American Historians, nor do they have the resources to check the factual accuracy or historical soundness of books that include hundreds of topics. Consequently, state and local textbook selection committees must make their own judgments, relying on teacher evaluations and reviews by political lobbyists. Laymen find it easier to make a judgment based on a book's appearance rather than its historical content. Surely these committees could do a better job of assessing textbooks if reputable scholars regularly reviewed them.

Textbooks are very important in American schools, especially in history. In most history classes, they *are* the curriculum. Many teachers are dependent on their textbook because they have not studied history. Today, most teachers of history in grades 7–12 have neither a major nor a minor in history; instead, they have a degree in social studies education, some other branch of pedagogy, a social science, or a completely unrelated field. Even those who do have a major or minor in history are unlikely to have a solid knowledge of every aspect of American or world history. Consequently, most teachers in this incredibly broad subject must rely of necessity on their textbooks to supply the organization and basic information for the course. Typically, students study American history in grades 5, 8, and 11, and they are likely to have a world history course in one year of middle school and another year of high school. Unless they are lucky enough to have a teacher who loves history and really knows it, what they are taught will be the material in the textbook.

For this book, I reviewed a dozen world history textbooks. The books overflow with artwork from civilizations around the world, but they suffer from superficiality. It is highly unlikely that children can absorb so many different epochs and civilizations. It is equally unlikely that there are more than a handful of teachers or college professors who know enough about the history of the world to teach such a course well. Students would learn more if they could spend an entire year, or even a semester, studying one civilization in depth rather than skimming across the history of the world.

In today's world history textbooks, complex events and ideas are reduced to vacuities because of space requirements. The nature of the books, with their forced march across civilizations and their lack of lively detail, makes it virtually impossible that any student would become enraptured with these studies. Certainly no one would read any of these books for pleasure. The best of them are excellent reference books, and the worst are incoherent, kaleidoscopic, and dull.[3]

The textbooks published in the late 1990s do, however, contain a coherent narrative. It is a story of cultural equivalence: All of the world's civilizations were great and glorious, all produced grand artistic, cultural, and material achievements, and now the world is growing more global and interconnected. Some bad things happened in the past, but that was a long time ago and now the cultures of the world face common problems.

In keeping with the imperative of avoiding ethnocentrism, no culture is "primitive." The idea of progress has disappeared, because no culture is more or less advanced than any other. Even those that had no literacy and only meager technology are described as advanced, sophisticated, complex, and highly developed. These are comparative terms, but cultures are never compared to one another.

Today's world histories, with rare exceptions, adhere closely to this line of cultural equivalence. The once traditional emphasis in textbooks on the growth of democratic institutions has nearly vanished. Glencoe's *World History: The Human Experience* is typical, with its upbeat descriptions of the "flowering of civilizations" in every part of the world. Students who learn about the world from these texts are unlikely to understand why some civilizations flourished and others languished, or why people vote with their feet to leave some places and go to others. Nor will they know that people in some regions have been trapped in grinding poverty for generations. Nor will they have any deep knowledge of the great ideological, political, economic, and military struggles between democratic nations and their totalitarian adversaries in the twentieth century. Nor will they perceive the critical importance of freedom, democracy, and human rights in the successful functioning of multiethnic, multireligious societies. Nor will they have any insight into the historic struggle to protect religious freedom and to separate religion from the state. Only one world history text focuses on the rise of democratic ideas, McDougal Littell's *Modern World History: Patterns of Interaction.*

In a significant variation on the cultural equivalence theme, Houghton Mifflin's world history text for middle school students, *To See a World,* implies that every world culture is wonderful except for the United States. It lauds every world culture as advanced, complex, and rich with artistic achievement, except for the United States. Readers learn that people in the United States confront such problems as discrimination, poverty, and pollution. Those who came to this country looking for freedom, the book says, found hardship and prejudice; the immigrants did all the hard work, but the settled population hated and feared them. Despite these many injustices, people kept trying to immigrate to the United States, but many were excluded because of their race or ethnicity. Compared to the other cultures in the world, the United States sounds like a frightening place. Why people keep trying to immigrate to this unwelcoming, mean-spirited culture is a puzzle.

The cultural equivalence narrative is so intent on shunning invidious comparisons that it elides hard questions. It celebrates everybody and omits many unpleasant historical facts. Cultural equivalence does not acknowledge that some societies developed democratic institutions based on the rule of law and others did not; it does not explain why some societies achieved a high standard of living for their people and others did not. It does not account for differences in literacy, public health, and technological development. It does not examine the relationship between a secular system of education and the development of civil society. When we read about the origins of democratic ideas, they turn out to be just another cultural "contribution," no more important in the grand sweep of history than art forms or trade routes in other civilizations. This zeal to respect all cultures and to overlook their form of government promotes selective ignorance about the past and the present.

The textbooks sugarcoat practices in non-Western cultures that they would condemn if done by Europeans or Americans. Seemingly, only Europeans and Americans were imperialistic. When non-European civilizations conquer new territories, the textbooks abandon their critical voice. They express awe toward the ancient empires of China, India,

Africa, and Persia but pay no attention to how they grew. Textbook after textbook tells the story of the "spread" of Islam. Christian Europe invades; Islam spreads.

The texts should have a consistent critical lens, in which gross violations of human rights—like slavery, cannibalism, genocide, human sacrifice, and the oppression of women—are recognized as wrong. To avoid moralism and presentism, the textbooks should encourage discussion of differences in historical and contemporary standards across cultures, while recognizing that our present-day values are based on democratic principles that evolved over time. However, the current textbooks are selectively critical. They condemn slavery in the Western world but present slavery in Africa and the Middle East as benign, even as a means of social mobility, by which slaves became family members, respected members of the community, and perhaps achieved prosperity and high office. The Aztec ritual of human sacrifice is glossed over as something that their religion required to ensure that the sun would rise the next day, a minor detail in what was otherwise a sophisticated and complex culture that valued education and learning.

The texts exaggerate women's roles, perhaps thinking that this will improve the self-esteem of female students. In text after text, we learn that women in non-Western societies enjoyed extensive rights and privileges. Women in ancient Egypt are said to have been the equals of their husbands; women in ancient Babylon had legal and economic rights; women in ancient China were very powerful within the household (later on, there was the unpleasant practice of foot-binding); women in ancient Japan played an important role in the arts; women in ancient Africa were the heads of their household; women in Incan culture were special attendants of the sun god; in certain Native American societies, women controlled the governing council. Even ancient India respected the "creative power of women," although a wife was sometimes required to throw herself on her husband's funeral pyre. Students might well wonder if the United States was the only culture in which women had to fight for equal rights.

The texts have difficulty criticizing tyranny unless it occurred before 1945. For example, some of them strive to find positive ways to describe Mao's murderous dictatorship in China. While admitting that he was responsible for the deaths of millions of people, they nonetheless try to look on the bright side by pointing to the great progress

that China made during his reign. Their message seems to be: Mao
may have killed millions, but he (like Mussolini) made the trains run
on time (or in Mao's case, improved education and health care).

From the texts we learn that Mao and the Communist Party redis-
tibuted land to the peasants; they built schools, bridges, canals, and
roads. They controlled inflation, reduced taxes, and fought corruption.
They pledged equality for women. They gained control by elections
and appointments, just as our officials do. They improved literacy and
public hygiene. They were reformers in a hurry. Students may infer
that if the land was "redistributed," the peasants actually gained ownership of the land; they may not realize that the state under Mao took
control of agriculture, businesses, and all other enterprises.

Some texts present Mao as a friendly, inclusive leader, who listened
to the peasants and won their support, just like our politicians. Most
texts point out that the Communist Party killed 1 million landlords
and that at least 20 million Chinese people died because of a famine
caused by Mao's disastrous Great Leap Forward. Some mention the
humiliation of teachers and professionals during the Cultural Revolution. But it often seems as though these were just unfortunate events
that occurred while Mao and the Communist Party were successfully
transforming China into a modern industrialized society. Not much is
said about thought reform, stigmatizing people by their social origins,
prison camps, the cult of personality, class warfare, the "anti-Rightist
campaign," the systematic oppression of political opponents, and other
ugly elements of totalitarianism. Students who read these texts will
have no understanding of China in the 1950s and 1960s. They might
well conclude that the Chinese Communist program had its ups and
downs, its good policies and its bad policies (just like ours), but overall
produced great gains for the Chinese people. It is an interesting and
depressing exercise to compare the textbooks' benign treatment of
Maoism with the chapter on Chinese Communism in *The Black Book
of Communism*.

Religion presents a special problem for the texts; they can't avoid
acknowledging its significance but they take care not to offend believ-
ers. Usually they do this by blurring the line between religious legends
and historical facts. Sometimes the texts explain these narratives by
a phrase like "as the Gospels say" or "according to Muslim belief."
But frequently, they simply state the origin myths and fundamental
beliefs of each religion as if historians had documented them. In

World History: Connections to Today, the transformation of Siddhartha Gautama from an ordinary man to the Buddha, the "Enlightened One," is respectfully and credulously told. In *To See a World*, Muhammad goes to the mountains, where, "according to Islamic tradition," he has a vision. The next paragraph says: "In the silence of the mountains, Muhammad was amazed to hear a voice. The voice seemed to come from everywhere at once. 'Recite!' the voice thundered. 'Recite in the name of thy Lord!' Twice more the message was repeated. Then Muhammad saw a figure looming against the sky. The figure told Muhammad that he had been chosen to be the prophet of God."[4] The reader of this world history textbook, a child in the sixth or seventh grade, may not understand that this story is religious belief, not a historical record of documented events.

The textbooks' treatment of religion is consistently deferential, even reverential; they seldom discuss the role of religious belief as a source of conflict. In their eagerness to show respect to all religions, the texts soft-pedal religious hatreds and the religious roots of many wars in history. In the textbooks' account, wars come and go, empires conquer one another, but religion hovers above all as a beneficent influence. The Crusades are briefly discussed, but their main importance seems to have been to whet the appetites of Europeans for rich goods from Asia. Children who read these books will not understand the passions stirred by religious differences, because such things don't seem to happen in textbook-land, where all religions coexist harmoniously.

The treatment of Islam, for example, lacks any critical analysis. The texts stress that Islam is tolerant and egalitarian; that its body of laws (the *sharia*) established a high standard of morality and ethics; and that Islam improved women's status. The texts appropriately describe Islamic civilization as the richest, most powerful, and most creative in the world during the Middle Ages, but they shed little light on the reasons for its loss of dominance to Europe.

The texts should honestly discuss the sources of conflict between different civilizations. Instead, they minimize differences by obscuring them. Thus, *World History: Connections to Today* says that the Koran "sets harsh penalties for crimes such as stealing or murder," but does not say that these penalties include hand amputation for stealing and public beheading for murder and are still imposed today in strict Islamic societies like Saudi Arabia.[5]

The Western democracies have recently become aware that their views of gender equality are not the same as those that prevail in the Muslim world. Again, the texts do not honestly portray the differences. Instead, they tell a remarkably consistent story of the improved status of women under Islamic rule. Houghton Mifflin's *Across the Centuries* asserts that Muslim women gained "clear rights in marriage and the right to an education. They had the right to control the earnings from their work, to make contracts, and to serve as witnesses in court."[6] Houghton Mifflin's *To See a World* says that Islam expanded the rights of women, allowing women to own and inherit property; even if a man has four wives, he must support all of them equally. If he divorces one of them, she is allowed to retain the property she had when she married him.[7] In Harcourt Brace's *World History: People and Nations*, we hear again about the enhanced status of Muslim women, who "gained certain rights with regard to property ownership."[8] In *World History: The Human Experience*, we read virtually the identical language about the enhanced position of women in Islamic societies. This text claims that the Iranian revolution of 1979 was a gain for women; it created new job opportunities for Iranian women because only women were permitted to tailor women's clothing and only women could teach in girls' schools. Prentice Hall's *World History: Connections to Today* states that "many educated Muslim women" have voluntarily returned to wearing traditional dress to show their "resistance to unpopular governments," their "refusal to imitate Western culture," or their "sincere loyalty to Muslim values and practices." An accompanying photograph shows women covered from head to toe "enjoy[ing] an afternoon of boating."[9]

Unable to say anything about religion unless it is positive, the textbooks become tongue-tied when dealing with Islamic fundamentalism. *World History: The Human Experience* says that Islamic fundamentalists want to "return to Muslim traditions" and compares them to conservative Protestants in the United States. It doesn't say what these traditions are, nor does it explain the difference between a society that protects diverse religious expressions and a theocracy that is ruled by religious authorities. Because the texts cannot write critically about Islamic fundamentalism, most ignore the aftermath of the Iranian revolution of 1979. In the textbook version of the story, the cruel and repressive Shah of Iran was replaced by a stern cleric, the Ayatollah Khomeini, who formed a government based on Islamic law. For most textbooks, the story of modern-day Iran ends there. Although a quarter-century has passed, the textbooks do not acknowledge that the theocratic reign of the ayatollahs has turned out to be as oppressive as the Shah's regime, just as willing to suppress dissent, and perhaps even more ready to hunt down and assassinate its enemies. Of course, none mentions the Ayatollah Khomeini's infamous fatwa against Salman Rushdie.[10]

The world history textbooks consistently shade or omit facts that might offend any racial, ethnic, or religious group. This does not occur by happenstance. Most of the books prominently identify an advisory board that includes representatives of religious and ethnic groups. Three publishers—Glencoe, Houghton Mifflin, and Prentice Hall—rely on the same individual from the Council on Islamic Education to review their Islamic content. This may account for the similarity of their material on Islam as well as their omission of anything that would enable students to understand conflicts between Islamic fundamentalism and Western liberalism. Some textbooks have multicultural advisory committees that include representatives of Jewish, Ukrainian American, Native American, Asian American, and Afrocentric organizations. Publishers that invite representatives of religious and ethnic groups to review their materials before publication are practicing self-censorship.

The sanitizing of world history texts has stripped them of their ability to present a critical, intellectually honest assessment of controversial subjects. On almost any subject relating to today's world, the texts strive so hard to be positive that they are misleading and inaccurate. The students who read most of the texts reviewed here would never know that there are serious political, social, and economic problems in the world.

For example, in 2002, prominent Arab intellectuals wrote a report for the United Nations Development Fund warning that their societies were being stifled by a lack of political freedom, the subjection of women, and a repressive social climate. Despite the region's vast oil income, the report said, per capita income was just above that of sub-Saharan Africa. Research, science, and technology were stagnant. Half the region's women were illiterate, and nearly all were denied opportunity for advancement. The authors of the report noted that the entire Arab world, in the thousand years since the reign of Caliph Mamoun, had translated as many books as Spain translates in just one year.[11]

American students, having read in their world history textbooks only about the glories of Islam, will have no understanding of contemporary realities in the Arab world. Unfortunately the same could be said of their misleading, adulatory treatment of other civilizations and cultures. It seems to be an unwritten rule not to admit that many nations today are undemocratic societies ruled by dictators and despots, where ordinary people have few rights or freedoms. This may be the consequence of publishers' guidelines that tell writers and illustrators to avoid showing anything negative about any group. Teachers and students who want an uncensored perspective should view the annual Freedom House survey, which ranks nations by the status of their political rights and civil liberties (www.freedomhouse.org/ratings/).

The one world history textbook that stands clearly outside the consensus of politically correct multicultural mush is Holt, Rinehart and Winston's *World History: Continuity and Change.* It deals honestly with controversial issues, without deferring to political sensitivities. It describes the removal of African slaves to the Arab world circa A.D. 1100 without invoking the customary exculpatory comments about the slaves' opportunities for advancement in their new land. Unlike the other texts, which tiptoe around the Iranian revolution of 1979, it explains that Ayatollah Khomeini's supporters required women to don the chador, and that they "imprisoned and executed many of their opponents."[12] Alone among the texts, it describes not only Nazi atrocities during World War II, but also Soviet and Japanese atrocities. While other texts appear to have been molded (i.e., censored) by their multicultural advisers, *World History: Continuity and Change* has an advisory board of historians, each of whom is a distinguished expert in his field. This is the textbook that I will keep on my shelf as a reliable reference book. I will place it alongside an extraordinary work that should be read by everyone who teaches world history: David S. Landes's *Wealth and Poverty of Nations,* which melds economic history, technological history, and cultural history, along with religion and geography. Landes's work abounds with the rich insights and anecdotes that demonstrate how exciting the study of world history might be and how stultifying, by contrast, the typical world history textbook is.

I evaluated U.S. history textbooks for students in different grades, most of them published in the late 1990s.[13]

The most salient characteristic of U.S. history textbooks published in the late 1990s is that they are splendid to the eye. They are also heavy; the average textbook has 1,000 pages. They are easy to look at, but hard to read. Like the world history titles, the American history texts assail the eye with splashy graphics, maps, and time lines, as well as historical cartoons, portraits, photographs, iconic images, section previews, section reviews, vocabulary tips, critical thinking questions, and suggested activities. The profusion of multicolor images and sidebars on every page is incredibly distracting, making it hard to follow the print. In most books, the graphics and study aids appear to take up more space than the text.

Unlike the graphics, the text is not splendid. In most books, the text is bland and colorless. Among the texts I examined, Joy Hakim's ten-volume middle-school series, *A History of Us*, is unusual in that it is written in a personal voice and is the work of a single author. It's hard to tell most of the other books apart. Their tone—that ubiquitous, smug tone of omniscience—seems to have come from the same word processor, the one that writes short declarative sentences and has a ready explanation for every event in history. This tone of certainty is very annoying, particularly because the books seem to share the same political orientation. Textbooks like Democratic presidents; textbooks don't like Republican presidents. Textbooks always know what should have been done in every crisis. Instead of presenting conflicting views and letting students debate ideas, the textbooks tell them what they are supposed to believe. They pretend to their readers that every historical question has an answer, and they know what it is.

With only a few exceptions, the textbooks are not good models of historical writing. They constantly moralize about the past, as though everyone in 1850 or 1900 or 1950 should have known what we know today and should have shared our enlightened values. They abound with anachronisms. Many imply that American women chafed under the burden of sexism at every point in history, not letting students know that feminists—in the contemporary sense—were an avant-garde until the 1970s. In addition, the books frequently quote historical figures or offer data without giving any sources for teachers and students who want to learn more, failing to demonstrate by deed the importance of presenting verifiable evidence. The reader must take it on faith that the information presented to them is accurate, because there is no way to check up on it.

Some books quote unnamed sources, which is unforgivable. *Ameri-*

can Odyssey quotes "a columnist" who said of President Eisenhower in 1959, "The public loves Ike. The less he does, the more they love him." Why not name the columnist so that readers can gauge the credibility of the source? *The Americans* cites a "Nahua witness" (presumably an Aztec) who "recalled" that the Spanish conquistadors "picked up the gold and fingered it like monkeys. . . . They hungered like pigs for that gold." Who was this mysterious eyewitness to one of history's great calamities, and where were his or her recollections recorded? *Call to Freedom* quotes "one woman" remembering dust storms on the Great Plains and "one voter" expressing "the views of the Silent Majority," without identifying either of them. Boyer's *The American Nation* freely cites quotes from unnamed sources, like "an Iowa farmer" who blockaded a highway to prevent food reaching the market in hopes of pushing up prices during the Depression, and "one shipyard worker" who described a general strike in Seattle as "the most beautiful thing I [had] ever seen!" Who were these people? In *The American Republic Since 1877*, a "sarcastic critic" makes a condescending comment about Levittown, but the reader is left to wonder whom that snob might be or whether the authors of the text want us to look down our noses at people who live in tract housing.[14]

Failing to cite sources is bad scholarship. Textbooks that indulge in this practice encourage their students to do the same. This is a corrupting lesson that directly contradicts one of the most important tenets in the study of history, which is that historians must base their conclusions on evidence that is available for review by others. Lapses in the transparency of a writer's sources are often a sign of distortion or fictionalization in the writing. *America: Pathways to the Present* includes references to its quotations. Others should do it as well.

Poor writing in textbooks is nothing new. What is truly new about American history textbooks of the late 1990s is their ideological slant. Like the world history texts, they too are committed to cultural equivalence. The old U.S. history narrative stressed the important contributions of England and the European Enlightenment to the new American nation. It centered on the rise of democratic institutions and the ongoing struggle to expand the rule of law. Those of us who were not of English descent nonetheless appreciated the unique contribution of England to our forming as a nation. The Magna Carta and the common law were part of our legacy from England, as were Shakespeare and Dickens. This approach is now considered "Eurocentric."

Older textbooks, even those written in the 1980s, reminded their readers that the United States was a country with a moral foundation grounded in values such as individual freedom and democratic institutions such as the rule of law. The great drama of American history, as traditionally told, was the conflict between the nation's ideals and its practices; over time, that conflict was increasingly resolved by elections, court decisions, legislative changes, a bloody civil war, heroic individuals, reform movements, and other advances in the realization of democratic institutions. Even when they were violated, the ideals were a constant set of goals toward which Americans continued to strive.

It was once customary for writers of American history textbooks to explain to their readers why it was important to study history. In the depths of the Depression, David Saville Muzzey told the readers of his popular high school text, *A History of Our Country:*

> You are growing up in this age of opportunity and responsibility. In a few years we of the older generation shall have passed on, leaving to you the duty of carrying on the American tradition of a free democracy, of preserving our ideals and remedying our faults. This is Your America. Whatever business or profession you may choose to follow, you are all, first and foremost, American citizens. Each of you should think of himself or herself as a person who has inherited a beautiful country estate, and should be proud to keep up that estate and to make such "modern improvements" as will increase its beauty and comforts. You would be ungrateful heirs indeed if you did not care to know who had bequeathed the estate to you, who had planned and built the house, who had labored to keep it in repair for your occupancy, who had extended and beautified its grounds, who had been alert to defend it from marauders and burglars. If you agree with me, you have already answered the question why you should be eager to study American history. . . .

Henry Graff opened his 1985 text, *America: The Glorious Republic,* with these words: "The United States shines among the nations as the 'land of opportunity.' Simply stated, the phrase means that Americans enjoy the freedom to pursue individual goals. As we study United States history, we quickly learn that this freedom was built into American life from the start . . . [and] has been the magnet drawing immigrants to the American continent ever since." Daniel Boorstin and Brooks Mather Kelley begin *A History of the United States:* "American history is the story of a magic transformation. How did people from everywhere join the American family?"[15] None of the textbooks written in the 1990s expresses such appreciation for American institutions, values, and ideals.

The new textbooks have adopted the "three worlds meet" paradigm that the UCLA history center advocated as part of its proposed national standards for U.S. history. In the new textbooks, democratic values and ideals compete with a welter of themes about geography, cultural diversity, economic development, technology, and global relations. In order to show how "three worlds" met, the texts downplay the relative importance of the European ideas that gave rise to democratic institutions and devote more attention to pre-Columbian civilizations and African kingdoms.

The drive to re-center American history around the theme of cultural equivalence has led to some strained assertions and overstatements. For example, the texts praise the technological accomplishments, the architecture, and the artistry of the Mayans, the Incans, and the Aztecs, but minimize or ignore human sacrifice and slavery in these societies. Only two texts (*A History of the United States* and *The American Journey*) point out that these civilizations had not invented the wheel and had no iron tools. None of the texts attempts to explain how the indisputable cultural achievements of these Meso-American civilizations influenced the culture or institutions of the United States. (The fact that Mayan civilization died out about A.D. 900, nearly 900 years before the establishment of the United States, suggests just how tenuous that influence was.)

Distortions appear as texts create new heroic figures and omit inconvenient facts. In *Call to Freedom* and *The American Journey,* one learns of the glorious Mansa Musa, the Islamic ruler of Mali, who undertook a pilgrimage (*hajj*) to Mecca in 1324 with a grand retinue that included many thousands of slaves. Neither text explains why Mansa Musa should be considered a major figure in the history of the United States, which did not exist until 450 years after his fabled *hajj*. Similarly the texts point to the great Islamic university in Timbuktu

(*The American Nation* claims that Timbuktu boasted three universities, but the other texts report only one), but it is hard to see any connection between the Islamic university in Timbuktu and the subsequent development of the United States. Most of the texts blame Europeans for African slavery, as if this horror were unprecedented before the arrival of the Portuguese on the west coast of Africa in the late fifteenth century. One of the better texts, *The American Republic Since 1877*, observes that "slavery had existed in Africa and other parts of the world for centuries," and that "West African slavery began to change with the arrival of Arab traders, who exchanged horses, cotton, and other goods for slaves. The gold trade also increased the demand for slaves." *World History: Continuity and Change* has the most thorough account of the slave trade, including an excellent map showing the numbers of people who were shipped across the Atlantic and their destinations (about 5 percent were sent to British North America, and the remainder to Brazil, the Caribbean, and Spanish America).[16]

Some textbooks engage in both overstatement and strategic omissions. For example, *American Odyssey: The United States in the Twentieth Century* describes the Anasazi Indians in mythical terms. The Anasazi lived in the southwest from about 900 to 1300, when they abandoned their homes. There is no attempt to explain how they influenced the United States, which was not established until nearly five hundred years after the Anasazi disappeared. The text implies that the Anasazi were far wiser than we, who think of ourselves as advanced. The Anasazi "fostered an egalitarian culture in which people functioned as equals. Without kings, chiefs, or other official authority figures to compel cooperation, members of Anasazi farming villages built dams, reservoirs, and irrigation systems," as well as four hundred miles of "roads and broad avenues." Because they had "leisure" and "prosperity," they produced "beautiful baskets and pottery, but their greatest creativity flowered in architecture." The book praises the Anasazi's multistoried "apartment complexes" and says: "Until a larger apartment building went up in New York City in 1882, the size of this Anasazi building of the tenth century remained unsurpassed in the world." It is worth recalling that the Anasazi were a prehistoric people who left no written records. How does the author know that they had no kings, chiefs, or other authority figures? Is it credible that a prehistoric civilization constructed roads, dams, and large dwellings with no one in charge? Were Anasazi structures really taller than any other building in the ancient or medieval world? *World History: Connections to Today* claims that "the Mayan pyramids remained the tallest structures in the Americas until 1903, when the Flatiron building, a skyscraper, was built in New York City." Since no text gives the height of any of these structures, it's anyone's guess which claim is right or why it matters. Why does no other textbook mention the remarkable feats of the Anasazi? They sound like the wise, egalitarian communes envisioned by campus radicals in the 1960s, having achieved "power to the people" without authority figures. This heroic description of the Anasazi fails to mention a heated debate among scholars in recent years over whether the Anasazi practiced human sacrifice and cannibalism. To do so would destroy the myth of the Anasazi as the New Age ideal, so the text omits this discussion, thereby denying readers a chance to grapple with a fascinating issue in pre-Columbian history.[17]

In the American history depicted in today's texts, the only civilization that seems to be not so very advanced is Europe's. Reviewing *In the Course of Human Events,* William J. Bennetta of the Textbook League, a relentless critic of both right-wing and left-wing politicization, asks, "What do you suppose the Europeans were doing while those Indians and Africans were erecting temples, instituting 'complex' societies, controlling fire, taking courses at Timbuktu U., and making sculptures?" They seem to have been "a uniformly dull lot, bereft of any cultural variations worth mentioning, who did little but to build ships, sail about, and engage in trade. There is not a single photo to depict European art or architecture. There is not a word about Dante, Erasmus, Brunelleschi, Bramante or Leonardo; not a word about Donatello, Giotto, Ghiberti or Botticelli; not a word about Raphael, Machiavelli, Gutenberg, Durer, or the van Eycks. All of these, and the cultures they represented, have been erased. All of Europe's universities, too, have been erased."[18]

The textbooks' jousting over whose ancestor was first and best is silly. If one tells the history of the land that is now the United States, then the story begins with the indigenous peoples who long predated European settlers. If one tells the origins of the American people as now constituted, then the story must draw upon world history. If one tells the history of the nation-state, then the story begins with the ideas of freedom and democracy that evolved in England and Europe. The textbooks confuse these stories, and in doing so, have nearly buried the narrative about the ideas and institutions that made our national government possible.

The important point that history teaches is almost lost in the textbooks' adherence to cultural equivalence. The capacity for good and evil is distributed across human societies, among all racial and ethnic groups and across genders as well. The age-old question that faces all societies is how to establish civilized norms grounded in the rule of law, justly administered. This should be the central theme of our histories, for it is the theme that connects history to civic understandings.

The texts published since 1995 show the influence of the publishers' bias guidelines, as well as the politicization that the guidelines represent. The words and phrases listed in the guidelines do not appear in the books. American Indians no longer are members of "tribes," but members of groups or nations. Slaves are now mainly "enslaved persons." Gender-specific adjectives and nouns have disappeared. The word *man* no longer is a synonym for humanity. There are no "Founding Fathers," no "brotherhood of man."

The changes go well beyond linguistic sanitizing. A specific politics has been injected into historical accounts. World War II sometimes seems to be as much about the fight for women's rights as it was about the struggle against Hitler and fascism. Several texts lionize the upheavals of the 1960s; they present the counterculture and student rebels as avatars of social justice, with no balanced discussion of the negative phenomena of that era, such as bombings, harassment of dissident professors and speakers on campus, and a sustained assault on social mores. The texts treat the Black Panthers as a beneficent social service organization, with little or no reference to their tactics of intimidation and violence.[19] Any number of other historical and contemporary topics, once controversial, have been flattened out, prettified, and watered down for mass consumption.

Nothing betrays the banality of the typical history textbook as much as the pages that publishers quickly pieced together to explain the events of September 11, 2001. These pages, written for the Texas state adoption process in the summer of 2002, provide less information and less penetrating analysis than a student might find in any newsmagazine published within a month of the terrorist attacks. At fault, however, were not the hapless writers and editors of these weighty tomes, who tried to maintain the customary mask of omniscience, but the expectation that a history textbook must teach both history and current events. With this demand, the states guarantee that the texts will conclude on a slick, superficial note, all the while pretending to be comprehensive and accurate for every event from 10,000 B.C. (or earlier) to yesterday.

There are a few good U.S. history textbooks. Boorstin and Kelley's *History of the United States* is the most literate title on the market, with the wisest perspective. Henry Graff's *America: The Glorious Republic* is well written and comprehensive. It would be best if teachers could use two different textbooks for the same subject and compare the differences between them. Appleby, Brinkley, and McPherson's *American Journey* and the same authors' *American Republic Since 1877* would be an ideal complement to Boorstin and Kelley or Graff. Then students would be able to see that authors and editors make choices and that textbooks disagree.

Under the best of circumstances, students should read both primary source documents and accounts written by historians with the vivid details and depth of perspective that bring history to life. This cannot happen until those who teach history are well educated in history. Students should also learn how historians piece their stories together from various kinds of records of the past, how historical interpretations differ and change, and how historians put their evidence out in the open to be judged by their readers and other historians. The textbooks should be only reference works.

Why do American students remember so little of the history that they are taught? When the National Assessment of Educational Progress tested for knowledge of U.S. history in 1994 and 2001, more than half of high school seniors scored below basic, which is as low as one can score. In no other subject—not in mathematics or science or reading—do American seniors score as low as they do in U.S. history. Maybe it is because their textbooks are so dull; maybe it is because so many of their history teachers never studied history and can't argue with the textbooks' smug certainty. Maybe it is because the students don't know why they are supposed to remember the parade of facts that are so glamorously packaged between covers. Or maybe it is because, with the teenagers' usual ability to spot a scam, they know that much of what is taught to them is phony and isn't worth remembering.

TEN

The Language Police: Can We Stop Them?

Don't you see that the whole aim of Newspeak is to narrow the range of thought? In the end we shall make
thoughtcrime literally impossible, because there will be
no words in which to express it.
—George Orwell, *1984*

RAY BRADBURY, a writer who smells trends long before anyone else,
saw what was happening in 1979. In a coda appended to the paperback
version of *Fahrenheit 451,* his classic novel about book burning, Bradbury wrote about his encounters with political censorship. He recalled
the letter he received from a college student who suggested that he
should add some female characters to his book *The Martian Chronicles;*
he also received a complaint that the blacks in the book were "Uncle
Toms," followed by a letter alleging that the story was prejudiced in
favor of blacks. Soon afterward, a publisher asked him for permission
to reprint a story in a high school anthology, but would he mind deleting references to a "God-light" and "the Presence"? He refused. Bradbury found another high school anthology that had compressed the
stories of classic authors: "Every story, slenderized, starved, blue-
penciled, leeched and bled white, resembled every other story. Twain
read like Poe read like Shakespeare read like Dostoevsky read like—in
the finale—Edgar Guest. Every word of more than three syllables had
been razored. Every image that demanded so much as one instant's
attention—shot dead."

He saw where the pressure to sanitize books and stories was coming
from, and he saw what it meant. Every minority, he said, whether
"Baptist/Unitarian, Irish/Italian/Octogenarian/Zen Buddhist, Zionist/

Seventh-day Adventist, Women's Lib/Republican, Mattachine/Four Square Gospel" was ready to burn books, and "every dimwit editor who sees himself as the source of all dreary blanc-mange plain porridge unleavened literature, licks his guillotine and eyes the neck of any author who dares to speak above a whisper or write above a nursery rhyme." When he discovered that his own publisher had quietly, and without his permission, removed seventy-five sections from *Fahrenheit 451*, he was outraged. He learned about it from students who wrote to tell him that his novel about censorship and book burning had been expurgated. He fumed, "If Mormons do not like my plays, let them write their own. If the Irish hate my Dublin stories, let them rent typewriters." He would not, he thundered, "go gently onto a shelf, degutted, to become a non-book."[1]

When Bradbury wrote his protest, he thought he was dealing with the aberrant acts of miscellaneous bluenoses, prudes, Pecksniffians, pharisees, and numbskulls. What he did not know was that he had experienced the early phase of a movement that was being institutionalized in educational publishing. It was no accident that chunks of his controversial novel silently dropped onto the cutting-room floor. This was not the result of arbitrary decisions made by a "dimwit editor." The system of silent editing was beginning to work. It was getting organized, becoming a regular process.

For twenty-five years, give or take a few, we have lived with this system of silent censorship. We have seen the refinement and perfection of this system, in which publishers have joined hands with state school boards to censor texts and tests. Now that the rules of censorship have been codified, editors, writers, and illustrators know well in advance what is not acceptable. No one speaks of "censoring" or "banning" words or topics; they "avoid" them. The effect is the same. Euphemisms are kinder and gentler than raw truths. By now, the rules and guidelines could be dismissed, and they would still function because they have been deeply internalized by the publishing industry. George Orwell and Franz Kafka would have understood this system perfectly; it works best when it permeates one's consciousness and no longer needs to be explained or defended.

The goal of the language police is not just to stop us from using objectionable words but to stop us from having objectionable thoughts. The language police believe that reality follows language usage. If they can stop people from ever seeing offensive words and ideas, they can prevent them from having the thought or committing the act that the words signify. If they never read a story about suicide or divorce, then they will never even think about killing themselves or ending their marriage. If they abolish words that have *man* as a prefix or suffix, then women will achieve equality. If children read and hear only language that has been cleansed of any mean or hurtful words, they will never have a mean or hurtful thought. With enough censorship, the language police might create a perfect world.

This is nonsensical, because the schools are not a total institution. They do not control every aspect of children's lives. Children are influenced not just by what they read in their textbooks and what they encounter on tests, but by their families, their friends, their communities, their religious institutions, and—perhaps more than anything else—the popular culture. Much as the censors may hope to limit what children see and hear, they do not have the means to do it.

Censorship in the schools, whatever its purposes, is censorship. It should be abhorrent to those who care about freedom of thought, to those who believe that minds grow sharper by contending with challenging ideas. How boring for students to be restricted only to stories that flatter their self-esteem or that purge complexity and unpleasant reality from history and current events. How weird for them to see television programs and movies that present life in all its confusing and sometimes unpleasant fullness, then to read textbooks in which language, ideas, and behavior have been scrubbed of anything that might give offense. How utterly vapid to expect that adolescents want to see themselves in everything they read, as if they have no capacity to imagine worlds that extend beyond their own limited experience, as if they will be emotionally undone by learning about the world as it is. How tedious it is for young people to find that school is an exercise in narcissism rather than an opportunity to discover the mysteries of time, space, and human nature.

The censorship that has spread throughout American education has pernicious and pervasive effects. It lowers the literacy level of tests because test makers must take care to avoid language as well as works of literature and historical selections that might give offense. It restricts the language and the ideas that may be reproduced in textbooks. It surely reduces children's interest in their schoolwork by making their studies so deadly dull. It undermines our common culture by imposing irrelevant political criteria on the literature and history that are taught.

Censorship distorts the literature curriculum, substituting political judgments for aesthetic ones. Because of the bias and social content guidelines, editors of literature anthologies must pay more attention to having the correct count of gender groups and ethnic groups among their characters, authors, and illustrations than they do to the literary quality of the selections. State education officials carefully scrutinize the former and ignore the latter. Once literary quality no longer counts, almost anything can be included in literature anthologies, such as television scripts, student essays, advertisements, and other ephemera, while indisputably major authors share equal billing with authors whose work will never be known outside the textbook industry. Quietly but inevitably, what we once considered our literary heritage disappears from the schools.

Censorship distorts the history curriculum by introducing political considerations into interpretations of the past, based on deference to religious, ethnic, and gender sensitivities. Forced into a political straitjacket, almost all history texts echo one another, with nary a fresh interpretation, idea, or anecdote, nor even a good argument to excite their readers' enthusiasms. Like books written by historians, history texts should have a point of view, but they should not all have the *same* point of view. That stultifying conformity guarantees that no sparks will be struck in young minds; it is a recipe for boredom.

The censorship regime has a chilling effect on writers, as Nat Hentoff pointed out. Most authors, editors, and illustrators whose work is affected by bias guidelines have accepted their permanence or have been reluctant to challenge them for fear of not getting any more assignments. No one wants to be accused of bias, so everyone acquiesces to political restrictions on his or her work. Compared to the larger society, where ideas are freely expressed and freely debated, the schools have become an island of censorship in a sea of freedom.

All this sanitizing of children's educational materials is meant to mold their minds and shield them from inappropriate language and thoughts. Censors always believe that their work is for the good of society. But is it? Who gave the schools and the publishers the right to decide how the next generation's minds should be molded? Because the censorship process developed so gradually and with so little public scrutiny, there has been no debate about whether it should be there at all. This is an issue that needs the light of day—that is, open and vigorous public discussion—shined upon it.

Rewarding groups that complain by allowing them to censor words and images that they don't like only encourages them. Censorship should be stopped, not rewarded with compliance and victories.

It must be said, not in defense of the publishers' bias guidelines, but as a way of seeing the climate in which they acted, that their bowdlerizing was in step with larger trends in society. They did not act alone. On hundreds of college campuses, administrators adopted speech codes and sexual harassment codes to punish anyone who told offensive jokes or said something that made another student feel uncomfortable. Students and faculty members were hauled before campus tribunals for saying the wrong thing, whether in jest, in the classroom, or on a date. In offices and universities across the nation, diversity trainers instructed workers and students about the language that they should and should not express. How natural, in this climate where political reeducation had a certain social validity, to expect that the schools would lead the way in building a new social order.

Jonathan Rauch criticized these attempts at cultural cleansing in his book *Kindly Inquisitors,* in which he argued passionately for freedom of thought. He wrote "No one has the right to be spared sacrilege—not Jews, not Muslims, not ethnic minorities, not me, and not you." What should we do about people who say offensive things? Rauch advises, "Ignore them." And what should we do to assuage the feelings of people who have been offended? Rauch says, "This and only this: *absolutely nothing.* Nothing at all." This is the burden of maintaining a free society. His advice to the offended is to be thick-skinned. No one has a right not to be criticized or offended. The campus speech codes, Rauch writes, aim to silence people with wrong opinions: "The agenda is always the same: stifle ideas you hate in the name of a higher social good." But in our society, the role of authorities is not to get rid of wrong opinions, but to protect the expression of opinion and the free exchange of ideas. A free society is not free unless it tolerates offensive words and unpopular opinions.[2]

Another way of expressing Rauch's view is the formula that parents used to teach their children. Whenever anyone says anything offensive, the correct response is: "Sticks and stones may break my bones, but words will never hurt me." Sometimes words do hurt, but we learn to live with that hurt as the price of freedom. The alternative is to submit our speech and our reading materials to bias guidelines, official censors, language police, and thought police.

Think about the strange contradiction in the life of a high school student today. At home, she watches television and sees news about terrorism, hijackings, massacres, famines, and political upheavals. She goes on-line, where the Internet gives her access to anything and everything. She goes to the movies, where she enters a world of fantasy, romance, passion, excitement, and action. She listens to music and hears the latest hip-hop, rap, or heavy metal performers. Before she falls asleep at night, she e-mails gossip to her friends.

Monday through Friday, she goes to school. There she will open her literature textbook to a story that has been carefully chosen for its inoffensive language. The teacher points out that the story was written by a woman; the student doesn't care. It's boring. She will read entries written by students her age. She will quickly skip over all the pedagogical junk about critical thinking, looking for something interesting. She won't find it. Then she moves to history class, where the class is studying the role of women in the Revolutionary War; the text says that twenty thousand women fought in the war. Really? Hmmm. Yawn.

Little, maybe nothing that happens in the classroom can compete with the powerful stimuli that she can easily find on television, in the movies, on her CDs, in video games, and on the Internet. For her and her friends, school is the Empire of Boredom. They do not know and surely do not care that an entire industry of bias reviewers has insulated them from any contact in their textbooks with anything that might disturb them, like violence, death, divorce, or bad language. They are safe, but they are bored.

No matter. When the school day is done, they will turn again to the videos and music and movies that feed them eroticized violence and surround them with language that knows no constraints. This is as wacky a combination as anyone might dream up: schools in which life has been homogenized, with all conflicts flattened out, within the context of an adolescent culture in which anything goes.

Schools cannot beat the entertainment industry at its own game. What they have to offer students is the chance for intellectual freedom, the power to think for themselves rather than gorge themselves on the media's steady diet of junk food.

But under the present regime of censorship, the schools themselves are not intellectually free. They cannot awaken young people's minds with great literature when the stuff in their literature textbooks is so banal, so ordinary, so engineered to appeal to childish narcissism. They cannot expect students to think critically about social issues and the world when their history textbooks do not demonstrate critical thinking. When their reading is constrained by the fine filter of bias and sensitivity codes, how can it possibly contribute to the forming of critical and independent minds? How can young people discover the drama of history when their textbooks anesthetize them with a relentless slog across the centuries, lumbering from one event to the next, from one culture to the next? Great history consists of great stories, surprising convergences, the conflict of powerful ideas, and the historian's insights into motivation and character that illuminate the life of a man or woman—but all of that has been sacrificed to the gods of coverage and cultural equivalence.

Something is terribly wrong here. The schools should be the great agencies of social and intellectual equality. This they cannot be unless they can give all children access to great literature and teach them the joy of reading. Reading is the key to future success; it builds vocabulary, it enriches the imagination, it opens new worlds. The novelist Mario Vargas Llosa has argued that new technologies will not replace literature. The new technologies are fast, and they are exciting, but they are only a means of getting information. What literature offers is a common denominator for understanding human experience; it allows human beings to recognize one another across time and space. By reading great literature, Vargas Llosa argues, we learn "what remains common in all of us under the broad range of differences that separates us. Nothing better protects a human being against the stupidity of prejudice, racism, religious or political sectarianism, and exclusivist nationalism than this truth that invariably appears in great literature: that men and women of all nations and places are essentially equal, and that only injustice sows among them discrimination, fear, and exploitation."[13] Literature, in other words, actually does what the bias and sensitivity codes claim to do: It teaches us about our common humanity. And it does so by speaking candidly to our souls, not by censoring what we read.

Great literature does not comfort us; it does not make us feel better about ourselves. It is not written to enhance our self-esteem or to make us feel that we are "included" in the story. It takes us into its own world and creates its own reality. It shakes us up; it makes us think. Sometimes it makes us cry.

The same is true of the study of history. It is possible to spend one's time learning only about one's own family or ethnic group. But there are worlds of adventure, worlds of tragedy awaiting us if we are willing to let go of our solipsism, our narcissism, our need to study only ourselves.

The flight from knowledge and content in the past generation has harmed our children and diminished our culture. As they advance in school, children recognize that what they see on television is far more realistic and thought-provoking than the sanitized world of their textbooks. The numbing nihilism of the contentless curriculum produced by the puritans of left and right merely feeds the appetite for the exciting nihilism of an uncensored and sensationalized popular culture, skillfully produced by amoral entrepreneurs who are expert at targeting the tastes of bored teenagers.

We do not know how these trends may yet affect the quality of our politics, our civic life, and our ability to communicate with one another somewhere above the level of the lowest common denominator. The consequences can't be good. As the technologies of the entertainment industry become more sophisticated, so too will its appeals to emotion, to feelings, to our basest instincts.

When we as a nation set out to provide universal access to education, our hope was that intelligence and reason would one day prevail and make a better world where issues would be resolved by thoughtful deliberation. The great goal of education was not to cultivate an elite, but to abolish class distinctions to the extent that education can do so. Here is the rub. Intelligence and reason cannot be achieved merely by skill-building and immersion in new technologies; elites have always known this and have always insisted on more for their children. Intelligence and reason cannot be developed absent the judgment that is formed by prolonged and thoughtful study of history, literature, and culture, not only that of our own nation, but of other civilizations as well.

That is not what our children get today. Instead, they get faux literature, and they get history that lightly skims across the surface of events, with no time to become engaged in ideas or to delve beneath the surface. Not only does censorship diminish the intellectual vitality of the curriculum, it also erodes our commitment to a common culture. It demands that we abandon our belief in *e pluribus unum,* a diverse people who are continually becoming one. The common culture is not static; it evolves to reflect the people we are becoming. But even as it changes, it preserves the memory of "we, the people" in song and story; whatever our origins, we too become part of the American story, neither its first nor its last chapter. We are not strangers, and we do not begin our national life anew in every generation. Our nation has a history and a literature, to which we contribute. We must build on that common culture, not demolish it. As our common culture grows stronger, as we make it stronger, so too grows our recognition that we share a common destiny.

The censorship that is now so widely practiced has become ubiquitous. Publishers do it. States do it. The federal government does it.

What can we do?

We can stop censorship. We must recognize that the censorship that is now so widespread in education represents a systemic breakdown of our ability to educate the next generation and to transmit to them a full and open range of ideas about important issues in the world. By avoiding controversy, we teach them to avoid dealing with reality. By expurgating literature, we teach them that words are meaningless and fungible.

The reign of censorship must end.

The strategy to achieve this goal is threefold: competition, sunshine, and educated teachers. The first and most important step in stopping censorship is to eliminate the state textbook adoption process. Currently, there are a score of states that have statewide adoptions, but the two that count most are California and Texas. What these two states decide has a huge impact on the fate of individual textbooks and their publishers. This is cartel-like behavior; the publishing marketplace has been warped by the adoption process, putting too much power into the hands of these two states. This concentration has raised the cost of publishing, favored the publishers with the deepest pockets, driven small publishers out of business, and concentrated the industry into four publishing giants, only one of which is American-owned. The dearth of competition has not been good for the textbook industry, which now operates like a procurement process rather than a competitive marketplace. It is easy for an aggressive pressure group—no matter how small and unrepresentative—to threaten a textbook company with public humiliation and the loss of market share. It is this leverage in the two big states that has enabled extremists to manipulate the states' requirements to fit their own political agenda.

So, first and above all, discontinue the state adoption process for textbooks. There is no reason why every school district in a state should be required to use the same textbooks or to choose their books from a list approved by state officials. The states should publish their standards for different academic subjects and then let schools and teachers decide how to spend their funds for materials. Some may want to buy textbooks; they should buy the ones they think are best. Some may decide to spend their money on trade books or software or other teaching tools. The state (and the districts) should not tell them which textbooks to buy.

Disestablishing and deregulating the textbook adoption process in the states would create a real market with real competition. It would encourage new writers and publishers to enter the market and create products for the schools. It would enable teachers to choose the materials they think are best for their students. It would empower teachers, rather than state officials, to make these decisions, which is the way college textbooks are chosen. The effect of deregulation would be to transform the highly political nature of textbook adoption. Political pressure groups would lose their leverage; they would no longer be able to threaten publishers at statewide hearings. They would have to make their case to millions of teachers and thousands of schools rather than the four big publishers. Bad textbooks would die a natural and unlamented death. Good books, whether texts or trade books, would have a chance to flourish.

Opening up the market to competition would free teachers to choose biographies, histories, or anthologies, rather than textbooks. Competition would encourage textbook publishers to seek out livelier writing. It would encourage writers to break free of the dull formulas that now make most of the textbooks look like peas in a pod, with interchangeable literary selections and conventional, politically safe opinions. With a real market, instead of state regulation, textbooks would be free to differ from one another.

Competition is the first prong of the strategy to end the reign of censorship in education.

The second strategy is sunshine. The strongest protection for censorship is public ignorance. The public needs to know what the publishers, the states, and the federal government are doing to educational materials. Whether it is textbooks or tests, we have a right to know what the authorities are censoring and to force them to bring their decisions into the open for public scrutiny. They do not believe that the public has a right to see their censorship practices. When I asked the Connecticut Department of Education to show me reading passages that had been rejected for bias and sensitivity reasons, the head of the state testing program wrote back to say that "it wouldn't be appropriate to share that material with you." Public outrage has a tonic effect. When the press revealed that the New York State Education Department was censoring literary excerpts on its examinations, officials were so embarrassed that they immediately pledged to stop doing it. As a result, the exams will be closely watched by the press in the future to see if the censorship does end.

That is why it is important to create mechanisms to expose censorship to public review. Many things that are done surreptitiously cannot withstand the light of day. So we must shine that light on the bias and sensitivity review process to make sure that it does not serve as a mechanism for imposing censorship and stopping "thoughtcrimes."

Every publisher and every state should publish, if they have not done so already, their bias guidelines.

They should publish on their Web sites the names of the members of their bias and sensitivity review panels, along with their curricula vitae.

Every bias and sensitivity review panel, whether analyzing textbooks or tests, should include teachers of the subject, not just diversity specialists. Teachers of English, history, science, and mathematics should be part of the review process.

Whenever bias and sensitivity reviewers propose the deletion of words, phrases, and stories, their recommendations should be reviewed by a panel of laymen (such as a state or local school board). Nothing should be deleted until it has passed the test of common sense.

The specific recommendations made by bias and sensitivity reviewers should be published on the Internet. The reading passages and test items that they reject should be released for the public to see. The public has a right to know what has been excluded from textbooks and tests and why.

State education officials should be required to divulge, in detail and with complete transparency, the names of the specific literary works that they have used as sources for examinations in the past. This information should be easily accessible on Web sites. Teachers and parents should know whether the state selects high-quality literature for its tests or whether such literature is regularly avoided.

Test developers should make public the results of DIF analysis and whether the analysis led to the deletion of test items, and if so, which items. DIF is the statistical analysis that shows whether some groups do better on specific test items than other groups. The public needs to know whether test developers are using DIF analysis to exclude test items about sports, the military, or agriculture, or items that incorporate charts or maps, or items that require spatial skills. If questions about geometry are excluded, for example, because blind children can't answer them, then the public should be told. These are decisions that affect everyone, and the public has a right to know about these decisions and how they affect American education.

At present, there is no public disclosure about DIF analysis or the bias and sensitivity review process; indeed, there is an atmosphere of furtive secrecy that hides these evaluations from public view. The public should be informed whether test items or literary passages have been censored because of DIF analysis or sensitivity review, and for what specific reasons.

One important way to bring sunshine into the world of textbook publishing is to make sure that textbooks are reviewed just like trade books. Broadening the purchasing decision by abolishing the state adoption process for textbooks would help; it would encourage the growth of an independent review media by creating a broad popular need, and hence a market, for reliable reviews. When nonfiction books are published, there is a large apparatus that assesses their value in the daily press, in weekly magazines, and in scholarly journals. Reviewers judge their accuracy, the soundness of their interpretations, their clarity and coherence. No such system exists for textbooks. Before teachers select a textbook, they should have in hand a sheaf of reviews by respected critics and scholars. They should know the strengths and weaknesses of the books in the opinions of a wide variety of reviewers before they choose them.

The third prong of the strategy to abolish censorship is better-educated teachers. In every subject area, we need teachers who are masters of what they teach. We need science teachers who would refuse to buy textbooks that are laden with errors and politicization. We need teachers of English who have read widely and know just the piece of literature—the fable, myth, legend, short story, novel, poem, or play—that will arouse young minds. We need teachers of history who will reject textbooks that are bland, boring, and misleading, and who will seek out histories, biographies, and primary documents that will make their students thirsty to learn more. We should insist that those who teach history have actually studied it (not social studies!) in college or can pass a college-level test of history.

In a perfect world, teachers would be so well educated that they wouldn't rely on textbooks. It is not a perfect world, however, and there will continue to be a need for textbooks to help teachers organize their courses. Textbooks will not disappear in our lifetimes. Even so, we must trust teachers to make the judgments about which books work best for them and for their students. I would rather trust teachers than leave these important decisions to the highly politicized process that now governs textbook publishing in America today.

I would also trust teachers to exercise good judgment in selecting readings for their students that are appropriate to their age and understanding. To expect third graders to read Shakespeare or Dickens would be foolish; a wise teacher knows what his or her students can grasp, and which readings are worthy of students' time.

The question before us, the battle really, is whether we have the will to fight against censorship. I, for one, want to be free to refer to "the brotherhood of man" without being corrected by the language police. I want to decide for myself whether I should be called a chairman, a chairwoman, or a chairperson (I am not a chair). I want to see *My Fair Lady* and laugh when Professor Higgins sings, "Why can't a woman be more like a man?" As a writer, I want to know that I am free to use the words and images of my choosing. As a grandmother, I want to feel sure that my grandchildren can read works of literature and history that have not been cleansed, sanitized, expurgated, and bowdlerized by the language police. As an American, I would like to be certain that future generations of children will no longer be robbed of their cultural heritage and their right to read—free of censorship.

Let us, at last, fire the language police. We don't need them. Let them return to the precincts where speech is rationed, thought is imprisoned, and humor is punished.

As John Adams memorably wrote in 1765, "Let us dare to read, think, speak, and write. . . . Let every sluice of knowledge be opened and set a-flowing."[4] Even in our schools.

Appendix 1

A Glossary of Banned Words, Usages, Stereotypes, and Topics

This is a compilation of words, usages, stereotypes, and topics banned by major publishers of educational materials and state agencies. They have been collated from various bias guidelines that editors, writers, and illustrators use when preparing textbooks and tests. This list would be even longer if I had been able to obtain the bias guidelines from every publisher, state testing agency, and professional association.

The first section is a dictionary of banned words, along with the recommended alternative when there is one. Each entry ends with a reference to its source, which is identified by its initials; the sources will be found at the end of this document. The sections that follow contain lists of banned usages, stereotypes, and topics.

Able-bodied (banned as offensive, replace with *person who is non-disabled*) [SF-AW]

Able-bodied seaman, able seaman (banned as sexist, replace with *crewmember*) [HRW1, NES]

Abnormal (banned as demeaning to persons with disabilities) [SF-AW, ETS2]

Actress (banned as sexist, replace with *actor*) [MMH, HM1, HAR2, NES]

Adam and Eve (replace with Eve and Adam to demonstrate that males do not take priority over females) [APhilA]

Afflicted/afflicted with/afflicted by/affliction (banned as a reference to persons with disabilities, replace with "a person who has . . .") [SF-AW, HAR2, ETS2]

Aged, the (banned as demeaning to older persons) [HM1]

Airman (banned as sexist, replace with *aviator*) [HRW]

America/Americans (use with care, because it suggests "geographical chauvinism" unless it applies to all people in North America, South America, and Central America; refer instead to *people of the United States*) [SF-AW, HM1, HAR2, NES]

American policy, American economy (replace with *U.S. policy, U.S. economy*) [NES]

Anchorman (banned as sexist, replace with *anchor person, newscaster*) [HM1, NES]

Arthritic patient (banned as offensive, replace with *person who has arthritis*) [SF-AW]

Authoress (banned as sexist, replace with *author*) [HMı, HRW3, NES, ETS2]

Average man (banned as sexist, replace with *average person*) [MMH, HMı, NES]

Average working man (banned as sexist, replace with *the average worker*) [SF-AW]

Aviatrix (banned as sexist, replace with *aviator*) [HMı, HARı, HRW3, NES, ETS2]

Babe (banned as sexist) [HMı]

Backward (banned as ethnocentric when it refers to a cultural or ethnic group) [HMı, SF-AW, AIR]

Backward country (banned as ethnocentric when referring to cultural differences) [SF-AW, ACT]

Backwoodsman (banned as sexist, replace with *pioneer*) [HRWı]

Ball and chain (banned as sexist, replace with *spouse, wife, partner, mate*) [MMH, ETS2]

Barbarian (banned as ethnocentric when it refers to a cultural or ethnic group) [HMı]

Baseman (banned as sexist, replace with *infielder*) [HRWı]

Batsman (banned as sexist, replace with *batter*) [HRWı]

Beast (banned as offensive when it refers to a person) [HMı]

Bellman (banned as sexist, replace with *bellhop*) [HRWı]

Best man for the job, the (banned as sexist, replace with *best candidate*) [ETS2]

Better half, the (banned as sexist, replace with *spouse, wife, partner, mate*) [HRW3, ETS2]

Biddy (banned as ageist, demeaning to older women) [SF-AW]

Birdman (banned as sexist, replace with *ornithologist*) [HRWı]

Birth defect (banned as offensive, replace with *people with congenital disabilities*) [SF-AW]

Bitch (banned as reference to female dog) [MMH]

Black/blacks (banned as a noun) [HAR2, SF-AW]

Black (banned as adjective meaning evil) [CT]

Blind, the (banned as offensive, replace with *people who are blind*) [SF-AW, HMı, HARı, NES, ETSı, ETS2, RIV]

Blind as a bat (banned as handicapism) [NYC]

Blind leading the blind (banned as handicapism) [NYC]

Boatman (banned as sexist, replace with *boat operator*) [NES]

Bookworm (banned as offensive, replace with *intellectual*) [HMı]

Border patrolman (banned as sexist, replace with *border guard*) [NES]

Boyish figure (banned as sexist, replace with *youthful figure*) [HMı]

Boys' night out (banned as sexist) [NES]

Brave (banned as offensive when it refers to a Native American person) [HRWı, HMı]

Brotherhood (banned as sexist, replace with *amity, unity, community*) [MMH, SF-AW, HRW3, CT, APhilA]

Brotherhood of man, the (banned as sexist, replace with *the human family, solidarity, affection, collegiality, unity, congeniality*) [APhilA]

Bubbler (banned as regional bias, replace with *water fountain*) [AIR]

Buck (banned as objectionable when referring to Native American male) [SF-AW]

Busboy (banned as sexist, replace with *dining room attendant*) [NES]

Bushman (banned as a relic of colonialism, replace with *San*) [NYC]

Businessman, businesswoman (banned as sexist, replace with *business person*) [MMH, HM1, HAR1, HRW1, HRW3, NES, ETS2]

Busman (banned as sexist, replace with *bus driver*) [HRW1]

Busybody (banned as sexist, demeaning to older women) [SF-AW]

Cabin boy (banned as sexist, replace with *ship's steward*) [HRW1]

Cameraman (banned as sexist, replace with *camera operator, camera technician*) [HAR1, NES]

Career girl (banned as sexist, replace with specific occupation) [NES, ETS2]

Career woman (banned as sexist, replace with specific occupation) [NES, ETS2]

Cassandra (banned as sexist, replace with *pessimist*) [AIR]

Cattleman (banned as sexist, replace with *cattle rancher*) [HRW1]

Caveman (banned as sexist, replace with *cave dweller*) [HM1, HRW3]

Chairman (banned as sexist, replace with *chair* or *chairperson* or *moderator* or *presiding officer*) [MMH, SF-AW, HM1, HAR1, HRW3, NES, ETS2, APA]

Chick (banned as sexist) [HM1]

Chief (banned as a noun referring to a Native American leader) [HRW1]

Chief Sitting Bull (banned as relic of colonalism, replace with *Totanka Iotanka*) [NYC]

Chippewa (banned as inauthentic, replace with *Ojibwa* or *Anishinabe*) [SF-AW]

Cleaning woman, cleaning lady (banned as sexist, replace with *housekeeper, custodian, janitor*) [HM1, HAR1, NES, ETS2]

Clergyman (banned as sexist, replace with *member of the clergy*) [HM1, HAR1, NES]

Codger, old codger (banned as demeaning to older men) [SF-AW, HM1]

Coed (banned as sexist, replace with *student*) [MMH, NES, ETS1, ETS2]

Colored (banned as offensive, refer to specific group) [HM1]

Confined to a wheelchair (banned as offensive, replace with *person who is mobility impaired*) [HAR1, ETS2]

Congressman (banned as sexist, replace with *member of congress, representative*) [SF-AW, HM1, HAR1, HAR2, HRW3, ETS2]

Costume (banned as offensive when referring to the clothing of a specific group, replace with *clothing*) [SF-AW]

Councilman (banned as sexist, replace with *council member*) [NES]

Courageous (banned as patronizing when referring to a person with disabilities) [ETS2]

Cover girl (banned as sexist, replace with *model*) [HRW1]

Craftsman (banned as sexist, replace with *craft worker, craftperson, artist*) [MMH, NES]

Craftsmanship (banned as sexist, no replacement) [NES]

Crazy, crazy person (banned as offensive, replace with *person with an emotional disability or a mental impairment*) [SF-AW, HM1, HAR1, NES]

Creature (banned when referring to people with disabilities) [SF-AW]

Credit to her/his race (banned as racist, replace with a *great American* or a *great person*) [SF-AW]

Cripple, crippled (banned as offensive, replace with *orthopedic disability, person with a mobility impairment*) [SF-AW, HM1, HAR2, NES, NYC, ETS2]

Crippled children (banned as offensive, replace with *children who are disabled*) [HAR1]

Cro-Magnon man (banned as sexist, replace with *Cro-Magnon people*) [MMH]

Crone (banned as demeaning to older women) [SF-AW]

Crotchety (banned as reference to older persons) [HM1]

Cult (banned as ethnocentric when referring to a religious group) [SF-AW, ETS2]

Culturally deprived (banned as ethnocentric when referring to a racial, ethnic, or cultural group) [HM1, ACT]

Culturally disadvantaged (banned as ethnocentric reference to cultural differences) [ACT]

Dame (banned as sexist, replace with *woman*) [HM1]

Dark Continent (banned as racist, replace with *Africa*) [SF-AW, AIR, RIV]

Deaf, the (banned as offensive, replace with *people who are deaf* or a *person with loss of hearing*) [SF-AW, HM1, NES, ETS2]

Deaf and dumb (banned as offensive) [SF-AW, HM1, NES, NYC]

Deaf-mute (banned as offensive, replace with *person who can't hear or speak*) [SF-AW, HM1, HAR1, NES]

Defective (banned when referring to people with disabilities) [SF-AW]

Deformed (banned as offensive, replace with *person with physical disability*) [SF-AW]

Delivery boy, deliveryman (banned as sexist, replace with *deliverer, messenger*) [HAR1, NES]

Devil (banned) [AEP]

Dialect (banned as ethnocentric, use sparingly, replace with *language*) [SF-AW]

Differently abled (banned as offensive, replace with *person who has a disability*) [SF-AW]

Dirty old man (banned as sexist and ageist) [NYC]

Disabled, the (banned as offensive, replace with *people with a disability*) [SF-AW, HAR1]

Dissenter (ethnocentric, use with caution) [ETS2]

Distaff side, the (banned as sexist) [ETS2]

Dogma (banned as ethnocentric, replace with *doctrine, belief*) [SF-AW]

Doorman (banned as sexist, replace with *door attendant*) [HRW1]

Down's syndrome (banned as offensive, replace with *Down syndrome*) [ETS2]

Draftsman (banned as sexist, replace with *drafter*) [NES]

Drunk, drunken, drunkeness (banned as offensive when referring to Native Americans) [SF-AW, HM2]

Duffer (banned as demeaning to older men) [SF-AW]

Dummy (banned as offensive, replace with *people who are speech impaired*) [SF-AW]

Dwarf (banned as offensive, replace with *person of short stature*) [SF-AW, HAR1]

Early man (banned as sexist, replace with *early human*) [HAR1, NES]

East, Eastern (banned as Eurocentric when used to discuss world geography; refer to specific continent or region instead) [HAR2]

Economically disadvantaged (banned as ethnocentric reference to racial, ethnic, or cultural group) [HM1]

Egghead (banned as offensive, replace with *intellectual*) [HM1]

Elderly, the (banned as ageist, replace with *older persons*) [SF-AW, APA]

Eskimo (banned as inauthentic, replace with *Inupiat* and *Yupik* or *Native Arctic peoples* or *Innuvialuit*) [SF-AW, ETS1] or replace with *Inuit, Inupiat, Yupik, Yuit* or *Native Arctic peoples;* note: *Yupik* and *Yuit* are "not interchangeable") [HAR2]

Exceptionalities (banned as patronizing to people with disabilities) [ETS2]

Exotic (banned when referring to Asian Americans) [SF-AW]

Extremist (banned as ethnocentric, replace with *believer, follower, adherent*) [SF-AW]

Factory foreman (banned as sexist, replace with *supervisor*) [ETS2]

Fair sex (banned as sexist, replace with *women* or *females*) [HM1, NES, AIR, ETS2]

Fairy (banned because it suggests homosexuality, replace with *elf*) [AEP]

Fanatic (banned as ethnocentric, replace with *believer, follower, adherent*) [SF-AW]

Fat (banned, replace with *heavy, obese*) [AEP]

Feebleminded (banned as offensive, replace with *person with mental disability*) [HM1, NES]

Fellowship (banned as sexist, replace with *friendship*) [HRW3]

Fellow worker (banned as sexist, replace with *coworker*) [NES]

Feminine wiles (banned as sexist, replace with *wiles*) [HM1]

Filly (banned as sexist, unless one means a female horse) [MMH]

Fireman (banned as sexist, replace with *firefighter*) [MMH, HM1, HAR1, HRW3, NES, AIR, ETS2]

Fisherman (banned as sexist, replace with *fisher, angler*) [MMH, HAR1, NES]

Forefathers (banned as sexist, replace with *ancestors, precursors*) [MMH, SF-AW, NES, CT]

Foreman (banned as sexist, replace with *supervisor, manager*) [MMH, HAR1, NES]

Founding Fathers (banned as sexist, replace with *the founders, the framers*) [HM1, HAR1, HRW3, APhilA]

Four eyes (banned as offensive to the visually impaired) [HM1]

Fraternity (banned as sexist, replace with *community, kinship, solidarity, collegiality*) [APhilA]

Fraternize (banned as sexist) [HRW3]

Freak (banned as demeaning to person with disability) [SF-AW]

Freshman (banned as sexist, replace with *first-year student*) [SF-AW, NES]

Frontiersmen (banned as sexist, replace with *pioneers, forebears, settlers*) [HAR1]

Gal (banned as sexist) [SF-AW, HM1]

Gal Friday, Girl Friday (banned as sexist) [HRW3, HM1, AIR]

Garbageman (banned as sexist, replace with *garbage collector, trash collector*) [HAR1]

Gay (banned, as it suggests homosexual, replace with *happy, lighthearted*) [AEP]

Geezer (banned as demeaning to older men) [SF-AW]

Geriatric patient (banned as demeaning to older persons) [SF-AW]

Gimp (banned as offensive to person with mental or physical disability) [SF-AW, HM1]

Girl (banned except for reference to females under sixteen) [MMH, SF-AW, HM1, HRW3, NES, ETS2]

Girlish laughter (banned as sexist, replace with *laughter*) [HM1]

Girls, the (banned as sexist) [NES]

God (banned) [AEP]

Golden Agers (banned as ageist, replace with *older persons* or *persons who are older*) [HM1, SF-AW]

Gringo (banned as offensive) [NES]

Groundsman (banned as sexist, replace with *grounds worker*) [NES]

Grow to manhood (banned as sexist, replace with *grow to adulthood*) [ETS2]

Handicap, the handicapped, handicapped person (banned as offensive, replace with *disability, person with a disability*) [HAR1, NES, ETS1, ETS2]

Handyman (banned as sexist, replace with *maintenance worker*) [NES]

He (banned as sexist, replace with *he or she* or *they*) [AIR]

Headman (banned as sexist, replace with *leader*) [HRW1]

Hearing-impaired (banned as offensive, replace with *deaf* or *hard-of-hearing*) [ETS2]

Heathen (banned as ethnocentric when referring to religion, replace with *nonbeliever*) [SF-AW, NYC, ETS2]

Heathen (banned when referring to American Indians) [SF-AW, HM1, HM2, NYC]

Heiress (banned as sexist, replace with *heir*) [HM1]

Hell (banned, replace with *heck, darn*) [AEP]

He-man (banned as sexist) [CT]

Henpecked husband (banned as sexist) [MMH, NES]

Heretic (use with caution when comparing religions) [ETS2]

Heroine (banned as sexist, replace with *hero*) [SF-AW, HAR2, NES]

Hispanic American (use with caution as some groups object to the term's suggestion of a shared European cultural heritage, replace with specific nationality) See **Latin American** [NES]

Homosexual (banned, replace with *person, child*) [AEP]

Hordes (banned as reference to immigrant groups) [CT]

Horseman, horsewoman (banned as sexist, replace with *equestrian*) [HRW1]

Horsemanship (banned as sexist, replace with *riding skill*) [NES]

Hottentot (banned as a relic of colonialism, replace with *Khoi-khoi*) [NYC]

Houseman, housemaid (banned as sexist, replace with *servant, housekeeper*) [HRW1]

Housewife (banned as sexist, replace with *homemaker, head of the household*) [SF-AW, HAR1, HAR2, NES, ETS2]

Hussy (banned as sexist) [SF-AW]

Huts (banned as ethnocentric, replace with *small houses*) [SF-AW]

Idiot (banned as offensive to person with mental disability) [SF-AW, HM1, NES]

Imbecile (banned as offensive to person with mental disability) [HM1, NES]

Inconvenienced (banned as patronizing to people with disabilities) [ETS2]

Indian giver (banned as offensive) [NYC]

Insane (banned as offensive, replace with *person who has an emotional disorder or psychiatric illness*) [SF-AW, HM1, NES]

Inscrutable (banned when referring to Asian Americans) [SF-AW, MMH]

Inspirational (banned as patronizing when referring to a person with disabilities) [ETS2]

Insurance man (banned as sexist, replace with *insurance agent*) [MMH, HAR1, HRW3, NES, ETS2]

Invalid (banned when referring to a person with disabilities) [ETS2]

Jewess (banned as sexist, replace with *Jew*) [NES]

Journeyman (banned as sexist, no replacement) [NES]

Jungle (banned, replace with *rain forest, savannah*) [AEP]

Junk bonds (banned as elitist) [ETS1, ETS2]

Junkman (banned as sexist, replace with *junk dealer*) [HRW1]

Kaffir (banned as a relic of colonialism, replace with *African*) [NYC]

King Philip (banned as reference to a Native American leader, replace with *Metacome*) [NYC]

Kinsman (banned as sexist, replace with *relative*) [HRW1]

Ladies, the (banned as sexist) [NES]

Lady (banned as sexist) [MMH, SF-AW, HM1]

Lady doctor (banned as sexist) [MMH]

Lady lawyer (banned as sexist) [HRW3, NES, ETS1, ETS2]

Ladylike (banned as sexist, replace with *feminine*) [HRW3]

Lame (banned as offensive, replace with *walks with a cane*) [SF-AW]

Landlord, landlady (banned as sexist, replace with *owner*) [NES]

Latin American (use with caution, as some groups resent the term's insensitivity to national differences, and some find it inaccurate, since not all such people speak a Latin-based language. Replace with specific nationality) See **Hispanic American** [NES]

Laundress, laundryman (banned as sexist, replace with *laundry worker*) [HRW1]

Layman (banned as sexist, replace with *layperson, nonexpert, nonspecialist*) [NES]

Lazy (banned as adjective when referring to American Indians) [SF-AW]

Letterman (banned as sexist, replace with *student who has won a letter*) [HRW1]

Limping along (banned as handicapism) [NYC]

Lineman (banned as sexist, replace with *line installer*) [MMH, NES]

Linesman (banned as sexist, replace with *sports official*) [HRW]

Little person (banned as offensive, replace with *person of small stature*) [SF-AW, HAR1]

Little woman, the (banned as sexist, replace with *wife, spouse, partner, mate*) [HM1, HRW3, ETS1, ETS2]

Longshoreman (banned as sexist, replace with *dock worker*) [NES]

Lumberman, lumberjack (banned as sexist, replace with *woodcutter*) [NES]

Lunatic (banned as offensive, replace with *person with a psychiatric illness*) [SF-AW]

Maid (banned as sexist, replace with *house cleaner*) [ETS2]

Mailman (banned as sexist, replace with *mail carrier*) [MMH, HRW1, HM1, HAR1, HRW3, NES, ETS2]

Majority group (banned as offensive reference to cultural differences) [ACT]

Male nurse (banned as sexist, replace with *nurse*) [MMH, SF-AW, HMI, NES, ETS]

Male secretary (banned as sexist, replace with *secretary*) [HMI]

Man (banned as a sexist verb, as in *man the sailboats* or *man the trucks*) [MMH, NES]

Man, mankind, men (banned as sexist, replace with *humankind, the human race, humanity, persons, people, figures, personalities, women and men, men and women*) [MMH, HMI, HARI, HAR2, NES, AIR, MA, NYC, ETS2]

Man's achievements (refer instead to *human achievement*) [MMH, NES, ETS2]

Man and wife (banned as sexist, replace with *husband and wife*) [MMH, SF-AW, HARI, ETS2]

Manhood (banned as sexist, replace with *adulthood, maturity*) [HMI, NES]

Man-hour (banned as sexist, replace with *work hour, total hours*) [HARI, NES]

Manhunt (banned as sexist, replace with *hunt for a person*) [HRWI]

Maniac (banned as offensive to persons with a psychiatric disability) [HMI, NES]

Mankind (banned as sexist, replace with *humankind, humanity, human beings, people*) [NES, NYC, ETS2, RIV]

Manly (banned as sexist) [MMH]

Man-made (banned as sexist, replace with *artificial, synthetic, manufactured*) [MMH, HMI, HARI, HRW3, NES, AIR, NYC, ETS2, CT]

Mannish (banned as sexist) [HRW3]

Man-of-war (banned as sexist, replace with *warship*) [HRWI]

Man on the street (banned as sexist, replace with *the average person*) [MMH, HMI, RIV, NES]

Manpower (banned as sexist, replace with *human power, workers, personal strength, workforce, human energy*) [MMH, SF-AW, HMI, HARI, NES, AIR, NYC, ETS2]

Man-size job (banned as sexist, replace with *big, enormous*) [HRW3, ACT, ETS2]

Masculine drive (banned as sexist) [HMI]

Massacre (banned as offensive when referring to Native Americans) [HM2]

Maven (banned as regional or ethnic bias) [ETSI]

Mental deficiency (banned as insensitive) [ETS2]

Mentally ill, the (banned as offensive, replace with *person with a mental or emotional disability*) [HMI, HARI, NES, ETS2, APA]

Mentally retarded (banned as offensive, replace with *person with mental retardation*) [SF-AW]

Middle East (banned as reflecting a Eurocentric worldview, replace with *Southwest Asia;* may be acceptable, however, as a historical reference) [HAR2]

Middleman (banned as sexist, replace with *go-between, intermediary*) [HRW3, NES]

Midget (banned as offensive, replace with *person of short stature*) [SF-AW, HARI]

Milkman (banned as sexist, replace with *delivery person*) [HRWI]

Minority group (banned as offensive reference to cultural differences) [ACT]

Mister, the (banned as synonym for husband) [HMI]

Mongoloid (banned as offensive, replace with *person with Down syndrome*) [SF-AW, HMI, NES, NYC]

Mother Russia (banned as sexist, replace with *Russia, vast land of rich harvests*) [HM1]

Mothering (banned as sexist, replace with *nurturing, parenting*) [APA]

Motherland, fatherland (banned as sexist, replace with *native land*) [HRW1]

Mrs., the (banned as synonym for wife) [HM1]

Mulatto (banned as racist) [NES]

Mute (banned as handicapism when used as a noun) [NYC]

Mysterious (banned when referring to Asian Americans) [SF-AW]

Myth (banned when referring to traditional beliefs of American Indians, replace with *story* or *narrative*) [SF-AW]

Native (banned when referring to a Native American person, banned also when used as a noun) [HM1, NYC]

Navajo (banned as inauthentic, replace with *Diné*) [SF-AW]

Newsboy (banned as sexist, replace with *newspaper carrier*) [NES]

Newsman (banned as sexist, replace with *newsperson, reporter*) [HRW1, NES]

Newspaperman (banned as sexist, replace with *reporter*) [HRW1]

Niggardly (banned, replace with *frugal, cheap*) [AEP]

Night watchman (banned as sexist, replace with *night guard*) [HRW1]

Nobleman (banned as sexist, replace with *member of the nobility* or *noble*) [HRW1]

Normal (banned as offensive, replace with *a person without disabilities*) [SF-AW, ETS2]

Office boy (banned as sexist, replace with *messenger, office helper*) [NES]

Old (banned as an adjective that implies helplessness, dependency, or other negative conceptions) [NYC]

Old folks (banned as ageist, replace with *persons who are older*) [HM1]

Old hag (banned as offensive) [NYC]

Old lady (banned as demeaning to older women) [SF-AW]

Old lady, the (banned as sexist when referring to one's wife) [HRW3]

Old maid (banned as both sexist and ageist) [SF-AW, HM1]

Old maidish (banned as sexist) [HRW3]

Old man (banned as demeaning to older men) [SF-AW, HRW3]

Old man, the (banned as synonym for husband) [HM1, HRW3]

Old witch (banned as offensive) [NYC]

Old wives' tales (banned as sexist, replace with *folk wisdom*) [NES, AIR]

Ombudsman (banned as sexist, no replacement) [NES]

One-man band (banned as sexist, replace with *one-person performance*) [MMH]

One-man show (banned as sexist, replace with *solo performance*) [MMH]

Orient, Oriental (banned as offensive, replace with *Asian, Japanese,* etc.) [SF-AW, MMH, HAR2, NES]

Overcoming a disability (banned as offensive when referring to a person with a disability) [ETS2]

Pagan (banned as ethnocentric when referring to religion, replace with *nonbeliever*) [SF-AW, HM1, ETS2]

Paper boy (banned as sexist, replace with *paper deliverer*) [HRW1]

Papoose (banned as demeaning to Native Americans) [MMH, SF-AW, HM1, HM2]

Paralytic (banned as offensive, replace with *person who uses crutches*) [SF-AW]

Paraplegic (banned as offensive, replace with *people with paraplegia*) [SF-AW]

Past one's prime (banned as demeaning to older persons) [SF-AW]

Peculiar (banned when it refers to religious practices or beliefs) [SF-AW]

Physically challenged (banned as patronizing to persons who have a physical disability) [SF-AW, ETS2]

Plainsman (banned as sexist, replace with *plains dweller*) [HRW1]

Poetess (banned as sexist, replace with *poet*) [SF-AW, HM1, HAR1, HRW3, NES, ETS2]

Policeman (banned as sexist, replace with *police officer*) [MMH, HM1, HAR1, HRW3, NES, AIR]

Pollyanna (banned as sexist, replace with *optimist*) [AIR]

Polo (banned as elitist) [ETS1, ETS2]

Pop (banned as regional bias when referring to soft drink, replace with *Coke, Pepsi* [however, note that brand names are banned by California social content review guidelines]) [AIR]

Postman (banned as sexist, replace with *mail carrier*) [MMH, HRW1]

Postmaster, postmistress (banned as sexist, replace with *post office director*) [HRW1]

Pressman (banned as sexist, replace with *press operator*) [NES]

Primitive (banned as ethnocentric when referring to racial, ethnic, religious, or cultural groups) [SF-AW, HM1, NES, NYC, AIR, ACT, ETS2]

Primitive man (banned as sexist, replace with *primitive peoples*) [HAR1, HAR2, NES]

Profoundly deaf (banned as offensive, replace with *person with loss of hearing*) [HAR1]

Provider, the (banned as synonym for husband) [HM1]

Public-relations man (banned as sexist, replace with *public-relations specialist*) [NES]

Red man (banned when referring to a Native American man) [HM1, AIR, RIV]

Redskin (banned when referring to American Indian) [SF-AW, HM1]

Regatta (banned as elitist) [ETS1]

Repairman (banned as sexist, replace with *repair person, maintenance person, plumber, carpenter, etc.*) [HRW1, HAR1, HAR2, NES]

Retard (banned as objectionable to people with disabilities) [SF-AW, HM1, NES]

Retardate (banned as offensive) [NES]

Retarded, the (banned as offensive, replace with *person who is developmentally disabled*) [HM1, HAR1, ETS2]

Right-hand man (banned as sexist, replace with *closest associate* or *assistant*) [HM1, HRW3, NES]

Roaming the land (banned as reference to Native Americans) [CT]

Rocking-chair brigade (banned as ageist) [HM1]

Roving the land (banned as reference to Native Americans) [CT]

Salesman, saleswoman (banned as sexist, replace with *sales representative*) [MMH, SF-AW, HRW1, HM1, HAR1, HRW3, NES, ETS2]

Satan (banned) [AEP]

Savages (banned when referring to Native Americans) [HM2]

Schoolgirl, schoolboy (banned as sexist, replace with *schoolchild*) [HRW1]

Sculptress (banned as sexist, replace with *sculptor*) [MMH, HM1]

Seaman (banned as sexist, replace with *sailor*) [HRW1]

Seamstress (banned as sexist, replace with *sewing machine operator, sewer, garment worker*) [NES]

Sect (banned as ethnocentric when referring to a religious group, unless it separated from an established religion) [SF-AW, ETS2]

Senile (banned as demeaning to older persons) [SF-AW, HM1]

Senility (banned as demeaning, replace with *dementia*) [APA]

Senior citizen (banned as demeaning to older persons) [SF-AW]

Serviceman (banned as sexist, replace with *member of the armed services, gas station attendant*) [HRW1]

Showman (banned as sexist, replace with *showperson, entertainer, producer*) [MMH, HRW1]

Sickly (banned as demeaning reference to person with disabilities) [ETS2]

Sightless (banned as offensive, replace with *people who are blind*) [SF-AW]

Sioux (banned as inauthentic, replace with *Lakota, Dakota,* or *Nakota*) [SF-AW]

Sissy (banned as demeaning) [MMH, SF-AW, NES, CT]

Sissified (banned as demeaning) [HRW3]

Slave (replace whenever possible with *enslaved person, worker,* or *laborer*) [AEP]

Sneaky (banned when referring to Asian Americans) [SF-AW]

Snow ball (banned for regional bias, replace with *flavored ice*) [AIR]

Snow cone (banned for regional bias, replace with *flavored ice*) [AIR]

Snowman (banned, replace with *snowperson*) [AEP]

Sob sister (banned as sexist, replace with *exploitive journalist*) [NES, AIR]

Soda (banned for regional bias, replace with *Coke, Pepsi* [however, note that brand names are banned by California social content review guidelines]) [AIR]

Songstress (banned as sexist, replace with *singer*) [HM1]

Sophisticated (banned when it refers to religious practices or beliefs) [SF-AW]

Soul food (banned as regional or ethnic bias) [ETS1]

Spastic (banned as offensive description; muscles are spastic, not people) [ETS2]

Special (banned as patronizing when referring to a person with a disability) [SF-AW, AIR, ETS2]

Spinster (banned as demeaning to older single women) [SF-AW]

Spinsterish (banned as sexist) [HRW3]

Spokesman (banned as sexist, replace with *spokesperson*) [MMH, HAR1]

Sportsman, sportswoman (banned as sexist, replace with *athlete, outdoor enthusiast*) [HRW1]

Sportsmanship (banned as sexist, replace with *sporting conduct*) [NES]

Squaw (banned as disparaging to Native American women) [MMH, SF-AW, HM1, HM2]

Statesman (banned as sexist, replace with *diplomat, legislator, leader, public servant*) [HRW1, HAR1, HAR2, NES]

Stewardess, steward (banned as sexist, replace with *flight attendant*) [HM1, HAR1, NES]

Stickball (banned as regional or ethnic bias) [ETS1]

Stone deaf (banned as handicapism) [NYC]

Strange (banned when it refers to religious practices or beliefs) [SF-AW]

Straw man (banned as sexist, replace with *unreal issue, misrepresentation*) [NES]

Subgroup (banned as offensive reference to cultural differences) [ACT]

Substandard English (banned as ethnocentric, replace with *slang* or *home language*) [SF-AW]

Sufferer of cerebral palsy (banned as offensive, replace with *person who has lost muscle control*) [HAR1]

Suffragette (banned as sexist, replace with *suffragist*) [MMH, SF-AW, HAR1, HAR2, NES, ETS2]

Swarms (banned as reference to immigrant groups) [CT]

Swarthy (banned as racist, replace with *dark, black, brown*) [SF-AW]

Sweet young thing (banned as sexist, replace with *young woman*) [ETS2]

Third World (banned as ethnocentric) [NES]

Tomboy (banned as sexist) [SF-AW, NES, AIR]

Tote (banned as regional bias, replace with *brown paper bag*) [RIV]

Tribe (banned as ethnocentric, replace with *ethnic group* or *nation* or *people*) [SF-AW, NYC]; however, HAR2 says that *tribe* is acceptable

Tribesman (banned as ethnocentric and sexist) [HM1]

Turning a deaf ear (banned as handicapism) [NYC]

Underdeveloped (banned as ethnocentric when referring to another country) [HM1, SF-AW]

Unfortunate (banned as negative judgment on person with disability) [ETS2]

Usherette (banned as sexist, replace with *usher*) [HM1, HRW3, ETS2]

Victim (banned as demeaning reference to person with a disability) [ETS2, RIV]

Victim of blindness (banned as offensive, replace with *persons who have lost their sight*) [HAR1]

Waitress (banned as sexist, replace with *server*) [MMH, HAR1, NES]

Wandering the land (banned as reference to Native Americans) [CT]

Warlike (banned when referring to American Indians) [SF-AW]

Warrior (banned as offensive when referring to a Native American person) [HRW1]

Weak sister (banned as sexist) [HRW3]

Weaker sex (banned as sexist, replace with *women, females*) [HM1, NES, ETS2]

Weatherman (banned as sexist, replace with *weather reporter, meteorologist*) [NES]

West, Western (banned as Eurocentric when discussing world geography, replace with reference to specific continent or region) [HAR2]

Wheelchair bound (banned as offensive, replace with a *person who is mobility impaired* or *wheelchair user*) [SF-AW, HAR1, ETS2, RIV]

White/whites (banned as a noun) [HAR2, SF-AW]

White (banned as adjective meaning pure) [CT]

Whole (banned as offensive when referring to a person's capability, replace with *person without disabilities* or *person who is nondisabled*) [SF-AW]

Wife, the (banned as synonym for wife) [HM1, HRW3]

Wild (banned when referring to American Indians) [SF-AW]

Woman doctor (banned as sexist, replace with *doctor*) [SF-AW, HM1, ETS2]

Woman driver (banned as sexist) [HRW3]

Womanish (banned as sexist) [HRW3, ETS2]

Woman's work (banned as sexist) [HRW3]

Women's libber (banned as offensive, replace with *feminist* or *supporter of the women's movement*) [HM1]

Workingman (banned as sexist, replace with *worker*) [MMH]

Workman (banned as sexist, replace with *worker, laborer, employee, staff member*) [HM1, HAR1, HRW3, NES]

Workmanlike (banned as sexist, replace with *competent*) [HM1, HRW3]

Workmanship (banned as sexist, no replacement) [NES]

Yacht (banned as elitist) [ETS2]

Yes-man (banned as sexist) [AIR]

Phrases and Usages That Must Be Avoided in Textbooks

Avoid *man, mankind, men.* [MMH, SF-AW, HM1, ETS2]

Avoid references to the *rise of man* (refer instead to *the rise of civilization or humanity*). [MMH]

Avoid references to *great men in history* (refer instead to *people who made history*). [MMH]

Avoid book titles like *Man and His World, Men of Science, Man and the State, Men and Nations.* [HRW3]

Do not say *you and your wife* (refer instead to *you and your spouse*). [ETS2]

Do not say *when you shave in the morning* (replace with *when you brush your teeth in the morning*). [ETS2]

Replace the masculine pronoun (*he* and *his*) with plural words (*they* and *their*) or by a nongendered word. For example, *Each citizen must pay his taxes* should be replaced by *All citizens must pay their taxes.* Or, *Each citizen must pay the tax.* [MMH, NES, ETS2]

Do not treat women as baggage, as passive actors who were brought along by their husbands, as in *Pioneers moved west, taking along their wives and children.* Replace with *Pioneer families moved west.* [NES, MMH, ETS2]

Spouses do not control each other. Do not say, *Carl lets his wife, Jane, work as a swimming instructor.* Say instead, *Jane works as a swimming instructor.* Do not say, *Jane permits her husband to play golf on Saturday afternoons.* Say instead, *Carl plays golf on Saturday afternoons.* [HRW3, ETS2]

Do not treat women as passive recipients of men's goodwill as in *Women were given the vote after the First World War.* Write instead, *Women won the vote after the First World War.* [MMH, SF-AW]

Do not use the feminine pronoun to refer to countries and boats; use *it* instead. Do not say, *England ruled the seas; her navy was huge,* but *its navy was huge.* [MMH]

Balance names like Mary, John, and Jane with names such as Jose, Lashunda, Che, Ling. [MA]

Do not compare humans with animals (especially with reference to Native Americans), e.g., *swift as a deer* or *eyes like a doe.* [NYC]

Use *it* to refer to animals, not *his* or *her.* Do not say, *The cat washed herself,* but *The cat washed itself.* Do not say, *The horse shook his mane,* but *The horse shook its mane.* [MMH, SF-AW, HM1]

An exclusive focus on Judeo-Christian contributions to literature or art is ethnocentric. [ETS1, ETS2]

Treat all religions with equal respect. [ETS2]

Do not imply or claim that the land called the United States was *discovered* by Europeans or that it was *empty land.* [SF-AW]

Do not refer to a U.S. cavalry victory as a *battle* and an American Indian victory as a *massacre.* [SF-AW]

Do not cast adverse reflection on any gender, race, ethnicity, religion, or cultural group. [CA]

Do not give a demeaning or negative portrayal of any group. [CT]

Do not use the following expressions:

Girls are sugar and spice and everything nice. [MMH]
Girls can't . . . [MMH]
Women can't . . . [SF-AW, MMH]
Women shouldn't . . . [SF-AW]
She acts like a lady. [SF-AW]
She (or he) runs like a girl. [SF-AW]
She thinks like a man. [SF-AW]
He acted like a woman. [MMH]
He took it like a man. [MMH, SF-AW]
He was as weak as a girl. [MMH]
I'll have my girl check that. [NES, ETS2]
She acted like a man. [MMH]
That was a manly act of courage. [MMH]
Smart as a man. [MMH, SF-AW]
Strong as a man. [MMH, SF-AW]

Stereotyped Images to Avoid in Texts, Illustrations, and Reading Passages in Tests

Girls and women/boys and men: Images to avoid:

Mothers and other females always wearing aprons [MMH]
Mother cooking or sewing while Father reads [MMH]
Mother bringing sandwiches to Father as he fixes the roof [MMH]
Mother running a vacuum cleaner, cooking, doing laundry, carrying food [MMH]
Mother seeing Father off to work [MMH]
Women finding achievement solely in marriage or motherhood [ETS1]
Women portrayed as teacher, mother, nurse, and/or secretary [CT]
Women portrayed as cute, fragile, delicate, helpless, doll-like [HRW3]
Women consistently portrayed as wives and mothers [AIR, RIV]
Women in jobs with less power than men [AIR]
Women dependent on men [AIR, NYC, RIV]

Women as catty, competitive with each other for male attention, preferring the company of men [NYC]

Women of achievement who are domineering, aggressive, lacking in desirable personal attributes [NYC]

Women aging less gracefully than men [AIR]

Women having consistently inferior math and science skills than men [AIR]

Women in stereotypical female jobs (teacher, nurse, secretary) [AIR]

Women as less rational and more intuitive than men [AIR, ETS1, ETS2]

Women needing less education than men [AIR]

Women as nurses, receptionists [RIV]

Women as more nurturing than men [AIR]

Women engaging in domestic chores more than men [AIR]

Mother shopping [MMH]

Mother showing shock, fear, horror [MMH]

Mother at vanity table [MMH]

Men as sole breadwinners for the family [AIR, RIV]

Men earning more money than women [AIR]

Men as active problem-solvers [AIR]

Men in positions of greater authority than women [AIR]

Men as capable leaders [RIV]

Men more rational than women [AIR]

Men more aggressive than women [AIR]

Men playing sports, working with tools [AIR, RIV]

Men as lawyers, plumbers [RIV]

Men and boys larger and heavier than women and girls [HRW3, NYC]

Men in stereotypical jobs like construction, police work, physician [AIR]

Men less able to complete domestic chores than women [AIR]

Father always driving the family car on outings [MMH]

Father taking children on adventurous outings [MMH]

Mother comforting children, giving sympathy, hugs, kisses, hot milk at bedtime [MMH]

Father expressionless or relaxed in trying circumstances [MMH]

Females backing off from center of action (e.g., a girl recoiling from a snake) [MMH]

Boys playing ball, while girls watch [MMH]

Boys playing sports [AIR]

Females wringing or fluttering their hands, covering their faces or mouths, making shrinking-back motions, lowering their heads, casting down their eyes [MMH]

Females using coy, flirtatious gestures, tilted heads, little shrugs, playing with hair, fingering dress [MMH]

Females usually sitting [MMH]

Girls playing in dresses or always wearing them to school [MMH]

Girls playing house [HRW3]

Girls deferring to boys [HRW3]

Girls always looking cute, wearing frills, ribbons, jewelry [MMH]

Women, girls who are weepy, fearful, and emotional [AIR, MA, NYC, RIV]

Women, girls as weak, frail, passive, docile, incompetent [MA, NYC]

Females more preoccupied with their appearance than males [MMH, AIR, MA, RIV, ETS1, ETS2]

Girls playing dress-up, buying clothes [MMH]

Women more concerned about home and family than about career [MA, NYC, ETS2]

Women, girls who love to gossip and talk all the time [MA]

Women, girls who lack leadership qualities such as self-confidence, ambition, assertiveness [MA]

Women shopping and spending money [MA]

Women who are not team players [MA]

Women, girls who lack mechanical abilities and basic mathematics abilities [SF-AW, MA]

Pink for girl babies, blue for boy babies [MMH]

Mothers always in dresses [MMH]

Girls playing with dolls, baby carriages, kitchen equipment [MMH, AIR]

Girls indoors or hovering near doorways, sheltered from the elements, carrying umbrellas while boys are out in the rain [MMH]

Pioneer women always cooking, sweeping, spinning wool, rocking babies [MMH]

Pioneer woman riding in covered wagon while man walks [MMH]

Lady of the manor doing needlepoint [MMH]

Women selling cakes at a fair [MMH]

Women as passengers on a sailboat or sipping hot chocolate in a ski lodge [MMH]

Women defined by the accomplishments of others, such as husband or children [AIR]

Women as nurses, elementary-school teachers, clerks, secretaries, tellers, hairdressers, librarians [MMH, HRW3]

Women or girls as fearful, squeamish, passive, dependent, weepy, mechanically inept, frivolous, shrewish, nagging, easily defeated by simple problems ("just like a girl" or "just like a woman") [HRW3]

Females as passive recipients, observers of actions, or victims in need of rescue by others [MA, NYC]

Men or boys who are brutish, violent, crude, harsh, insensitive [HRW3]

Men or boys in active, problem-solving roles [MMH, SF-AW]

Girls as frightened, weak [SF-AW, NYC]

Girls as gentle, silly, illogical [SF-AW, ETS2]

Girls as shrewish, nagging [SF-AW]
Girls as indecisive, uncertain, confused [SF-AW]
Girls suppressing anger [SF-AW]
Girls as conformist, dependent, passive, cooperative [SF-AW, HRW, NYC]
Girls as peaceful, emotional, warm [SF-AW]
Girls as poor at math, science [SF-AW]
Girls as neat [SF-AW, HRW3, MMH]
Girls as shorter, smaller than boys [SF-AW]
Men and boys as strong, brave, silent [AIR, RIV]
Boys as strong, rough, competitive [SF-AW]
Boys as curious, ingenious, able to overcome obstacles [NYC]
Boys as intelligent, logical, mechanical [SF-AW, NYC]
Boys as quiet, easygoing [SF-AW]
Boys as active, brave, decisive problem-solvers [SF-AW, NYC]
Boys as messy, unconcerned with appearance [SF-AW, NYC]
Boys as independent, autonomous, loners [SF-AW, NYC]
Boys as adventurous leaders, innovators [SF-AW, NYC]
Boys expressing anger [SF-AW, AIR]
Boys as unemotional, cold [SF-AW, NYC]
Boys as athletic, outdoor-oriented [NYC]
Boys as good at math, science [SF-AW]
Boys as confident, concerned with achievement, career-oriented [SF-AW, NYC]
Boys as violent [SF-AW]

People of color: Images to avoid:

People of color as universally athletic [AIR]
Minority children or adults as passive recipients, observers of action, or victims in need of rescue by others [MA]
People of color who become successful by accepting discrimination and working hard [NYC]
People of color who abandon their own culture and language to achieve success [NYC]
People of color as exotic, childlike, folkloric [NYC]
People of color as gangsters and criminals [NYC]
People of color living in poor urban areas [AIR, ETS1]
People of color being angry [AIR]
People of color as politically liberal [AIR]
People of color belonging to any one religion [AIR]
People of color valued as tokens or valued by whites as professional peers [AIR]
People of color sharing a common culture or preferences [AIR]
People of color sharing common dress [AIR]
People of color sharing common personality traits [AIR]
People of color sharing a common heritage, including language, dance, music, food preferences [AIR]

African American people: Images to avoid:

African Americans as great athletes, physically powerful [HRW1, AIR, MA, RIV, ETS1, ETS2]

African Americans sharing common tastes in food [AIR]

African Americans as musical, great sense of rhythm, terrific entertainers [MA]

African American women as graceful [MA]

African Americans speaking "black" language [MA]

African Americans being lazy and shiftless, don't want to work [MA]

African American men who desert their families [MA]

African American children having children and becoming welfare mothers [MA]

African Americans as less intelligent than other groups [MA]

African Americans who have white features or all look alike [MMH]

African Americans who all have the same skin color [MMH, HRW1]

African Americans with the same hairstyles and hair textures [MMH, HRW1]

African Americans with exaggerated facial features [MMH]

African Americans always wearing loud colors, straw hats, white suits, or conversely, standard, middle-class clothes [MMH]

African Americans driving big cars and wearing flashy clothes [MA]

People in Africa wearing native dress or wearing Westernized version of African costumes [MMH, HRW1]

African Americans in crowded tenements on chaotic streets, big bright cars, abandoned buildings with broken windows and wash hanging out, or living in innocuous, dull, white-picket-fence neighborhoods [MMH]

African Americans in low-paying jobs, unemployed, or on welfare [HRW1, AIR]

African Americans in urban ghettos [HRW1, AIR, MA, ETS1, ETS2]

African Americans who are unaware of their African heritage [ETS2]

African Americans who are uneducated (high school dropouts) [HRW1]

African Americans as maids [RIV]

African American woman as powerful "black matriarch" [NYC]

African Americans living in urban environments [RIV]

African Americans who are baggage handlers [HRW1]

African Americans who are cleaning women/men [HRW1, NYC]

African Americans in photos in the background or as the only minority in the photo [MMH, SF-AW, HRW1]

African Americans playing only with toys from the mainstream or
  only with toys from their own culture [HRW1]
African cultures portrayed as primitive or uncivilized [ETS1]

Native American people: Images to avoid:

Native Americans who speak broken English [MMH, HM2]
Native Americans performing a rain dance [MMH]
Children "playing Indian" [HM2]
Native American males acting like fierce savages [MMH]
Native Americans in low-paying jobs, drunk, unemployed, or on
  welfare [HRW1, AIR]
Native Americans living in shacks on reservations, with outdoor
  water tanks and bleak landscapes [MMH, HRW1, ETS1]
Native Americans who are uneducated [HRW1, ETS1, ETS2]
Native Americans who are not part of the American mainstream
  [HRW1]
Native Americans living in rural settings on reservations [HRW1,
  ETS1, ETS2]
Native Americans with "how" gestures, warlike stances, look-alikes,
  caricatures [MMH, HRW1]
Native Americans depicted in teepees, with totem poles, pinto
  horses with buffalo thundering by [MMH, HRW1]
Native Americans with sameness of facial features, impassive
  expressions [MMH]
Native Americans with long hair, braids, headbands [MMH,
  HRW1]
Native Americans wearing full headdresses, feathers, beads, buffalo
  robes, war paint, holding bow and arrows [MMH, HRW1]
Native Americans with red skin [MMH, HRW1]
Native Americans hunting or in war parties or passing the peace
  pipe [MMH, HRW1]
Modern Native Americans working on ranches, in menial jobs, or
  doing construction work [MMH, HRW1]
Native Americans who are dependent on Caucasians [HM2]
Native Americans playing only with toys from the mainstream
  culture or only with toys from their own culture [HRW1]
Native American females sewing buffalo hides, grinding corn,
  carrying papooses [MMH, HRW1]
American Indians portrayed as people who live in harmony with
  nature [AIR]
American Indians portrayed as "closer to nature" than other
  Americans [ETS1, ETS2]
American Indians as alcoholics, warriors, or thieves [AIR]
American Indians who are craftspeople [HRW1]
American Indians as primitive or warlike [AIR]

Asian American people: Images to avoid:

Asian Americans as very intelligent, excellent scholars [MA]

Asian Americans with look-alike features for all ages: short, skinny, slanted eyes, wear glasses [MMH, MA]

Asian Americans as a "model minority," repressed, studious, goody-goody [SF-AW, RIV, HM2, MMH, MA]

Asian Americans as ambitious, hardworking, and competitive [MA]

Asian Americans as having strong family ties [MA]

Asian Americans as quiet, polite, concerned with proper form [MA]

Asian Americans as inscrutable, mysterious, concerned with saving face [MMH, MA]

Asian Americans as frugal, passive, rigid, submissive, unathletic [SF-AW]

Asian Americans as musical prodigies or class valedictorian [HM2]

Asian Americans unable to speak English or uninvolved in mainstream America [HRW1]

Asian Americans working as laundry workers, engineers, waiters, gardeners, health workers [HRW1]

Asian Americans living in ethnic neighborhoods [AIR, ETS2]

Asian Americans as predominantly refugees [AIR, ETS2]

Asian Americans working in a laundry [AIR, RIV]

Asian American males as peasants, coolies, waiters, laundry owners, math students [MMH, HRW1]

Asian Americans working at vegetable stands [HRW1]

Asian American females as doll-like, geisha-girl image, ingratiating to males [MMH, HRW1]

Asian Americans playing only with toys from the mainstream culture or only with toys from their own culture [HRW1]

Chinese people living and working only in Chinatown or in China working in rice fields [MMH, HRW1]

Asian Americans shown with eyes as single, slanted lines; look-alikes; straight black hair with bangs; buck teeth [MMH, HRW1]

Modern Chinese males wearing pigtails and glasses [HRW1]

Modern Chinese women wearing high-collared cheong dresses [HRW1]

Modern Chinese males with inscrutable grins, with folded or clasped hands or always wearing glasses and looking serious and polite [MMH, HRW1]

Chinese people who have great food [MA]

Chinese people who own or run laundries and restaurants [MA, NYC]

Chinese people who love to gamble [MA]

Chinese people who are cruel [MA]

Modern Asian Americans wearing dark business suits and glasses [MMH]

Hordes of Japanese with suits and cameras [MMH]

Modern Japanese women wearing kimonos or carrying babies on
 their backs [HRW1, MMH]
Japanese people who are law-abiding [MA]
Japanese people who are great imitators [MA]
Japanese people who are sneaky [MA]
Japanese women who are servile and obedient [MA]
Korean Americans owning or working in fruit markets [NYC]

Hispanic-American people: Images to avoid:

Latinos who are lazy or passive [HM2, MA]
Latinos who are migrant workers [HM2]
Latinos who have broken English [HM2, ETS1, ETS2]
Latinos who wear serapes and sombreros [HM2]
Latinos who are dependent on Caucasians [HM2]
Hispanics with same facial features, skin color, size, hairstyles, men
 with mustaches [MMH, HRW1]
Hispanic men who are excessively demonstrative and swaggering,
 women and girls who are shy and docile [MMH, HRW1]
Hispanics who are warm, expressive, and emotional [MA]
Hispanics who most often work in service or agricultural jobs [MA]
Hispanics who refuse to learn English [MA]
Hispanics who don't value education [MA]
Hispanic men who are macho, dominate women [MA]
Hispanics who are lazy and shiftless [MA]
Hispanics who are not punctual and frequently procrastinate [MA]
Hispanics who don't care if they are on welfare [MA]
Hispanics who are violent, hot-tempered, and bloodthirsty [MA]
Hispanics in low-paying jobs, unemployed, or on welfare [HRW1,
 AIR]
Hispanics in urban settings (ghettos or barrios) [HRW1, AIR,
 ETS1, ETS2]
Hispanics unable to speak English or uninvolved in mainstream
 America [HRW1]
Hispanics as clothing workers [HRW1]
Hispanics as farm laborers [HRW1]
Hispanics as cleaning women/men [HRW1]
Hispanics wearing bright colors, older women in black, girls always
 in dresses [MMH]
Mexican men always wearing ponchos and wide-brimmed hats
 [MMH, HRW1]
Mexicans always living in huts or men sleeping under huge hats
 [MMH, HRW1]
Hispanics living in shacks or crowded tenements [MMH, HRW1]
Mexicans grinding corn [MMH, HRW1]
Hispanic young people always working on secondhand cars
 [MMH]
Mexicans riding donkeys [MMH, HRW1]

Mexicans employed in menial jobs, such as crop picking, delivering goods, waiting on tables [MMH, HRW1]

Hispanics playing only with toys from the mainstream culture or only with toys from their own culture [HRW1]

Jewish people: Images to avoid:

Jews as diamond cutters, jewelers, doctors, dentists, lawyers, classical musicians, tailors, shopkeepers [HRW1]

Jews with hooked noses; dark, kinky hair; hunched-over postures; heavy makeup and fancy hairstyles [HRW1]

Jewish-princess image [HRW1]

Jews always wearing business suits, glasses, and carrying briefcases [HRW1]

Jews either in urban tenements or in wealthy neighborhoods, with nothing in between [HRW1]

Jews playing only with toys from the mainstream culture or only with toys from their own culture [HRW1]

Persons who are older: Images to avoid:

Older people as meddlesome, demanding, childish, unattractive, inactive, victims of ridicule and violence [MMH, NYC]

Older people in nursing homes or with canes, walkers, wheelchairs, orthopedic shoes, or eyeglasses [HRW1]

Older people as helpless and dependent on others to take care of them [AIR, NYC, ETS2, RIV]

Older people as ill, physically weak, feeble, or dependent [AIR, NYC, ETS1]

Older people as funny, absent-minded, fussy, or charming [NES]

Older people who have twinkles in their eyes, need afternoon naps, lose their hearing or sight, suffer aches and pains [NES]

Older people who are retired, are at the end of their careers, have lived the most fruitful years of their lives, or are engaged in a life of leisure activities [NES, NYC]

Older persons who are either sweet and gentle or irritable and pompous [HM1]

Older people with gray hair and in juvenile or faddish clothing or in worn, outdated clothing [HRW1]

Older people in rocking chairs, knitting, napping, or watching television [HRW1]

Older people who are isolated, inactive, or lonely [HRW1]

Older people who are poor or living on welfare [HRW1]

Older people as nonproductive members of society [HRW1, AIR, ETS2]

Older people as senile, forgetful, or eccentric [HRW1, ETS2]

Older people who are irritable, senile, withdrawn from the world [ETS2]

Older people who are sickly, fragile, sedentary [ETS2]

Older people living with their offspring or with other relatives [HRW1]

Older people with peers, people of the same sex, or only with children [HRW1]

Older people who are fishing, baking, knitting, whittling, reminiscing, rocking in chairs [SF-AW, NES, AIR, RIV]

Older persons who are bent, bespectacled, dentured, dowdy, feeble, frail, gnarled, hard-of-hearing [SF-AW]

Older persons who are hobbling, shuffling, stooped, trembling, white-haired, wheezing, wrinkled [SF-AW]

Older persons who are cute, dear, docile, little, mild-mannered, spry, sweet, well-meaning [SF-AW]

Older persons who are bitter, cantankerous, crabby, cranky, difficult [SF-AW]

Older persons who are grumpy, meek, nagging, rigid, selfish, silly, stubborn [SF-AW]

Older persons who are bored, dependent, inactive, sick, unhappy, weak, weary [SF-AW]

Older persons who need government assistance because of financial problems [ETS2]

Older persons who need or want to be pitied or patronized [ETS2]

Older persons who suffer from physical deterioration [AIR]

Persons with disabilities: Images to avoid:

Disabled people as helpless, passive, dependent, naïve, childlike [HM1, AIR]

Disabled people as segregated from mainstream society [AIR]

Disabled people interacting only with other disabled people [AIR]

Disabled people as victims [HM1, AIR, ETS2]

Disabled persons as objects of pity or curiosity [HM1]

Disabled persons as sinister characters; for example, pirates, witches, criminals [HM1, MMH]

Nearsighted persons bumping into things [HM1]

People with disabilities as saintly like Tiny Tim [NYC]

People with disabilities as victims of violence [NYC]

People with disabilities as laughable, the brunt of jokes [NYC]

People with disabilities as their own worst enemy [NYC]

People with disabilities as sinister or evil, like Dr. Strangelove, "whose physical disability symbolizes moral depravity" [NYC]

People with disabilities endowed with magic powers, "e.g., the crippled newsboy who says the magic word and becomes Captain Marvel Jr., or the little Lame Prince who finds a magic carpet" [NYC]

People with disabilities should be presented with an emphasis on their positive accomplishments, not their disabilities. [MA]

People with disabilities being unproductive [AIR, ETS1, ETS2]

People with disabilities sharing common needs or problems [AIR]
People with disabilities as a burden to others [AIR]
People with disabilities portrayed only as white and middle-class [AIR]
People with disabilities as heroic, inspirational, or courageous because of their disability [AIR, SF-AW, ETS1, ETS2]
People with disabilities "overcoming" the disability or achieving "in spite of" it [SF-AW, ETS2]
People with disabilities portrayed as invalids, patients, bitter, sickly, or victims [SF-AW, ETS1]

Persons who are homosexual: Images to avoid:

Gays and lesbians as universally artistic [AIR]
Gays and lesbians as outcasts [AIR]
Gays and lesbians as living only in urban areas [AIR]
Gays and lesbians as having emotional problems [AIR]
Gays and lesbians as pedophiles [AIR]

Miscellaneous stereotypes to avoid:

Dumb athletes [MMH]
Stupid, beautiful women [MMH]
Skinny intellectuals wearing glasses [MMH]
Fat social misfits [MMH]
Old ladies with twenty cats [MMH]
Narrow-minded, prejudiced working-class people [MMH]
Exemplary upper-class people of bygone days [MMH]
Working-class people who are poor, lazy, intellectually inferior, and prone to violence [MMH]
Working-class people who make ethnic or racial jokes or slurs [NYC]
Working-class people who speak English ungrammatically and use vulgar language [NYC]
Irish policemen [AIR, RIV]
Caucasians living in affluent suburbs [AIR, RIV]
Children as healthy bundles of energy [AIR]

Topics to Avoid in Textbooks

Anthropomorphism in nonfiction [HM2]
Behavior that will lead to dangerous situations, e.g., children should not go with strangers [HRW2]
Bodily functions [HRW2]
Brand names, corporate logos, or trademarks [HRW1, CA]

Conflict with authority (parents, teachers, law) [HRW2]

Controversial people, such as Malcolm X [HM2]

Creation myths that present alternatives to biblical creation [HRW2]

Crime [HRW2]

Dialect (especially black dialect) [HRW2, HM2]

Divorce [HRW2]

Drinking [HRW2, CA]

Drugs [HRW2, CA]

Ethnic groups in desperate situations [AEP]

Euthanasia [HRW2]

Evolution presented as fact rather than as scientific theory [HRW2]

Fighting [HRW2]

Fire hazards [CA]

Guns, shooting [HRW2]

Illegitimacy [HRW2]

Irreverent references to the Deity [HRW2]

Liquor [HRW2, CA]

Lying, or duplicity of any kind [HRW2]

Name-calling [HRW2]

Nudity [HRW2]

Obscene or profane language [HRW2]

Physical violence [HRW2]

Poor nutrition, poor eating habits, junk food [HRW2, CA]

Questions that ask students to describe their feelings. Say instead, "How do you think a person would feel if . . . ?" [HRW2]

References to Christmas, Easter, Hanukah [HRW2]

References to humanism that might be interpreted as giving it the status of a religion [HRW2]

Religion [HRW2]

Selections that imply that "white" behavior standards are needed for success [HAR1]

Sex or sexuality [HRW2]

"Situation ethics" in which the right or wrong of a given act is based on the situation in which it occurs rather than on an absolute standard of behavior [HRW2]

Smoking [HRW2, CA]

Stealing [HRW2]

Stories about slavery, slaves [HM2]

Suicide [HRW2]

Unflattering comparisons between the sexes [HM1]

Unpunished transgression [HRW2]

Winter holidays [AEP]

Foods to Avoid in Textbooks

(as compiled by the California State Nutrition Unit, 1981, and cited in Holt, Rinehart and Winston, *Guidelines for Literature Selection*, 1984 [HRW2])

Alcoholic drinks
Bacon, salt pork
Butter, margarine, lard
Cakes
Candy
Coffee
Condiments
Corn chips
Cream
Cream cheese
Doughnuts
French fries
Fruit punches
Gravies
Gum
Honey
Jam, jelly, preserves
Ketchup
Juice drinks
Pickles
Pies
Potato chips
Pretzels
Salad dressings, mayonnaise
Salad oil, shortening
Salt
Snack chips
Soda pop
Sour cream
Sugar (all kinds)
Sweet rolls
Tea
Water (Italian) ices
Whipped cream

Acceptable Foods

(as compiled by the California State Nutrition Unit, 1981, and cited in Holt, Rinehart and Winston, *Guidelines for Literature Selection*, 1984 [HRW2])

Meat (preferably unfried)
Fish

Poultry (unfried)
Shellfish
Eggs
Cooked beans, peas
Nuts
Nut butters
Seeds
Milk
Cheese
Yogurt
Cottage cheese
Fruits
Vegetables
Fruit and vegetable juices (100 percent)
Enriched and whole-grain breads, rolls, muffins, biscuits
Enriched and whole-grain cereal
Enriched and whole-grain pastas
Enriched and whole-grain rice
Bulgur
Cornmeal
Enriched and whole-grain crackers
Hamburgers
Hot dogs
Pizza
Burritos
Fish sandwiches
Tacos

Topics to Avoid on Tests

(because they might upset and distract some students,
unless the topic is relevant to the subject being tested)

Abortion [AIR, MA, NYS, ETS1, RIV]
Addiction [AIR, RIV]
AIDS [AIR]
Alcoholism [RIV]
Animal abuse [AIR, RIV]
Animal rights [AIR]
Aspirin or any other drug [AIR]
Birth control, condoms [NEB, MA]
Birthday celebrations [AIR, RIV]
Blizzards [AIR]
Brand-name products or corporate logos [AIR, CA]
Cancer (or other serious illnesses) [AIR, RIV]
Catastrophes (such as fires or earthquakes; a tornado or hurricane
    may be acceptable if it is not too frightening) [AIR, RIV]

Child abuse [AIR, MA, RIV]
Child neglect [NEB, MA]
Children mistreating each other [AIR, RIV]
Christmas (or other religious holiday celebrations) [AIR]
Coming-out parties [AIR]
Cotillions [AIR]
Creatures that are scary or dirty (e.g., rats, mice, roaches, snakes,
     lice) [AIR, RIV]
Death [AIR, NYS, RIV]
Dinosaurs (implies evolution) [AIR]
Disease [AIR, RIV]
Disobedient children [AIR, RIV]
Disrespect for authority [AIR, RIV]
Disrespectful or criminal behavior [AIR, RIV]
Divorce [AIR, MA, RIV]
Drugs and alcohol [AIR]
Euthanasia [AIR, ETS1]
Evolution, the origins of the universe [AIR, RIV]
Extraterrestrials [AIR, RIV]
Family issues (feelings about parents, siblings) [NEB, MA]
Farms (specialized terms like *gilt*) [ETS1]
Finances (specialized terms like *arbitrage*) [ETS1]
Fossils (implies evolution) [AIR, RIV]
Gambling [AIR, RIV]
Gangs [AIR]
Ghosts [AIR, RIV]
Giving birth, whether people or animals [AIR, RIV]
Gratuitous gore, such as animals eating other animals [AIR, RIV]
Guns, gun control [AIR, RIV]
Halloween [AIR, RIV]
High-priced consumer goods, such as a brand-new ten-speed
     bicycle or a family vacation [AIR, MA, RIV]
Homelessness (may or may not be suitable) [MA]
Hurricanes [AIR]
Incest [NEB, MA]
Injury [AIR]
Junk bonds [AIR]
Junk foods [AIR, CA]
Knives [RIV]
Law (specialized terms like *tort*) [ETS1]
Magic [AIR, RIV]
Masks (tainted by association with Halloween) [AIR, RIV]
Military topics (terms such as *smart bomb, stealth bomber, rapier,
     muzzle*) [AIR, ETS1]
Murder [AIR, MA (may or may not be suitable)]
Native American religious references (animal gods, plants with a
     spirit, etc.) [AIR, RIV]
New Age religion [AIR]

Nonstandard English (slang, dialect, trendy expressions) [AIR]
Nudity, implied nudity [AIR, RIV]
Occult [MA]
Oppression [AIR]
Paganism [AIR, RIV]
Parapsychology [AIR, RIV]
Parents quarreling [AIR, RIV]
Personal appearance (e.g., height and weight) [AIR, RIV]
Personal information about self or family [RIV]
Politics [AIR, RIV]
Politics (specialized terms like *alderman*) [ETS1]
Pornography [AIR]
Poverty [AIR]
Pregnancy [RIV, MA (may or may not be suitable)]
Profanity [MA]
Pumpkins (tainted by association with Halloween) [AIR]
Questioning parental authority [MA]
Race relations [AIR]
Racial prejudice [AIR, RIV]
Rap music [AIR, RIV]
Rape [NEB, MA]
Rats, mice, roaches, snakes, lice [RIV]
Religion [AIR, RIV]
Religious holidays [AIR, RIV]
Rock and roll music [AIR, RIV]
Satanism [AIR, RIV]
Science (specialized terms like *enzyme*) [ETS1]
Secular humanism [AIR]
Serious car accidents [AIR]
Sexuality [AIR, NEB, MA]
Sexual preference or orientation [MA]
Sexually transmitted diseases [NEB, MA]
Situation ethics [AIR]
Slavery (except in historical context) [AIR]
Smoking [AIR]
Social register [AIR]
Someone getting fired or losing their job [AIR, RIV]
Sports (except for incidental references to a ball, game, score, or
    match) [AIR, ETS1]
Suicide [AIR, MA]
Supernatural [AIR, RIV]
Technology (specialized terms like *spreadsheet*) [ETS1]
Teen pregnancy [AIR]
Thanksgiving (because it is a religious holiday) [AIR, RIV]
Tools and machinery (specialized terms like *flange*) [ETS1]
Transportation (specialized terms like *flatcar*) [ETS1]
Typhoons [AIR]
Unemployment [AIR, RIV]

Unsafe situations (such as keeping dangerous animals or doing dangerous things) [AIR, RIV]

Vacations in faraway places, ski trips, and other expensive items beyond the reach of all [AIR]

Violence [AIR, ETS1, RIV]

War [AIR, NYS, ETS1]

Weapons (avoid mention of guns, knives, except in historical context) [AIR, MA, RIV]

Witchcraft, witches (except in historical context in Massachusetts) [AIR, MA, RIV]

Yachting [AIR]

Material to avoid on tests:

Any language or content that suggests economic, regional, cultural, or gender bias [NYS]

Any language, content, or context that might be emotionally upsetting [NYS]

Any language, content, or context that is offensive to males or females [NYS]

Any language, content, or context that favors one racial or ethnic group over another [NYS]

Any language, content, or context that portrays one or more racial or ethnic groups in a pejorative fashion [NYS]

Any language, content, or context that favors one religion and demeans others [NYS]

Any language, content, or context that portrays one or more religion or religious leaders in a pejorative manner [NYS]

Any language, content, or context that is not accessible to one or more religions [NYS]

Any language, content, or context that requires the parent, teacher, or student to support a position that is contrary to their religious beliefs [NYS]

Any language, content, or context that portrays one or more age groups in a pejorative fashion [NYS]

Any language, content, or context that is offensive to one or more age groups [NYS]

Any language, content, or context that degrades people on the basis of their physical appearance or their physical, cognitive, or emotional challenge [NYS]

Any language, content, or context that focuses on a person's disability rather than the whole person [NYS]

Any language, content, or context that makes assumptions about what a disabled person can or cannot do [NYS]

Any language, content, or context that requires a student to take a position that challenges parental authority [NYS]

Any language, content, or context that presents violence

gratuitously, disproportionately, or in an overly graphic manner [NYS]

Any language, content, or context that presents inflammatory or highly controversial themes such as death, wars, abortion, etc. [NYS]

Any language, content, or context that suggests that affluence is related to merit [NYS]

Any language, content, or context that contains sexual innuendoes [NYS]

Any language, content, or context that fails to denounce criminal, illegal, or dangerous behavior [NYS]

Any older text or paintings that portray women in stereotypical or demeaning ways [ETS]

Sources:

[ACT]=*Fairness Report for the ACT Assessment Tests, 1999–2000* (ACT, 2000)

[AEP]=Association of Education Publishers on-line newsletter, speech by Jonathan Rosenbloom of TIME Learning Ventures, September 3, 2002

[AIR]=American Institutes for Research, *AIR Principles for Bias, Sensitivity, and Language Simplification*, fall 2000

[APA]=American Psychological Association, *Publication Manual*, 4th ed. (APA, 1994), pp. 46–60

[APhilA]=American Philosophical Association, *Guidelines for Non-Sexist Use of Language*, www.apa.udel.edu/apa/publications/texts/nonsexist.html," 2001

[CA]=California Department of Education, *Standards for Evaluating Instructional Materials for Social Content: 2000 Edition* (California Department of Education, 2001)

[CT]=Connecticut Department of Education, *Fairness/Bias Review Guidelines for the Connecticut Mastery Test*, 2002

[ETS1]=Educational Testing Service, *Overview: ETS Fairness Review* (ETS, 1998)

[ETS2]=Educational Testing Service, *Sensitivity Review Process: Guidelines & Procedures* (ETS, 1992)

[HAR1]=Harcourt, *Striving for Fairness* (unpublished document, for internal use by publishing company, 2001)

[HAR2]=Harcourt Horizons, *Editorial Guidelines* (unpublished document, for internal use by publishing company and reviewers of its textbooks, 2001)

[HM1]=Houghton Mifflin, *Eliminating Stereotypes* (Houghton Mifflin, 1981)

[HM2]=Houghton Mifflin, *HMR 2001: Guidelines for Literature Search* (unpublished, for internal use by publishing company, 2001)

[HRW1]=Holt, Rinehart and Winston School Department, *Guidelines for the Treatment of People and Related Issues*, 1981

[HRW2]=Holt, Rinehart and Winston School Department, *Guidelines for Literature Selection*, 1984

[HRW3]=Holt, Rinehart and Winston School Department, *The Treatment of Sex Roles*, 1975

[MA]=Massachusetts Department of Education, *Guidelines for Bias Review of the Massachusetts Comprehensive Assessment System*, March 3, 1998

[MMH]= Macmillan McGraw Hill, *Reflecting Diversity* (1993)

[NEB]=Nebraska Department of Education, *A Guide to Aid Nebraska School Districts in Addressing the Quality Components in the District Assessment Plans*, April 2000

[NES]=National Evaluation Systems, *Bias Issues in Test Development*, 1991

[NYC]=New York City Board of Education, *Promoting Bias-Free Curriculum Materials: A Resource Guide for Staff Development*, 1988

[NYS]=New York State, *Sensitivity and Bias Review of New York State Assessment* (Albany: 2000), including "New York State Sensitivity Review Guidelines," 2000

[RIV]=*Bias and Sensitivity Concerns in Testing* (Riverside Publishing, 1998)

[SF-AW]=Scott Foresman–Addison Wesley, *Multicultural Guidelines*, 1996

Appendix 2

THE ATKINSON-RAVITCH SAMPLER OF CLASSIC
LITERATURE FOR HOME AND SCHOOL

After a generation or more in which textbooks have been censored by pressure groups and state boards of education, there are many people of all ages who have only the most fleeting acquaintance with good literature. Sadly, many adults and children never had the chance to read the works that inspired previous generations. Happily, this is a condition that can easily be remedied.

This list is intended for parents, teachers, and students who want to become familiar with some of the leading classics of literature, especially those written for children. The list highlights modern classics (enduring works that were published within living memory) and older works that reflect a common literary and cultural heritage: the fables, songs, fairy tales, hero stories, plays, poems, essays, and novels that once were commonplace in homes and schools. The reading of such books should be complemented by the best in contemporary literature. Such works may easily be found in bookstores, in libraries, or on-line.

Our list is purposely open-ended. Readings are suggested for grades 3–10 only, and the grade-level recommendations are not only arbitrary but interchangeable in many cases. The King Arthur legends are as good at high school as they are at seventh grade, for example, and some titles suggested for high school might well be deferred until a later age. It is truly a matter of "user's choice."

Classics furnish excellent opportunities for an adult and child to enjoy a book or poem together. When children are expected to read a classic on their own, the unfamiliar style and vocabulary can be off-putting. Longfellow and Andrew Lang do not read the way modern-day conversation sounds, for example; but when children hear an adult read aloud works by these authors, the "aural imprint"— the sound, the rhythm, the patterns of language, the sense—develops familiarity. This principle is demonstrated in everyday life. Very young children learn Mother Goose rhymes by hearing them, despite archaic pronouns and phrases.

It is both amusing and disheartening to meet adults today who express regret that they never read (or heard) works like *Aesop's Fables* or *Heidi;* or to hear a recent high school graduate complain that she spent nearly four years in English class without reading a classic English novel; or to hear of classrooms where popular teen literature is required reading, but the literary classics are not; or to hear of a library that discards *Little Women* because it is too hard for children to read and its place on the shelf could be better used by books with higher circulation rates. If our list helps to mitigate such situations, then its intentions will have been fully realized.

—Rodney Atkinson and Diane Ravitch

Rodney Atkinson has worked for nearly thirty years in California public schools as a teacher, administrator, and a specialist in children's literature.

Grade Three

Andersen, Hans Christian. Selected tales.

Andersen's tales should be read throughout primary and intermediate grades, and beyond. Beautifully illustrated editions of individual stories are available. A good, one-volume collection of Andersen suitable for reading aloud is *Hans Christian Andersen: The Complete Fairy Tales and Stories,* translated by Erik Christian Haugaard. Some of the most beloved stories include:

The Emperor's New Clothes	The Snow Queen
The Little Fir Tree	The Steadfast Tin Soldier
The Little Match-Seller	Thumbelina
The Little Mermaid	The Tinder Box
The Nightingale	The Ugly Duckling
The Red Shoes	The Wild Swans

Classic Fairy Tales.

In discussing the spiritual value of fairy tales, Katharine Lee Bates once noted that children "are quick to catch the noble strain even in the wildest of their fairy-tale heroes whose exploits life will give them many a chance to emulate." In Joseph Jacobs's classic *English Fairy Tales,* and in recent collections, such as Berlie Doherty's *Fairy Tales* and Naomi Lewis's *Classic Fairy Tales to Read Aloud,* old favorites—"Jack and the Beanstalk," "Goldilocks and the Three Bears," "The Frog Prince"—and less familiar tales retain perennial appeal. Adults who enjoy scavenging secondhand bookstores may find it worth the effort to locate Bates's own *Once Upon a Time: A Book of Old-Time Fairy Tales.* See also third-grade entries for Perrault and fourth-grade entries for Andrew Lang and the Brothers Grimm.

Collodi, Carlo. *The Adventures of Pinocchio.*

Disregarding the wise counsel of Gepetto, the Blue Fairy, and the talking Cricket, the wooden marionette makes his way through life with mishap and travail. But he learns that following good advice is a most advisable thing, and his odyssey leads to his conversion from a recalcitrant puppet to a quickened human being of tears and joys. As a storyteller, Collodi was blessed with humor, tolerance, understanding, and wit.

de la Mare, Walter. *Rhymes and Verses: Collected Poems for Young People.*
Perhaps no children's poet better cultivates the love of language—sound, mood,
melody. In upper primary grades, popular de la Mare poems include:

The Buckle	The Cupboard
Silver	The Lost Shoe
Bunches of Grapes	The Little Bird
Someone	The Chicken
Somewhere	

Dickinson, Emily. Selected poems.
Children are strongly responsive to some of Dickinson's poems. To complement a
child's introduction to Emily Dickinson, see *Emily Dickinson's Letters to the
World,* written and illustrated by Jeanette Winter; and the fanciful *Mouse of
Amherst* by Elizabeth Spires. A few of the poems that resound with child
audiences:

Beclouded	A Book
If I Can Stop One Heart from Breaking	Chartless
"Hope" Is the Thing with Feathers	A Bird
The Locomotive	I'm Nobody! Who Are You?

Field, Eugene. Selected poems from *Lullaby Land* and *Poems of Childhood.*
A newspaper poet of the late 1800s, Field contributed several enduring poems
that children enjoy:

The Duel	The Night Wind
Jest 'Fore Christmas	The Rock-a-by Lady
Little Boy Blue	So, So, Rock-a-by So!
Wynken, Blinken, and Nod	

Hughes, Langston. Selected poems.
Hughes is noteworthy for his range, which spans humor and satire, lyricism, political comment, and social protest. Among poems suited for this age group are:

African Dance	Cycle
April Rain Song	Heaven
City	Snail
In Time of Silver Rain	

Lear, Edward. Selected poems.
An amusing and inventive master of nonsense, Lear is especially known for his
polished limericks. Adults and children can chuckle together.

Calico Pie	The Owl and the Pussycat
The Jumblies	The Scroobious Pip
There Was an Old Man in a Tree	The Pobble Who Has No Toes

Perrault, Charles. *The Complete Fairy Tales of Charles Perrault.*
Perrault's collection of Mother Goose tales first appeared in 1697. Like other great
storytellers, Perrault retold classic tales in lively form. Today, many people
know these stories in a bowdlerized (Disneyized) version. Children can
understand them as they were written and will find that the morals apply to
their own lives. Little Red Riding Hood, for instance, is not saved by a friendly
woodchopper at the end of the story; she is gobbled up by the wolf, and the
moral is "Don't talk to strangers," which is timeless advice for young children.
Perrault's stories include:

Bluebeard	Puss-in-Boots
Cinderella	Sleeping Beauty
Little Red Riding Hood	

Potter, Beatrix. Selected tales.
This gifted author and illustrator created many stories and verses for children,
drawing upon her observations of the animals near her home in the Lake District of England. Her most famous story is *The Tale of Peter Rabbit,* but *Jemima
Puddle-Duck, Squirrel Nutkin, The Tale of Mrs. Tittlemouse,* and other stories
give Peter good company. Readers should experience the stories in the early
formats—tiny books that fit easily in the hands of a child.

Prokofiev, Sergei. *Peter and the Wolf.*
Storybook editions complement Prokofiev's famous musical work, in which each
character is signified by a particular instrument and melodic phrase. With the
help of friendly animals, Peter overcomes the threat of the wolf, and the farm-
yard creatures celebrate—even the devoured duck makes joyful comment.

Rossetti, Christina Georgina. *Sing-Song: A Nursery Rhyme Book* and other poems.
Rossetti was one of three siblings who became distinguished in the fields of
poetry and art. Among her works are some of the loveliest and most intense
children's poems. A few of her poems that are frequently anthologized:

Boats Sail on the Rivers	Lambkins
Caterpillar	My Gift
Color	The Swallow
Coral	When the Cows Come Home
Wrens and Robins	

Spier, Peter. *The Star-Spangled Banner* and *The Erie Canal.*
In two separate picture books, Spier illustrates two famous American songs—
illustrates not only in the sense of providing pictorial decoration or interpretation, but also of illuminating the meaning of the words. Francis Scott Key's
lyrics for our national anthem were spurred by an event of the War of 1812, and
Spier gives pictorial treatment for three of the four stanzas. "Erie Canal" is a
well-known folk song stemming from a colorful era in U.S. history.

Stevenson, Robert Louis. *A Child's Garden of Verses.*

Years ago, in many homes and schools, selections from this classic collection were considered almost to be a child's birthright. Attractive editions are still issued today, and the following poems may serve as a place to begin:

At the Seaside	Looking Forward
Bed in Summer	My Bed Is a Boat
The Cow	My Shadow
Farewell to the Farm	Singing
The Lamplighter	The Swing
The Land of Counterpane	The Wind

Traditional Tales from World Cultures.

Children should read widely to gain a greater sense of the world's diversity and common humanity. Here are a few examples.

The Girl Who Loved Wild Horses by Paul Goble (American Indian, Plains)

Mufaro's Beautiful Daughters by John Steptoe (Zimbabwe)

Lon Po Po by Ed Young (China)

Suho and the White Horse by Yuzo Otsuka (Mongolia)

Magic Spring by Nami Rhee (Korea)

Momotaro, the Peach Boy by Linda Shute (Japan)

The Bravest Flute by Ann Grifalconi (Mayan)

Anansi Finds a Fool by Verna Aardema (Ashanti, Africa)

Wilder, Laura Ingalls. *Little House on the Prairie* and *Farmer Boy,* from the Little House stories.

The Little House saga comprises eight volumes, beginning with *Little House in the Big Woods* and *Little House on the Prairie.* Less well known, *Farmer Boy* tells of the Wilder boys growing up on their New York farm.

Williams, Margery. *The Velveteen Rabbit.*

First appearing in 1926, this story of "how toys come to life if they are loved enough" has proven its timelessness with generations of children. Its emotional appeal is reminiscent of Andersen. A child's beloved toy is thoughtlessly tossed out while the child is ill, but love redeems in ways that are undying.

Grade Four

Aesop's Fables.

The root word for *fable* originally meant "to give light," and generations of children have gained wisdom and insight from this treasury of fables. Good editions are available, and the fables lend themselves to discussion between adults and children. Examples:

The Ant and the Dove	The Town Mouse and the
The Lion and the Mouse	Country Mouse
The Ants and the Grasshopper	The Goose and the Golden
The Milkmaid and Her Pail	Egg
Belling the Cat	The Two Pots
The North Wind and the Sun	The Hare and the Tortoise
The Farmer and His Sons	The Wolf and the Crane
The Shepherd Boy and the Wolf	The Wolf and His Shadow
The Fox and the Grapes	

Biographies of Famous and Notable People.
Through biography children acquire a sense of history and learn the nature of life. Biographies can help children to form decent lives of their own. Good writers of biography include David Adler, Ingri and Edgar P. D'Aulaire, Jean Fritz, James Cross Giblin, Robert Lawson, Elizabeth Yates, and—for slightly older readers—Marc Aronson, Dennis Fradin, Russell Freedman, Kathryn Lasky, and the Random House Landmarks series.

Benét, Stephen Vincent and Rosemary. *A Book of Americans.*
These humorous and thoughtful verses about American historical figures, ranging from George Washington, Johnny Appleseed, Dolley Madison, Nancy Hanks, and P. T. Barnum to Captain Kidd, appeal to children.

Dunbar, Paul Laurence. Selected poems.
Dunbar was a gifted poet who received national regard by the time of his death in 1906. Some of his poems reflect African American domestic life of the nineteenth century. Dunbar's "Sympathy" ("I know why the caged bird sings . . .") is suggested for older students. Among poems suggested for fourth grade:

Amanda Kneading Dough	Nobody's Town
Candle-Lightin' Time	On the River

Brothers Grimm. Selected tales.
The "household tales" collected by two scholar brothers are among the world's most loved stories: "Hansel and Gretel," "The Goose Girl," "Mother Holle," "The Musicians of Bremen," "Rumpelstiltskin," and many others. Having enjoyed the most familiar tales, children can explore some of the less well-known ones. Naomi Lewis offers fresh and elegant retellings in *The Twelve Dancing Princesses and Other Tales from Grimm.* Wanda Gág's *Tales from Grimm* and *More Tales from Grimm,* though currently hard to come by, are still available through libraries and are recommended.

Harris, Joel Chandler. *The Complete Tales of Uncle Remus* or
The Favorite Uncle Remus.
Harris scholarship has changed since the tumultuous 1960s and 1970s, and the almost unanimous condemnation of him is being softened now by a more thoughtful reconsideration of his achievements. The dialects that Harris tried

to capture and preserve on paper, however, are difficult for some readers. For this reason, Julius Lester's retellings, such as *The Tales of Uncle Remus: The Adventures of Brer Rabbit,* are also recommended. "The Wonderful Tar-Baby" remains one of the most beloved stories in children's literature.

Kipling, Rudyard. *Just So Stories.*
A wizard with words, Kipling nowhere better displays his gift for fanciful language than in such beloved stories as "The Elephant's Child," "How the Leopard Got His Spots," and "The Butterfly That Stamped." See also Kipling's *Jungle Book,* including "Rikki-Tikki-Tavi."

Lang, Andrew. *The Blue Fairy Book* and other volumes in the Fairy Book series.
This classic series of folktales from many lands offers retellings noteworthy for their language and well suited for reading aloud. Some children have been known to progress through volume after volume, reading a story a night. Among the famous stories in *The Blue Fairy Book*:

Beauty and the Beast	The History of Whittington
East of the Sun and West of the Moon	Prince Darling
The History of Jack the Giant Killer	A Voyage to Lilliput

Lawson, Robert. *Watchwords of Liberty.*
Lawson highlights famous sayings and mottoes from U.S. history and gives background information on their genesis and meaning. Children enjoy memorizing the sayings, then quizzing one another for proper identification.

Longfellow, Henry Wadsworth. Excerpts from *Hiawatha.*
Longfellow's poem is an artistic blending of disparate elements from different North American Indian cultures. See illustrated versions by Susan Jeffers and Errol LeCain. Another Longfellow classic suitable for this age, *Paul Revere's Ride,* has been given excellent picture-book treatment by Ted Rand.

MacDonald, George. *The Light Princess.*
This amusing story tells of a princess who has no gravity and, unless she is moored to earth, floats in the air. Her frivolous and superficial view of life changes, however, when she learns to love. Life and gravity take on new meaning. Some critics regard MacDonald's works as the foundation of modern fantastic literature.

Osborne, Mary Pope. *American Tall Tales.*
Some old standards are here—Paul Bunyan, John Henry, Pecos Bill—along with less familiar figures like Stormalong. Adrien Stoutenburg's *American Tall Tales* adds Mike Fink, Davy Crockett, and Joe Margarac to the mix.

Riley, James Whitcomb. Selected poems.
Few regional poets are as well loved as Riley, the great Hoosier poet. Among the Riley poems enjoyed by children are:

The Circus-Day Parade	Out to Old Aunt Mary's
Extremes	The Raggedy Man
When the Frost Is on the Punkin	Little Orphant Annie

Ruskin, John. *King of the Golden River.*

Treasure Valley is a lovely and verdant land through which flows the Golden River. But the greed and selfishness of Hans and Schwartz demean the peace and bounty of the valley; and their brother, the kindly Gluck, must endure harsh treatment from their hands. When the dwarfish King of the Golden River instigates a quest to change the river to gold, the outcomes are unexpected but just. This Victorian fairy tale lends itself to reading aloud. Some editions, such as the 1974 Dover reprint, retain the original illustrations by Richard Doyle.

Grade Five

American Patriotic Songs and Anthems.

The texts of favorite patriotic songs furnish much to acknowledge, celebrate, and reflect upon: Samuel F. Smith's "America (My County, 'Tis of Thee)," Katharine Lee Bates's "America, the Beautiful," Francis Scott Key's "The Star-Spangled Banner," Irving Berlin's "God Bless America," Julia Ward Howe's "Battle Hymn of the Republic," Woody Guthrie's "This Land Is Your Land," and the civil rights anthem "We Shall Overcome." Texts may be found in Diane Ravitch's *The American Reader*. Melodies and chord accompaniments for some of the songs may be found in *Heritage Songster* by Leon and Lynn Dallin and similar collections.

The Arabian Nights. Selected tales.

This unforgettable collection, which evolved over the centuries, contains the marvelous exploits of Ali Baba, Aladdin, Sinbad, and others. For young readers, recommended editions include *The Arabian Nights: The Best-Known Tales,* edited by Kate Douglas Wiggin and Nora Smith, with illustrations by Maxfield Parrish, and *The Arabian Nights Entertainments,* edited by Andrew Lang.

Brink, Carol Ryrie. *Caddie Woodlawn.*

How does a girl grow to become a resilient and independent young woman? Caddie's own life offers insights into the question. The historical substance of the book—the hardships and pleasures of frontier life, and the picture of work and family—all contribute to Caddie's wonderful spirit. Since its first appearance in the 1930s, this pioneer story has been loved for its strong female protagonist, the inspiration for which was Brink's own grandmother.

Burnett, Frances Hodgson. *The Secret Garden.*

After the death of her parents, neglected and selfish little Mary Lennox finds spiritual healing in an abandoned garden. Her restoration leads to the rejuvenation of those she has come to love. See also Burnett's *Little Princess.*

Carroll, Lewis. *Alice in Wonderland* and *Through the Looking Glass.*
From such writers as Lewis Carroll and W. S. Gilbert, we learn the truth that lies
in topsy-turvy things. Whether down the rabbit hole or through the mantel
mirror, readers join Alice in mad adventures to illogical lands. The Cheshire
Cat, the Mad Hatter, and the March Hare are just a few of the fascinating
characters, and we still prefer John Tenniel's illustrations. Special attention
should be given to Carroll's wonderful poems (e.g., "The Walrus and the Carpenter," "Jabberwocky"). Like other great works, these books can be read again
and again with pleasure as one grows older.

Eliot, T. S. *Old Possum's Book of Practical Cats.*
Is your favorite cat a Rum Tum Tugger? A Macavity? Andrew Lloyd Webber's
musical *Cats* has brought new popularity to this delightful collection. Each
poem is witty and knowing.

Franklin, Benjamin. "The Whistle."
A delightful bit of Poor Richard's wisdom resides in this anecdote of Franklin's
youth. Written in 1779, and once commonly included in elementary school
textbooks, today the story may be found in *The Autobiography and Other Writings by Benjamin Franklin,* edited by Peter Shaw.

Gates, Doris. *Blue Willow.*
The human need for beauty and belonging are inherent in this moving story. A
migrant worker's daughter dreams of a permanent home of her own, complete
with a mantel on which she may display her prized Blue Willow plate. When a
landlord threatens eviction, Janey sacrifices her treasured possession for the
family's welfare. By doing so, she gains what she has longed for.

Grahame, Kenneth. *The Wind in the Willows.*
Spacious, leisurely, and full of whimsical humor, this story celebrates the halcyon
countryside and the pleasures and annoyances of friends and neighbors. As
with *Alice in Wonderland* and other classics, the age levels at which children first
love *Wind in the Willows* vary widely; some of us learned to love it as adults.

Henry, Marguerite. *Misty of Chincoteague.*
On a tiny island off the eastern shore of Virginia, Paul and Maureen dream of
capturing and taming the wild horse Phantom, and riding her during Pony
Penning Day. They are successful in their quest, and though Phantom rejoins
her stallion and the wild freedom of the island, her colt Misty becomes her
legacy to the family. Along with Walter Farley (e.g., *The Black Stallion*), Henry
is outstanding for her books about horses, including *King of the Wind* and
Justin Morgan Had a Horse.

Hurlbut, Jesse Lyman. *Hurlbut's Story of the Bible.*
Bible personages and events figure extensively in famous literature, music, and
art. Students should become familiar with stories of Joseph and his brethren,
Moses, David, Ruth, Queen Esther, and other major figures from Hebrew history; the nativity, selected parables, and other portions from the New Testa-

ment. *Hurlbut's* is only one of several Bible story collections that have been issued over the years. Adults are encouraged to seek retellings that are literate and dignified rather than updated and dressed-down.

Longfellow, Henry Wadsworth. *The Children's Own Longfellow.*
Among the Longfellow poems most popular with young readers, "The Wreck of the Hesperus" and "The Village Blacksmith" are within the grasp of fifth graders.

MacDonald, George. *At the Back of the North Wind.*
MacDonald recounts the many adventures of poor little Diamond and the North Wind. The adventures veer between the magical or dream world and the world of harsh reality. MacDonald's interest—children who must face sorrows, suffer hardships, yet who acquire moral responsibility with courage—is conveyed through soaring fantasy. A somewhat complicated story with a "sad happy ending," this novel is perhaps best read by adult and child together. See also MacDonald's *The Golden Key* and *The Princess and the Goblin.*

Salten, Felix. *Bambi.*
"A Life in the Woods" is *Bambi's* subtitle, and though the wonders of nature figure strongly in the story, Salten was more than a naturalist. *Bambi* says much about coming of age and the acquisition of wisdom from elders. Tinged with allegory, Salten's work is moving and meaningful to readers of different ages. Adults are encouraged to seek out creditable translations of the story, as opposed to commercialized versions.

Sewell, Anna. *Black Beauty.*
Black Beauty tells his own life story, from happy child years, through times of human cruelty and heedlessness, to his days as a London cab-horse, and finally as a lady's carriage horse. Sewell accomplished much toward mitigating the cruel treatment of horses, and her book helps children better understand the value of sympathy and loyalty. Sewell's own life is inspiring to children.

Sketches and Vignettes of Famous People and Events in U.S. History.
Tales of heroism, bravery, and achievement amid obstacles, fear, and sacrifice for great causes—these used to be common fare in storybooks and elementary readers. During the past thirty years, the casualties of the curriculum wars have included Ethan Allan and the Green Mountain Boys, "Mad" Anthony Wayne at Stony Point, Francis Marion ("the Swamp Fox"), John Paul Jones, and Thomas Edison, among others. Such books as Eva March Tappan's *American Hero Tales* have few comparable counterparts today, but happily, American hero stories are beginning to reappear. William Bennett's estimable *The Book of Virtues: A Treasury of Great Moral Stories* and *The Moral Compass: Stories for a Life's Journey* offer stories of Patrick Henry, Nathan Hale, Rosa Parks, Susan B. Anthony, Columbus, Pocahontas, Washington, Molly Pitcher, Betsy Ross, Francis Scott Key, Jackie Robinson, and Margaret Haughery. The paperback *Classic American Readers: Stories of the American Revolution* contains stories of Franklin, Jefferson, and Washington. In place of a "tales" approach, Dennis

Denenberg and Lorraine Roscoe offer a magazine-style page layout, with engaging, informational essays and photographs, in their *50 American Heroes Every Kid Should Meet.*

Songs of American Heritage.
All students should learn such songs as "Home on the Range," "On Top of Old Smoky," "Clementine," "Erie Canal," "I've Been Working on the Railroad," Stephen Foster's "Oh, Susanna," Albert Von Tilzer and Jack Norworth's "Take Me Out to the Ball Game," and George M. Cohan's "You're a Grand Old Flag." Most are collected in Diane Ravitch's *American Reader,* Leon and Lynn Dallin's *Heritage Songster,* or similar collections.

Twain, Mark. *The Adventures of Tom Sawyer.*
Since 1876, this novel has become one of the all-time favorites of American literature. Generations of schoolchildren not only have read the book but have participated in dramatizations of it. The title alone calls to mind fondly remembered episodes—the whitewashing scene, the Sunday School scene, Tom and Huck's witness to a nocturnal murder, their escape to Jackson's Island and their disquieting return, Tom's care for Becky Thatcher, Muff Potter's trial, and the frightening cave sequence. Tom epitomizes the spirit of boyhood.

Grade Six

Alcott, Louisa May. *Little Women.*
Familial love is a major theme of this wonderful novel—love that binds and grows amid separation, deprivation, hardship, death, and growing up. Alcott was blessed with a warm sense of humor, a love of fun, and keen powers of observation. So artful is her character portraiture that readers have personal favorites among the family and regard them as special friends. If some children find *Little Women* too lengthy, they may read it as nineteenth-century youngsters first did—in two separate parts, with several months intervening (it was originally published this way, in two volumes). Children are encouraged to complete the March saga by reading *Little Men* and *Jo's Boys* as well.

Creswick, Paul. *Robin Hood.*
With King Richard away at the Crusades, tyrannical Prince John usurps the power of the throne. Robin of Locksley forms an outlaw band to help the poor and regain lands seized by the evil prince. Howard Pyle's *Merry Adventures of Robin Hood,* also recommended, combines into one story the various fragments of Robin Hood lore.

DeJong, Meindert. *The House of Sixty Fathers.*
During the time of the Japanese invasion of China, Tien Pao is separated from his parents during a storm when their boat is swept downriver. DeJong tells of the boy's harrowing struggle to be reunited with his family, despite the threats from nature and wartime enemies. In a more lighthearted mood, DeJong's

Wheel on the School also centers on children who must overcome challenges to win a quest for happiness.

Folktales from World Cultures.

The study of folktales from around the world continues as students proceed into junior high school. Students should explore the variety of religious and moral tales, animal tales, and wisdom and "fool" tales, becoming familiar with character and story types. Older students are encouraged to read from the collections in such series as the *Oxford Myths and Legends* and the *Pantheon Fairy Tale and Folklore Library,* devoted to tales from Arabia, India, Africa, Russia, Ireland, Spain, and other lands. Among folktales suggested for upper intermediate grades are:

> *The Flame of Peace* by Deborah Nourse Lattimore (Aztec)
> "Tales of the Heike," in *Japanese Tales and Legends,* edited by Helen and William McAlpine
> *The Tale of the Mandarin Ducks* by Katherine Paterson (Japanese)
> "The Squire's Bride," in *Norwegian Folk Tales* by P. C. Asbjornsen and Jorgen Moe
> *Zlateh the Goat and Other Stories* by Isaac B. Singer (Yiddish)
> "Stories of the Firebird" and "Vassilissa" in *Russian Folk Tales* by Gillian Avery

Frost, Robert. Selected poems.

Clarity, conversational ease, and memorability mark the work of this San Francisco–born New England poet. Frost's poems help students to cultivate the intellectual pleasure of reading and discussing poetry. Among selections suggested for this grade:

Christmas Trees	Nothing Gold Can Stay
The Road Not Taken	The Pasture
Dust of Snow	The Need of Being Versed
Stopping By Woods on a Snowy	A Time to Talk
Evening	The Tuft of Flowers
Fire and Ice	

Greek Mythology.

Greek myths are fundamental to understanding literature, art, psychology, everyday vocabulary—even advertisements. Ingri and Edgar D'Aulaire's *Book of Greek Myths* is well suited to intermediate students. Doris Gates's *Fair Wind for Troy,* Padraic Colum's *Children's Homer,* Olivia Coolidge's *Trojan War,* and Roger Lancelyn Green's *Tale of Troy* are recommended for slightly older readers. In the out-of-print category are *A Child's Book of Myths and Enchantment Tales,* illustrated by Margaret Evans Price, and Edna Barth's more sophisticated *Cupid and Psyche.* A good, general-purpose reference for adults is H. A. Guerber's *Myths of Greece and Rome.*

Hamilton, Virginia. *The People Could Fly: American Black Folktales.*
The stories in this collection reflect the burdens and sorrows of slavery. Tales range from animal stories to ones of the supernatural. The title story is a particular favorite with many readers.

Henty, G. A. *In the Reign of Terror.*
Historian Gordon Craig once attributed his youthful interest in history to the works of this prolific novelist. A nineteenth-century English writer of historical romances for young readers, Henty is gaining new attention. The resurgence is attributable to his romantic style: a clear, strong story line that upholds the cardinal and martial virtues; a resourceful young hero; a colorful depiction of historical events, well researched as to background and details. Henty's prejudices and historical viewpoints are those of his own time and place but should not prevent the reader from appreciating the stories.

Knight, Eric. *Lassie Come-Home.*
Confronted with hard times, the owners of a prize dog sell her to a wealthy family. She is taken hundreds of miles away. But Lassie's dutiful and unconditional love for young Joe Carraclough prompts a long and weary journey back. Television and motion picture versions have tended to overshadow Knight's poignant original story.

Lewis, C. S. *The Lion, the Witch, and the Wardrobe* and other Narnia stories.
The Pevensie children discover that a doorway in the back of an old wardrobe leads to the wondrous land of Narnia, held in thrall by the evil White Witch. Eventually the children become engaged in the battle between good and evil. The characters of Aslan the Lion and Edmund are perhaps the most compelling ones in Lewis's story.

Pearce, Philippa. *Tom's Midnight Garden.*
Tom's drab life takes an unexpected turn when he is sent for a long visit to his aunt and uncle's home. A mysterious clock sounds in the night, and Tom discovers a strange and lovely garden that never materializes by day. His new world is a time warp to the past, leading to a new friendship and an affinity that surpasses time and generations. Nearly fifty years old, this beautiful story is recognized as a modern classic and deserves wide readership.

Seton, Ernest Thompson. *Wild Animals I Have Known.*
A writer, traveler, and naturalist prominent in the first part of the twentieth century, Seton combined factual material with narrative elaboration, achieving a unique kind of writing that is halfway between literary realism and natural history. His story of Lobo became the basis for a motion picture. See also Seton's *Animal Heroes.*

Sketches and Vignettes of Famous People and Events in World History and Legend.
If John Paul Jones and Oliver Hazard Perry have lost places of honor in storybooks for children, so have some of the heroes of world history and legend—

Darius of Persia, Prometheus, Pericles, Cincinnatus, Mucius of the burning hand, Horatius, Hannibal, Julius Caesar, Thor, Rama, Siegfried, and Joan of Arc, to name only a few. Louis Untermeyer's *The World's Great Stories: 55 Legends That Live Forever* and *The Firebringer and Other Great Stories: 55 Legends That Live Forever* offer a corrective. For readers who enjoy ferreting out old treasures in secondhand bookshops and libraries, Eva March Tappan's *Old World Hero Tales*, *The Story of the Greek People*, and *The Story of the Roman People* comprise a worthy introduction to classical history.

Spyri, Johanna. *Heidi.*
A five-year-old orphan is sent to live with her grandfather, high in the Swiss mountains. Though the old man is disagreeable, she finds new happiness until an aunt whisks her off to Frankfurt to tend a sick child. In time, Heidi returns to the Alpine home of her grandfather and is rejoined by her new friend, Clara. There, the mountain air, fresh milk, and clear skies work their healing influence. Heidi's story is one of goodness and faith in the midst of travail. The Books of Wonder edition has the advantage of Jessie Wilcox Smith's illustrations.

Grade Seven

Birch, Beverly. *Shakespeare's Stories.*
By reading and hearing the stories of Shakespeare's plays, young people gain a pleasurable introduction to the Bard second only to witnessing the plays themselves. Birch's retellings appear in three slender volumes—*Comedies, Histories*, and *Tragedies*. Just as commendable is Leon Garfield's *Shakespeare Stories*, in one volume. In lieu of these, readers may consider such classics as E. Nesbit's *The Children's Shakespeare* (also known as *The Best of Shakespeare*), and Charles and Mary Lamb's *Tales from Shakespeare*.

Conkling, Hilda. Selected poems.
The daughter of a poet, Conkling is said to have "spoken poems" before she was six years old, her mother writing them down and publishing them. The free form and brevity are easily grasped by young people, and several of her poems speak well to early adolescents. Suggested poems include:

Goldfish	River
I Keep Wondering	Song for Morning
My Mind and I	Water

Dickens, Charles. *A Christmas Carol.*
Because of this famous story, the name Ebenezer Scrooge is synonymous with penny-pinching bad humor. Scrooge's penuriousness, his maltreatment of Bob Cratchit, his encounter with the three ghosts, and his conversion to a year-round spirit of goodwill make for fond reading, year after year. This story is an

agreeable (and not too lengthy) introduction to Dickens, his times, and his works.

Doyle, Sir Arthur Conan. Sherlock Holmes stories.
Every adult familiar with Holmes has favorites among the stories. As an introduction to the adventures of the great Victorian detective, readers might start
with stories reflecting different phases of Holmes's career:

The Copper Beeches	The Speckled Band
The Dancing Men	The Final Problem
The Solitary Cyclist	The Empty House

Fisher, Leonard Everett. *Gutenberg.*
The development of movable type is one of the most important developments in
the evolution of the modern world. Fisher's works—*The Great Wall of China,
Pyramid of the Sun–Pyramid of the Moon, The Tower of London,* and *The Wailing
Wall,* among others—are enjoyed by middle-grade students for their factual,
historical presentations and sophisticated approach to the picture book.

Garfield, Leon. *Smith.*
Twelve-year-old Smith is a pickpocket who darts through the streets of eighteenth-
century London. Shortly after filching a document from an old man, Smith
unexpectedly witnesses the murder of his own victim. The killers, it seems, are
after the very item now in Smith's possession. Smith's plucky investigation
leads to the London underworld and to his own change of heart and mind.

Hawthorne, Nathaniel. Selections from *A Wonder Book* and *Tanglewood Tales.*
"The Miraculous Pitcher," Hawthorne's retelling of the Baucis and Philemon
story, was at one time standard fare in junior high school textbooks. There are
many riches here.

Irving, Washington. "The Legend of Sleepy Hollow" and other selections from
The Sketch Book.
Ichabod Crane still rides in this beloved American classic. Arthur Rackham's
illustrated version of "Rip Van Winkle" is also recommended.

Kipling, Rudyard. "If."
Young people—boys *and* girls—can find encouragement and strength in
Kipling's counsel for a forthright and serene life that adheres to fortitude and
principle. See also Longfellow's poem "A Psalm of Life."

Legends of King Arthur.
Retellings abound of Camelot and the exploits of its noble-hearted king.
Through such legends, young people come to know something of honor and
faithfulness. Different treatments include Roger Lancelyn Green's *King
Arthur and His Knights of the Round Table;* Sidney Lanier's *Boy's King Arthur;*
Howard Pyle's *Story of King Arthur and His Knights;* Rosemary Sutcliff's

Arthurian trilogy: *The Light Beyond the Forest, The Sword and the Circle,* and *The Road to Camlann;* and J. R. R. Tolkien's *Sir Gawain and the Green Knight.*

Marrin, Albert. Biographies and histories.

Few contemporary authors write history as engagingly for young readers as Albert Marrin. His biographies are especially suited to junior high school students, and they include interesting and well-researched books on Hitler, Stalin, Sitting Bull, Sir Francis Drake, George Washington, Ulysses S. Grant, Abraham Lincoln, and Robert E. Lee. As students proceed through subsequent grades, they can profit from his *War for Independence: The Story of the American Revolution, America and Vietnam: The Elephant and the Tiger,* and *Aztecs and Spaniards: Cortes and the Conquest of Mexico.*

Montgomery, Maud. *Anne of Green Gables.*

Charming and spirited Anne Shirley, an orphan girl, is brought to live with a stern-visaged old couple. Though she suffers personal setbacks, Anne is a salutary influence on Aunt Marilla and others. As she grows into young womanhood, she manages to forgive and to fall in love with Gilbert Blythe, who had teased her about her red hair. Students who love this book often proceed to other Anne novels or to Montgomery's *Emily of New Moon,* set in America.

Our Country's Founders: A Book of Advice for Young People. Edited by William J. Bennett.

What does it mean to "keep a republic"? This collection highlights the letters, speeches, poems, and articles of such personages as Washington, Jefferson, Franklin, Abigail Adams, and others. Their advice on civility, friendship, education, justice, patriotism, and piety comprise timely lessons that young people welcome. Bennett's *Our Sacred Honor: Words of Advice from the Founders in Stories, Poems, Letters, and Speeches* is recommended for high school students.

Stevenson, Robert Louis. *Treasure Island.*

While tending his mother's inn, Jim Hawkins befriends a mysterious and raucous old sailor and learns the location of buried treasure. When the old salt is foully murdered, Jim seeks the aid of Dr. Livesey and Squire Trelawney. Together the three set out to find the treasure, fitting out a schooner and hiring a crew. But danger awaits: Unbeknownst to Jim and his elders, their crew includes the pirate Long John Silver and his men, who are themselves after the treasure. The adventure is on! Seventh graders will appreciate the rising dilemma as Jim bonds with Silver, a villain who is at once colorful, likable, gregarious, and treacherous. See also Stevenson's *Black Arrow,* set at the time of England's War of the Roses.

Verne, Jules. *Twenty Thousand Leagues Under the Sea.*

Captain Nemo's *Nautilus* and his awestruck guests have furnished young readers with many hours of romantic pleasure. Verne is great not only as a storyteller but as an uncannily accurate technological seer. Other Verne works—*Around the World in Eighty Days* and *Journey to the Center of the Earth,* for example—have been enjoyed by young teens.

Wells, H. G. *The Time Machine.*
Scientific speculation is entertainingly disguised in this classic work of science fiction. When the inventor of a time machine moves forward across innumerable centuries, he witnesses different phases in the degeneration of life: The evil, underground Morlocks, descendants of industrial workers, prey upon the lovely Eloi; giant crabs rule the earth; the planet and the sun wane and die. Wells's ending is hopeful but his evolutionary predictions were grim, earning the skeptical disapproval of President Theodore Roosevelt, among others.

Grade Eight

The American Reader: Words That Moved a Nation. Edited by Diane Ravitch.
This compendium of primary source material complements studies of U.S. history: documents, poetry, speeches, songs, and so forth. Comprehensive and eclectic, *The American Reader* contains much profitable reading, including the Mayflower Compact, Chief Logan's lament, Thomas Paine's "The American Crisis," Washington's Farewell Address, Frederick Douglass's Independence Day speech at Rochester, and Lincoln's Cooper Union speech.

Benét, Steven Vincent. *The Ballad of William Sycamore.*
In this poem Benét's hero symbolizes the spirit of the pioneer. Sycamore, the son of a mountaineer, tells his own story: boyhood, marriage, children, sorrows, and death. Rejecting modernity as cities begin to encroach upon the prairie, Sycamore rests beneath a great tree, contented that "my buffalo have found me."

Bierhorst, John. *In the Trail of the Wind.*
This is an excellent collection of authentic American Indian poetry, with helpful bibliographical information. Selections are culled from societies in both North and South America, and the contents include ritual orations and song texts.

Bunyan, John. *Pilgrim's Progress.* Retold by James Reeves.
The most influential allegory in all of English literature, *Pilgrim's Progress* has been read with affection by generations of readers in many lands since it was first published in 1678. Its focus is the development of the soul, from the City of Destruction, through the Slough of Despond, Vanity Fair, and the House Beautiful, to the Celestial City. Reeves preserves the dignity of the original, deleting lengthy passages of debate. Bunyan's original may be reserved for high school or adult reading.

Forbes, Esther. *America's Paul Revere.*
Based upon Forbes's Pulitzer Prize–winning biography of Revere and illustrated with distinction by Lynd Ward, this biography for young readers presents the life and times of one of America's important patriots. Forbes's *Johnny Tremain*, based upon historical records, is a high point in American historical fiction, a deeply moving novel of the War for Independence. Johnny, a silversmith's apprentice, comes to embody the words of James Otis: "We give all we have, that a man can stand up."

Halliburton, Richard. *The Royal Road to Romance.*
Adventure is the hallmark of this unique and enduring travelogue. Fresh from
Princeton University, Halliburton and a pal set out in the early 1920s to view
other parts of the world, and *Royal Road* is an account of that unforgettable
first trip. Writers attest to Halliburton's formative influence, and readers still
are caught by the freshness, wanderlust, and charm that mark this work.

Harte, Bret. Selected short stories.
The rugged, luck-oriented life of the California gold rush era is caught in Harte's
most famous stories, some of which were based on actual newspaper reports of
the time. "Tennessee's Partner," "The Luck of Roaring Camp," and "The Outcasts of Poker Flat" capture a significant era now gone.

Hope, Anthony. *The Prisoner of Zenda.*
An Englishman passing through a tiny Balkan country is mistaken for its king.
Because of prevailing political intrigues and the need to protect the crown, he
agrees to pose as the king until the machinations of the evil Rupert of Hentzau
can be overcome. This leads to danger, heroism, and romance.

Jackson, Helen Hunt. *Ramona.*
In 1881, concerned about the plight of the American Indians, Jackson wrote a cri-
tique of the U.S. government's policies entitled *A Century of Dishonor.* The
book made little impact. Still compelled to portray the tragedy, Jackson recast
her sympathies in the form of a romantic novel, *Ramona,* which remains a
classic. This tragic love story is set in Southern California during the days of
the Spanish grandees, just as the old regime is passing away.

Lindbergh, Charles. *We.*
In his own words, the famous hero of the air relays the story of his life and his
transatlantic flight. Of particular interest today are his experiences as a stunt
flier during the early days of aviation and his views on the then-future of aviation. An unassuming book, *We* is an engrossing story of a young man's impressive accomplishments.

London, Jack. *The Call of the Wild.*
Strong and dignified Buck—part Saint Bernard, part shepherd dog—guards
Judge Miller's family and farm in the Santa Clara Valley of California. But he
is callously stolen and sold to black-market brokers who deal in sled dogs for
the Yukon gold country. Fierce cruelty and learn-as-you-go survival in the
midst of potentially fatal conditions comprise Buck's new life. Each gripping
episode hardens Buck and cultivates the spirit of the wolf within him. See also
London's *White Fang* and his sea story, *The Sea-Wolf.*

Longfellow, Henry Wadsworth. *Evangeline* or *The Courtship of Miles Standish.*
Both these famous narrative poems display Longfellow's versatility in story-
telling, description, and characterization. The tragic *Evangeline* is based upon
the expelling of the Acadians from Nova Scotia by the British and the separation of a young couple who love each other. In *The Courtship of Miles Standish,*

Captain Standish of Plymouth Settlement sends John Alden to win Priscilla
Mullins for him, but Priscilla prefers John. Only when Standish is reported
killed do John and Priscilla plan their wedding. But Standish is not dead, and
he returns in time to bless their union. The poems are engaging and compara-
tively easy for good readers to understand. If they cannot be read in their
entirety, the poems are approachable with judicious excerpting and supportive
explanation. Grade schools used to present dramatic versions of these poems,
with Longfellow's lines serving as part of the dialogue.

Orczy, Baroness Emmuska. *The Scarlet Pimpernel.*
During the French Revolution, the elusive Pimpernel (a nobleman in disguise)
aids the innocent to escape from the unjust and hideous fate of the guillotine. This is a capital adventure-romance, one that youths enjoy once they get
into it.

Poetry of Youth. Selected and annotated by Edwin Markham.
In its seriousness of purpose and the quality of its selections, perhaps no better
anthology ever existed for middle and high school students. Regrettably, the
book is no longer in print, but copies are obtainable through libraries and secondhand bookshops. The contemporary selections stop with the mid-1930s,
but the range of poetry reflects over three centuries of literary heritage. Poems
are categorized in terms that youths can understand, and each selection is
introduced with just enough explanation so that students can connect with the
work as they begin to read. This anthology deserves to be reprinted—and
sought out by teachers and parents.

Pyle, Howard. *Men of Iron* and *Otto of the Silver Hand.*
Set in medieval England, *Men of Iron* tells of young Myles Falworth, who, when
he learns that his father is falsely accused of plotting against the king, sets out
to free him. Myles's efforts to learn the ways of knighthood and master his
own faults of character are an important aspect of the story, as is his friendship
with Gascoyne. Pyle's *Otto of the Silver Hand* is set in medieval Germany during the time of the robber barons—a grim and suspenseful tale. Otto, raised in
the peaceful monastery, returns to his family's domain, only to be caught up in
the bitter blood feud between his father and a rival house. Pyle was a unique
talent: an outstanding artist, illustrator, author, and teacher.

Service, Robert W. Selections.
Best known for his poems and stories of the Yukon, this Canadian poet has written thoughtfully about the Great War as well.

The Cremation of Sam McGee	Grand-Père
Fleurette	The Spell of the Yukon

Sloane, Eric. *The Diary of an Early American Boy: Noah Blake, 1805.*
An authentic diary from 1805, in which a young boy noted all of his chores and
social activities, is the basis for Sloane's extensive drawings and explanations
of ordinary daily life long ago. Through the alternation of diary excerpts

and Sloane's pictorial descriptions of milling, stump-pulling, ink-making, and so forth, readers gain insight and appreciation for early American life and people.

Grade Nine

Aldrich, Bess Streeter. *A Lantern in Her Hand.*
Based on actual pioneer and family history, this novel relays the life of Abbie Deal, who accompanies her family to the Nebraska prairie and settles in a sod house. A sequel, *A White Bird Flying*, brings the generational story into the twentieth century. Aldrich's warm, homely *The Cutters* tells of a traditional American family living on the thin line between tightly budgeted subsistence and financial failure.

Barrie, Sir James M. *The Admirable Crichton.*
Crichton is a faithful and humble family servant. When the family's yacht goes down in a sea storm, the passengers seek refuge on a desert island, where Crichton proves himself to be a gifted and resourceful leader. The gentry acquiesce to his superior gifts until the rescue ship arrives. Barrie offers perceptive and touching insights into human nature. Though Barrie is best known for *Peter Pan,* such plays as *What Every Woman Knows, Dear Brutus,* and *A Kiss for Cinderella* are also worth reading.

Bontemps, Arna. Selected poems.
Bontemps is one of several outstanding writers of the Harlem Renaissance whose works include prose as well as poetry.

A Black Man Talks of Reaping	Nocturne of the Wharves
God Gives to Men	Reconnaissance

Bradbury, Ray. *Dandelion Wine.*
In the summer of 1928, young Douglas Spaulding comes alive to everything around him and to life itself. Family relationships, celebrations, fears and joys, even the mundane tasks of living take on marvelous significance. The story is set in Green Town, an invented name for Bradbury's own hometown of Waukegan, Illinois. A beautifully thoughtful book, *Dandelion Wine* can serve as a foil for *Main Street,* Sinclair Lewis's aloof portrayal of small-town life in the 1920s. Bradbury's breadth and versatility are seen in *Fahrenheit 451,* his one-act plays, and other works.

Browning, Elizabeth Barrett. Selections from *Sonnets from the Portuguese.*
Presented as a gift to the poet's husband, Robert Browning, these sonnets are an excellent introduction to love poetry. Sonnets 14 ("If thou must love me, let it be for naught . . .") and 43 ("How do I love thee? Let me count the ways . . .") are perhaps the most famous; numbers 1 and 20 are suggested as well.

Clark, Walter Van Tilburg. *The Ox-Bow Incident.*
In the days of the Old West, a posse brutally hangs three men presumed to be
guilty of cattle rustling. Few American novels penetrate the human proclivity
for rumor, self-righteousness, and mob psychology as well as this. Though
Clark's novel is different from William Golding's *Lord of the Flies,* there are
aspects in common.

Conrad, Joseph. *Lord Jim* and *Heart of Darkness.*
Lord Jim, Conrad's first important book (published in 1900), is a perceptive analysis of a man's failure to meet a crisis at sea and his ultimate recovery of self-
respect through honor and death. In *Heart of Darkness,* Conrad tells of the
brutal colonial exploitation in what was, in 1902, the Belgian Congo. Conrad
uses the character of Marlow as a narrator for both stories and as a kind of
commentator on moral dilemmas.

Cooper, James Fenimore. *Deerslayer* and other "Leatherstocking Tales."
Cooper was the first important novelist to address the American character. In
Books That Build Character, William Kilpatrick and Gregory and Suzanne
Wolfe note that Natty Bumppo "is a rebel against the corruption in society," a
man whose morality "is more true to the historical and practical realities of life
than that of representatives of 'civilization' around him." The novels remain
timely: The germ of today's environmental debate may be seen in *The Pioneers,*
for example; *The Last of the Mohicans* shows the arrogant folly of people who
disregard the dangers and evil that surround them.

Cullen, Countee. Selected poems.
A classically educated writer, Cullen took inspiration from Keats and other
romantic poets, eschewing the avant-garde.

For a Lady I Know	Heritage
For a Poet	Incident
From the Dark Tower	The Loss of Love
Fruit of the Flower	Simon the Cyrenian
Youth Sings a Song of Rose Buds	

Dickens, Charles. *David Copperfield* and *Oliver Twist.*
The novels of Dickens offer a wealth of memorable characters and character
types. The ones in *David Copperfield* include some of the most famous, ranging from the malevolent to the eccentric and lovable—Murdstone, Uriah
Heep, Steerforth, Betsey Trotwood, Mr. Micawber, Little Emily, and others.
The story relates David's harsh upbringing, his school years and young manhood, and his ultimate happiness. In both *David Copperfield* and *Oliver Twist,*
Dickens's infectious humor is tempered by his outrage at hypocrisy and the
malign treatment of children during the England of his day.

Golding, William. *Lord of the Flies.*
Survivors of a plane crash after an atomic war, a group of boys is stranded on an
island. They struggle to achieve order and to govern themselves. Despite their

presumed "age of innocence," the youngsters resort to pride, savagery, murder, and the drive for domination. Golding, who described his novels as "fables," leads readers to reflect on human nature, evil and sin, and the fragility of civilization.

Goldsmith, Oliver. *She Stoops to Conquer; or, The Mistakes of a Night.*
This comedy of manners is one of the most heartily humorous plays ever written. Mischievous Tony Lumpkin jokingly directs two young men to a house that he says is an inn, but that actually is the private home of the Hardcastle family. The young men proceed to order the family members about as if they were servants in a hostelry. One of the men, Marlowe, feels comfortable only in the company of servant girls, not genteel young ladies. Mistaking the eligible Kate Hardcastle for the former type, he indicates a romantic interest in her. She returns his interest and, seeing in him the makings of a man of quality, maintains the mistaken identity, thereby "stooping" in rank and by pretense to win his hand. Much comedy is furnished by the elder Hardcastles and by the denizens of the Three Jolly Pigeons alehouse.

Hudson, W. H. *Green Mansions.*
This poetic and almost mystical tale of the tropics deals with Mr. Abel and his love for Rima, the orphaned girl of the birds. Essentially a story of sorrow and loss amid the beauties and wildness of nature, Hudson's tale is a haunting one, and the character of Rima remains fresh and fascinating.

Huxley, Aldous. *Brave New World.*
First published in 1935, this novel depicts life under a world state in the future. With a gimlet eye, Huxley portrays the social and spiritual void that exists under a supposedly utopian regime. The calm, imposed efficiency of "community, identity, stability" is disturbed with the discovery of a self-educated "savage" whose mind and soul are not possessed by prevailing powers. Moral worth, a true sense of home, and a naturally thriving community are among the things that keep the world from becoming the state that Huxley shows.

Jager, Ronald. *Eighty Acres: Elegy for a Family Farm* and *Last House on the Road.*
Having been raised in an agrarian society, Jager sees life and community with different depth perception than do the heads of the media age. In his thoughtful memoir, *Eighty Acres,* he reflects upon his family and childhood; chapters 6 and 17, "Enlarging the Family" and "And Don't Lick the Hoarfrost Off the Pump Handle," are suggested as excerpts. In the amusing *Last House on the Road,* Jager ruminates on his experiences in restoring an old home; chapter 18, "Chicken Dinner: The Unwritten Recipe," stands alone as recommended high school reading.

Kipling, Rudyard. "L'Envoi to *The Seven Seas*" and "The Gods of the Copybook Headings" from *Rudyard Kipling's Verse: Definitive Edition.*
The splendid images and phrases in Kipling's "When Earth's last picture is painted and the tubes are twisted and dried . . ." are memorable. With the second poem, readers reflect on the historical rise and decay of civilizations and

the perennial hardiness of world-common moral fundamentals that C. S. Lewis once named the Tao.

Melville, Herman. *Typee.*

For years, *Moby-Dick*'s popularity was far outshone by that of *Typee,* a fictionalized account of Melville's life in the Polynesian islands. Through his portrayal of Edenic innocence coexisting with evil, readers come to examine their own world and the nature of humanity itself. See also *Billy Budd* and *Moby-Dick.*

O'Neill, Eugene. *Seven Plays of the Sea.*

Based upon O'Neill's personal experiences as a seaman, these plays are rich with atmosphere and dramatic intensity. Suggested for reading are "Bound East for Cardiff," "Ile," "In the Zone," and "Where the Cross Is Made." These are the plays that made the Provincetown Playhouse—and O'Neill—famous.

Poe, Edgar Allan. Selected tales and poems.

Poems suggested for high school readers include "To Helen," "The Bells," "Israfel," "The Raven," and "Annabelle Lee." Among the short stories: "The Telltale Heart," "The Pit and the Pendulum," "The Murders in the Rue Morgue," and "The Fall of the House of Usher."

Rawlings, Marjorie Kinnan. *The Yearling.*

This tragic coming-of-age story transpires during one year in the life of a backwoods boy and his father and mother. It is a compelling depiction of the decisions and painful choices that force maturity. Though the novel is commonly thought of as children's literature, Rawlings's intended audience was adult readers. Atheneum's reissued Scribner Illustrated Classics edition contains N. C. Wyeth's 1939 paintings, newly rephotographed.

Saroyan, William. *The Human Comedy.*

During World War II, the Macauley family strives to keep things together, even though the father has died and the eldest son, Marcus, is away in the service. High-school-age Homer helps to support the family through his job as a telegram delivery boy. On his routes he must bear news of war casualties to families, which prepares him for contending with life. Much of the appeal of this story stems from the depiction of wartime Ithaca, a fictional city firmly based on the author's own hometown of Fresno, California. This is an unassuming and sweetly poignant story.

Scott, Sir Walter. *Ivanhoe.*

Though Scott has been banished from many English classrooms, *Ivanhoe* still commands a readership. The father of modern historical fiction, Scott is exceptional in his ability to fashion a grand story with historical color, atmosphere, and picturesque detail. In *Ivanhoe,* he builds upon the noble and chivalrous aspect of the Middle Ages. The story is set in the period following the Norman conquest and centers on the love of Wilfrid, knight of Ivanhoe, for Rowena, his father's ward, and the love of Rebecca the Jewess for Ivanhoe. When Rebecca is falsely accused of sorcery, she demands a trial by combat, and Ivanhoe fights on her behalf. Richard the Lionhearted and Robin Locksley are well integrated into the story. Among many memorable events are the archery match at Ashby, the pageantry of the tournament, and the siege of Torquilstone Castle. Scott's novels of Scottish life—*The Heart of Midlothian, The Antiquary, Rob Roy*, for example—are considered to be his best works.

Selections from Proverbs, Ecclesiastes, and Psalms.

The King James version of the Bible contains some of the most majestic passages in the English language, and the formative influence of its wisdom literature is perennial. Representative selections include the pastoral Psalm 23, the jubilatory Psalm 100, and the honorary Psalm 103; the book of Ecclesiastes in its entirety; and Proverbs, chapters 1 and 10–20.

Shakespeare, William. Selected plays.

A Midsummer Night's Dream, As You Like It, and *Much Ado About Nothing* are comedies congenial for ninth graders, but some students prefer the lyrical tragedy of *Romeo and Juliet*. If students watch on videocassette Kenneth Branagh's film version of *Much Ado About Nothing* after having read it, they can discuss the significant ways in which the producer altered the play. The reading of a Shakespearean play is nicely motivated when there exists a prospect of seeing it performed by a good company.

Stevenson, Robert Louis. *Kidnapped* or selected short stories, poems, and essays.

Cheated out of his inheritance, David Balfour falls victim to the scheme of his evil uncle: he is kidnapped and taken to sea. David's survival and his perilous journey to find his way back are the substance of the novel. The story is set amid the political intrigues of eighteenth-century Scotland. See also Stevenson's "Markheim" or other stories, "Travels with a Donkey," the poem "The Celestial Surgeon," or selected essays (e.g., "Character of a Dog," "On the Enjoyment of Unpleasant Places").

Stratton-Porter, Gene. *A Girl of the Limberlost.*

In her poem "The Butterfly," Alice Freeman Palmer writes, "God give me courage to trust/I can break my chrysalis too!" Something of this same spirit dwells in Stratton-Porter's novel. Elnora Comstock finds a haven from her sorrows in the forest of Indiana's Limberlost swamplands. Nature furnishes her with the inspiration she needs to penetrate her mother's unyielding bitterness and to resolve her own inner conflicts and resentments. Elnora is a heroine of grace, self-reliance, and resolve. Her story provokes an unexpectedly warm and positive response from many young readers today.

Twain, Mark. *Life on the Mississippi.*

"The Mississippi is well worth reading about. It is not a commonplace river, but on the contrary is in all ways remarkable." With these words, Twain begins his memoir of his youthful days as a steamboat pilot, an account rich in humor, color, and action, with an abundant array of characters and waterfront life. Amid the tall tales and true tales, readers gain insight into human ingenuity, skill, and interreliance, as well as an appreciation for the life that thrives along the nation's greatest river. See also Twain's *Roughing It.*

Grade Ten

By the end of tenth grade, students should be reading some of the principal American and English novelists, poets, essayists, and dramatists. Their reading should include works that touch on themes of coming of age, personal loss, transitions, first love, virtue, and responsibility. By the time they graduate from high school, students should have surveyed the development of American and English literature, including representative samples from the great writers.

Austen, Jane. *Pride and Prejudice.*
The story concerns Mrs. Bennett's efforts to land suitable husbands for her five daughters. Austen's wittily comic style superbly captures the usual dilemmas of youth and courtship, as well as the manners and mores of her time. Austen, said William Vaughn Moody and Robert Morss Lovett in *A History of English Literature,* "accept[s] the world in an ironical spirit, and . . . find[s] in it such amusement as it offers."

Bowen, Catherine Drinker. *Miracle at Philadelphia.*
Bowen's account of the 1787 Constitutional convention in Philadelphia is a fairminded, engaging, and well-documented presentation. It may be read as preliminary to, or in conjunction with, a study of the U.S. Constitution and the debates between the Federalists and Anti-Federalists.

Brontë, Charlotte. *Jane Eyre.*
Shy Jane Eyre leaves her unhappy school days behind to enter the home of the troubled Rochester and serve as governess to his ward. Jane's feelings for this disturbed man grow into love, but his brusque and erratic nature offsets any prospect for an even course. A mixture of Gothic mystery and intense realism, *Jane Eyre* is one of the greatest novels of the nineteenth century. Readers who enjoy Charlotte Brontë may seek out her *Villette,* a book that contrasts with *Jane Eyre.* See also sister Emily's *Wuthering Heights.*

Brooke, Rupert. "The Soldier."
Brooke's lines speak eloquently for soldiers who have fought and died for freedom. It was in that spirit that Brooke joined the armed forces in the Great War. His entry into that terrible conflict led to his untimely death. "The Soldier" is anthologized frequently, and may be found in *The Oxford Book of War Poetry* edited by Jon Stallworthy.

Cather, Willa. *My Ántonia.*
Jim Burden tells the life of his friend, Ántonia Shimerda, an immigrant girl who passes from girlhood into maturity on the prairie. Published in 1918, Cather's novel is a tribute to the generous and wholesome strength of America's immigrant settlers.

Crane, Stephen. *The Red Badge of Courage.*
Crane intended his novel to be a study in the psychological effects of fear. Set at
the time of the Civil War, the story tells of young Henry Fleming, who dreams
of heroism and grandeur in battle. But his first taste of war shatters all illusions
and reduces him to cowardice. His subsequent experiences form him as a man,
fellow soldier, and hero.

Dana, Richard Henry, Jr. *Two Years Before the Mast* and "Twenty-four Years After."
This is an engrossing, accurate, and authentic narrative of two years in the life of a
common sailor. In 1834, an unhappy young man left his genteel Boston home
to pursue a career as a seaman. Dana's memoir recounts his voyage round Cape
Horn to the California coast, and back. He pictures the day-to-day routine of
sailors, their hardships, the brutalities inflicted upon them, and the character
of island and coastal towns. Dana proved himself under the most exacting and
perilous conditions. Some editions include Dana's 1869 appendage "Twenty-
four Years After," which relays the fate of his old comrades and acquaintances.

Defoe, Daniel. *Robinson Crusoe.*
Heedlessly disregarding the loving counsel of his parents, young Crusoe sets out
from home, determined to go to sea. He experiences capture, enslavement,
escape, shipwreck, and solitary survival on a lonely island. The hardships Crusoe faces lead to his spiritual and intellectual development. His motives and
ambitions, as described in the first chapter, are readily understood by teens
today. The story was based on the real-life experiences of a rescued castaway,
Alexander Selkirk (1676–1721). Avoid expurgated versions.

Dickens, Charles. *A Tale of Two Cities* and *Great Expectations.*
These two novels are among Dickens's finest achievements. *Great Expectations*
contains elements of a romantic mystery story, but it is a sharp and perceptive
portrayal of Pip's growth from a somewhat superficial lad to a man of character. Self-knowledge is one of the best legacies one could have in life. *A Tale of
Two Cities,* perhaps better known, tells the story of a cluster of people caught
up in the fury of the French Revolution.

Douglass, Frederick. *Narrative of the Life of Frederick Douglass.*
Writer, orator, and diplomat, Douglass rose from slavery to become a leader in the
fight for emancipation. His autobiography is an eloquent self-portrait as well
as a work of history. Because of its comparative brevity, the *Narrative* lends
itself to classroom study. His *Life and Times of Frederick Douglass* is more comprehensive. Both books contribute to a deeper understanding of American life
and heritage.

Du Bois, W. E. B. *The Souls of Black Folks.*
This poetic and forthright set of essays incorporates a well-calculated argument
in the cause of black America, circa 1903. A sharp critic of Booker T. Washington's "Tuskegee Machine," Du Bois believed in the power of logic and strove
to appeal to the national conscience. Young readers benefit by studying this
book in tandem with Washington's *Up from Slavery* (see author listing in this
grade level).

Dumas, Alexandre. *The Three Musketeers.*
The term *musketeers* refers to the personal guards of King Louis XIII of France. The story is concerned with three musketeers in particular—Athos, Porthos, and Aramis; how they come to be joined by a gallant and dashing Gascon D'Artagnan; and their magnificent adventures in outwitting Lady de Winter and Cardinal Richelieu. This outstanding historical romance and its sequels are said to have been based upon the actual exploits of an actual M. D'Artagnan. See also *The Count of Monte Cristo* and *The Man in the Iron Mask.*

Eliot, George. *Romola.*
The dramatic historical background of this novel is fifteenth-century Florence, encompassing the expulsion of the Medici and the invasion by France. The central characters include courageous Romola, her selfish and deceitful husband, Tito Melma, and the charismatic monk, Savonarola, whose excommunication and execution figure in the story.

Eliot, George. *Silas Marner.*
For many years, this book was a standard part of sophomore reading but eventually was replaced by teen-focused literature. Too bad, because *Silas Marner* is one of the great stories of materialism, greed, personal loss, and suffering. Youngsters, even those who balk at reading it, will remember it long after humdrum teen lit has been long forgotten.

Ellison, Ralph. *Invisible Man.*
Ellison's great novel describes the journey of its narrator, a nameless black man, as he moves through a landscape of intolerance, unable to establish his identity. It is a moving book about race in America, but it is also a book about our common humanity as well.

Emerson, Ralph Waldo. Selected essays.
Two series of essays contain Emerson's most notable work. "Self-Reliance" and "Compensation" are perhaps the best known. Emerson's address "The American Scholar" was of great influence, encouraging scholars and writers to pursue native aims in place of European models or associations. Such works offer much for young people to discuss with adults. Does a good exist for every evil? Is the pursuit of originality commendable for its own sake? Is it truth or over-statement to say, "Whoso would be a man must be a nonconformist," or "Do your work, and I shall know you"?

Fitzgerald, F. Scott. *The Great Gatsby.*
The inscrutable Gatsby was at once a dreamer and a materialist, riding high amid the giddy, life-is-a-party "Jazz Age"—a segment of the 1920s rather than an "age." What did he intend to accomplish by it all? This is a lingering and unsettled question among Fitzgerald's readers. This remains one of the most popular novels both in- and outside of classrooms.

Franklin, Benjamin. *Autobiography.*
Franklin's writing of his autobiography was the whim of an idle moment while visiting an English home. It was written for his son, with no apparent thought

of publication. Though it was written intermittently at different phases of his career, the result was a distinctly American work reflecting Franklin's wide sphere of interests and experience: printer, statesman, postmaster, scientist, philosopher, diplomat, inventor, and more.

Hawthorne, Nathaniel. *The House of the Seven Gables* or other selected stories from *Mosses from an Old Manse* and *Twice-Told Tales.*
Romanticism pervades *The House of the Seven Gables,* for which a famous house in Salem, Massachusetts, furnished inspiration. (The house still stands.) The characters of Hepzibah, Clifford, Phoebe, and Jaffrey are beautifully limned, and the sunny ending stands in contrast to Hawthorne's other great novel, *The Scarlet Letter,* also recommended. Such stories as "Earth's Holocaust," "Rappaccini's Daughter," "The Celestial Railroad," and "Feathertop" are within the range of high school sophomores.

Henry, O. Selected short stories.
A master of his art, and known for his sentiment and gentle irony, William Sydney Porter excels as a writer of short stories. The stories fall into four geographic groupings: stories of the South, the Southwest, South America, and New York City. His characters are ordinary folk whom one might encounter in the everyday and "fringe" worlds. Among suggested stories are "The Gift of the Magi," "A Chaparral Christmas Gift," "The Last Leaf," "A Municipal Report," "A Retrieved Reformation," and "An Unfinished Story."

Hurston, Zora Neale. *Dust Tracks on the Road.*
Hurston was one of the major contributors to the Harlem Renaissance. Her essays about growing up in the South express a unique and independent perspective, and her novel *Their Eyes Were Watching God* has increasingly gained recognition as a classic of American literature.

Orwell, George. *1984.*
Orwell's futuristic novel about a totalitarian regime rings true today. His selection of the year 1984 was off-the-cuff, but his apprehension of worrisome trends has proven to be prescient. Privacy, propaganda, and thought control are lively topics at the beginning of the twenty-first century. Though the years since its publication have brought overwhelming change, Orwell's sobering satire remains timely and important. His *Collected Essays,* especially "Politics and the English Language," are gems.

Parkman, Francis. *The Oregon Trail.*
An eyewitness account of America's westward movement, Parkman's vivid account stands as a work of literature as well as a historical and geographical record. Though some of Parkman's attitudes toward American Indians are typical of his time, he foresaw the demise of indigenous cultures and strove to correct commonly held misconceptions. Chapter 7, "The Buffalo," is sometimes selected as a stand-alone introduction to Parkman's work.

Plutarch. *Parallel Lives.*

The classic Greek biographer (ca. A.D. 46–126) compared twenty-three pairs of
Greek and Roman statesmen and soldiers, focusing on personal character and
showing the relationship between private and public lives. The work is often
published under different titles—*Lives of the Noble Greeks, Makers of Rome,* for
example. Modern Library provides in two volumes the Clough-Dryden translation, with the original pairings. Selections rather than the entire work are
advisable at this age level, and the chapters on Solon, Cato, Demosthenes,
Pericles, and Cicero are a place to begin. America's founding fathers studied
their Plutarch to learn what to emulate and what to avoid in leadership.

Presidential Writings.

Why should students study excerpts from the writings of Adams, Jefferson, Lincoln, and Washington? They should study them to better understand such
issues as federalism, the new and old liberalism, the foundational ideas of
American government, slavery, the poor, and the rights of women. They
should study them to gain a realistic understanding of the nation's most
famous leaders, recognizing them as human beings rather than stilted figures
of history, and to better understand the thinking behind important documents, such as the Declaration of Independence and the Gettysburg Address.
They should learn to recognize some of the mischaracterizations and misun-
derstandings common today. If not read in tenth grade, presidential writings
should be integrated with later studies of American history and government,
perhaps during eleventh or twelfth grade, preferably under the guidance of a
knowledgeable adult. Popular editions include *Abraham Lincoln: His Speeches
and Writings,* edited by Roy P. Basler; *George Washington: A Collection,* edited
by W. B. Allen; and *The Portable Thomas Jefferson,* edited by Merrill D. Peter-
son. Although it was written years before his presidency, James Madison's
Notes of Debates in the Federal Constitution of 1787 complements presidential
readings. A "common reader" or popular edition of John Adams's writings is
needed, but recent Adams biographies and C. Bradley Thompson's *The Revolutionary Writings of John Adams* will suffice for the time being. The writing
styles of these great men are individual, often elegant, and in some cases, worthy of study as literature.

Runyon, Damon. Selected short stories.

Once upon a time, in a midnight land lit by neon and lulled by Klaxon horns,
there lived a now-vanished society of bookies, touts, apple sellers, hoods,
sharps, and chorines who had hearts of gold. Their lingo was a music all its
own, and some of the characters, like the Lemon Drop Kid and Miss Ade-
laide, live on in such works as "Little Miss Marker" and *Guys and Dolls and
Other Stories.*

Shakespeare, William. Selected plays.

The reading of Shakespeare's plays should continue throughout high school:
*Richard III, King Lear, Henry V, Julius Caesar, The Tempest, Hamlet, Antony and
Cleopatra,* and others.

Shaw, George Bernard. *Pygmalion.*

In this witty and polished comedy, Professor Henry Higgins makes a casual wager that he can turn a lowly flower girl into a lady of society by teaching her to speak proper English. Eliza, the flower girl, strives to achieve his aim but, though triumphant, earns little of his regard or respect. The ending of the play, characteristically Shavian and unromantic, was altered for both the 1938 film version and the 1956 musical, *My Fair Lady.* The final act prompts discussion among audiences even today.

Smith, Betty. *A Tree Grows in Brooklyn.*

Smith's story of life in Brooklyn in 1912 has been a first "adult" book for many adolescent readers. "Beloved" and "poignant" are two words commonly applied to this novel about a young girl growing up amid the American melting pot and coping with adversity.

Steinbeck, John. *The Grapes of Wrath.*

This is the famous story of the Dust Bowl era and the Joad family's journey from the choking, sand-swept air of Oklahoma to the orchards of California. The novel remains a powerful testament to the suffering and resolve of migrants who faced loss and complete defeat. See also *The Red Pony.*

Synge, John Millington. "Riders to the Sea," from *The Complete Plays of John M. Synge.*

This one-act tragedy is set in a fishing village on the Aran Islands and was inspired by events that occurred while Synge was visiting there. "The smoking fog has passed over and given me a strange sense of exile and desolation," he wrote, and the fate of Maurya's sons and daughters is portrayed in this same spirit. A moving and evocative audio performance of the play was once recorded by the Abbey Players (Spoken Arts, #743).

Tey, Josephine. *The Daughter of Time.*

While Alan Grant of Scotland Yard is hospitalized with a minor injury, his friend brings him a packet of portraits to amuse him. One is the infamous villain Richard III. Grant sees something in the man's face that intrigues him. With a detective's keen eye for detail, the bedridden Grant sets out to solve one of history's most notorious crimes. It is a dazzling novel that is a model of the creative power of skeptical thinking.

Thackeray, William Makepeace. *Vanity Fair.*

The title, taken from John Bunyan's *Pilgrim's Progress,* refers to society itself—a fair "where is sold all sorts of vanity, and where is to be seen juggling, cheats, games, plays, fools, apes, knaves, rogues, and that of every kind." So is society today. With wisdom and mordant humor, Thackeray probes every kind of frivolity and superficial pretense, exposing those segments of society that strain for recognition from social lions and "who stint in private to shine in public." The coil for his satirical shafts is the story of conniving, competent Becky

Sharp, whose efforts to rise in society are as clever as they are wanton. In today's vernacular, *Vanity Fair* is of "summer reading length," ideal for the young reader who wants to tackle an expansive Victorian novel.

Thoreau, Henry David. *Walden.*
A restless and independent spirit, Thoreau repaired to a cabin in the woods around Walden Pond in an effort to "front only the essential facts of life." His observations of nature and his meditations on "higher laws" and "brute neighbors" result in a plea for a simplified life, one that is free from preoccupation with material things. "Only that day dawns to which we are awake." See also Thoreau's essay on civil disobedience.

Thurber, James. *My Life and Hard Times.*
Thurber's ability to meld the mundane and the cuckoo makes his brand of humor distinctive. "The Night the Bed Fell" links humor and autobiography, as does his tale of Muggs the Airedale in "The Dog That Bit People." The laughable, repetitive mistakes of bureaucracy are portrayed in "Draft Board Nights." The reading of this book can lead to forays into literary humor—Robert Benchley, Langston Hughes, Ring Lardner, S. J. Perelman, and others.

Tocqueville, Alexis de. Selections from *Democracy in America.*
In the 1830s, two French aristocrats visited the United States with the intention of studying American prisons. One of them, Tocqueville, wrote his impressions of the country, its people, and its traditions. His book endures as the most discerning reflection on the nature of democracy and on the connection between a citizenry's character and the welfare of a nation and its communities. Far from celebratory, *Democracy in America* is a sober and frequently melancholy evaluation of democracy's prospects for survival. Suggested excerpts include Tocqueville's discussion of "the three races that inhabit the territory of the United States" (volume 1, part 2, chapter 10); "How the Americans Combat Individualism with Free Institutions," "On the Use That the Americans Make of Associations in Civil Life," and "How the Taste for Material Enjoyments Among Americans Is United with Love of Freedom and with Care for Public Affairs" (volume 2, part 2, chapters 4, 5, and 14). The new translation by Harvey C. Mansfield and Delba Winthrop is now supplanting that of Phillips Bradley. A good introduction or companion to the work is the video *Traveling Tocqueville's America,* produced by C-SPAN.

Twain, Mark. *Adventures of Huckleberry Finn.*
Published in 1885, just twenty years after the close of the Civil War, this great novel touches on themes of friendship, flawed humanity, and injustice. Escaping a drunken father and the confinement of Jackson's Island, Huck pairs up with Jim, a runaway slave. As they float down the Mississippi River on a raft, making occasional stops along the way, they encounter a range of characters and experiences. From these—and from Jim—Huck's outlook on life and his fellow man is formed.

Washington, Booker T. *Up from Slavery.*

During his time, no black American was as powerful or influential as Washington. His 1901 autobiography indicates the greatness of the man and his accomplishments in education, politics, and culture.

Whitman, Walt. Selected poems.

In addition to Whitman's more frequently read "I Hear America Singing," the poems "Sea Drift," "Passage to India," and "Song of the Exposition" have much to offer young readers in their reflections on valor in the voyages of life.

Wilde, Oscar. *The Importance of Being Earnest.*

Wilde's drawing-room comedy is rich with epigrams, wry observations, and sly satire on social conventions. Since the mannered style of the play is completely unfamiliar to young readers, it helps to view a video or DVD of Anthony Asquith's film production starring Michael Redgrave and Margaret Rutherford.

Wilder, Thornton. Selected plays.

In addition to his major plays—*Our Town, The Skin of Our Teeth,* and *The Matchmaker*—this distinguished playwright has written memorable, although less well known, one-act plays that are suitable for reading and discussion: "Pullman Car Hiawatha," "The Long Christmas Dinner," and "The Happy Journey to Trenton and Camden." See also Wilder's novel *The Bridge of San Luis Rey.*

Yeats, William Butler. Selections from *The Collected Poems of W. B. Yeats.*

The leader of the Irish Renaissance, Yeats was a great Irish nationalist. His plays and poems reveal his fascination with lore and the occult. Some of the more accessible poems for high school readers include:

Among School Children	The Fiddler of Dooney
The Ballad of Moll Magee	The Happy Townland
The Cap and Bells	The Stolen Child
Down by the Salley Gardens	When You Are Old

Notes

THREE: *Everybody Does It: The Textbook Publishers*

1. *Scott Foresman–Addison Wesley Multicultural Guidelines* (Scott Foresman–Addison Wesley, 1996).
2. Susan Chira, "Writing Textbooks for Children: A Juggling Act," *The New York Times,* January 17, 1990.
3. *Reflecting Diversity: Multicultural Guidelines for Educational Publishing Professionals* (Macmillan/McGraw-Hill, 1993).
4. "Excerpts from Harcourt Horizons Editorial Guidelines" (2002); Harcourt, "Striving for Fairness" (2001).
5. *Eliminating Stereotypes* (Houghton Mifflin, 1981).
6. "Guidelines for Literature Search" (Houghton Mifflin, 2001).

FOUR: *Everybody Does It: The Testing Companies*

1. Donald Ross Green, "Methods Used by Test Publishers to 'Debias' Standardized Tests," *Handbook of Methods for Detecting Test Bias,* edited by Ronald A. Berks (Johns Hopkins University Press, 1982), pp. 233–35.
2. William H. Angoff, "Perspectives on Differential Item Functioning Methodology," in *Differential Item Functioning,* ed. Paul W. Holland and Howard Wainer (Lawrence Erlbaum Associates, 1993), p. 4.
3. Kathleen A. O'Neill and W. Miles McPeek, "Item and Test Characteristics That Are Associated with Differential Item Functioning," *Differential Item Functioning,* pp. 255–76.
4. Lloyd Bond, "Comments on the O'Neill & McPeek Paper," *Differential Item Functioning,* pp. 277–79.
5. Elizabeth Burton and Nancy W. Burton, "The Effect of Item Screening on Test Scores and Test Characteristics," *Differential Item Functioning,* pp. 333–335.
6. Julie Noble, Mark Davenport, Jeff Schiel, and Mary Pommerich, "High School Academic and Noncognitive Variables Related to the ACT Scores of Racial/Ethnic and Gender Groups" (ACT Research Report, 1999).

7. Paul A. Ramsey, "Sensitivity Review: The ETS Experience as a Case Study," *Differential Item Functioning*, pp. 376–78.

FIVE: *Censorship from the Right*

1. Sally J. Taylor, *Stalin's Apologist: Walter Duranty, the* New York Times *Man in Moscow* (Oxford University Press, 1990).
2. Ronnie Dugger, "What Corrupted Texas?" *Harper's*, March 1957, p. 73.
3. *The Houston Post*, March 27, 1957.
4. See Jonathan Zimmerman, *Whose America? Culture Wars in the Public Schools* (Harvard University Press, 2002); Jonathan Zimmerman, " 'Each "Race" Could Have Its Heroes Sung': Ethnicity and the History Wars in the 1920s," *The Journal of American History*, June 2000, pp. 92–111. Also, Jack Nelson and Gene Roberts Jr., *The Censors and the Schools* (Little, Brown, 1963), pp. 24–34.
5. Diane Ravitch, *Left Back: A Century of Battles Over School Reform* (Simon & Schuster, 2001), pp. 312–14.
6. Stephen Bates, *Battleground: One Mother's Crusade, the Religious Right, and the Struggle for Control of Our Classrooms* (Poseidon Press, 1993), p. 319. Another excellent source for these issues is Joan DelFattore, *What Johnny Shouldn't Read: Textbook Censorship in America* (Yale University Press, 1992).
7. Lee Burress, *Battle of the Books: Literary Censorship in the Public Schools, 1950–1985* (Scarecrow Press, 1989), pp. 180–81.
8. The "Ten Most Challenged Books of 2000," according to the American Library Association (www.ala.org/pio/presskits/midwinterawards2001/challenged.html), were:

> The Harry Potter series by J. K. Rowling, for occult/Satanism and anti-family themes
> *The Chocolate War* by Robert Cormier, for violence, offensive language, and being unsuited to age group
> Alice series, by Phyllis Reynolds Naylor, for sexual content and being unsuited to age group
> *Killing Mr. Griffin* by Lois Duncan, for violence and sexual content
> *Of Mice and Men* by John Steinbeck, for offensive language, racism, violence, and being unsuited to age group
> *I Know Why the Caged Bird Sings* by Maya Angelou, for sexual content, racism, offensive language, violence, and being unsuited to age group
> *Fallen Angels* by Walter Dean Myers, for offensive language, racism, violence, and being unsuited to age group
> Scary Stories series by Alvin Schwartz, for violence, occult themes, and being unsuited to age group
> *The Terrorist* by Caroline Cooney, for violence, occult themes, and being unsuited to age group
> *The Giver* by Lois Lowry, for sexual explicitness, occult themes, and violence

SIX: *Censorship from the Left*

1. Burress, *Battle of the Books,* pp. 116–34; DelFattore, *What Johnny Shouldn't Read,* p. 9.
2. Lionel Trilling, *American Literature* (Ginn, 1964), p. 509, cited in Burress, p. 96.
3. Jocelyn Chadwick-Joshua, *The Jim Dilemma: Reading Race in Huckleberry Finn* (University Press of Mississippi, 1998).
4. Council on Interracial Books for Children, "Ten Quick Ways to Analyze Children's Books for Sexism and Racism," *Guidelines for Selecting Bias-Free Textbooks and Storybooks* (CIBC, 1980); originally published in the Council on Interracial Books for Children, *Bulletin,* vol. 5, no. 3, 1974, pp. 1–6.
5. Robert Moore, "Toward Unbiased Textbooks," CIBC *Bulletin,* vol. 8, no. 2, 1977; Howard Meyer, "Neutralism Isn't Neutral," *The New York Times,* July 24, 1980, in CIBC *Bulletin,* vol. 11, no. 6, 1980.
6. American Library Association, "Diversity in Collection Development," *Intellectual Freedom Manual* (American Library Association, 1982), p. 124.
7. " 'Censorship' or Selection: The Search for Common Ground," CIBC *Bulletin,* vol. 7, no. 4, 1976, p. 3.
8. American Library Association, "Diversity in Collection Department," p. 127.
9. CIBC *Bulletin,* vol. 3, no. 4, 1971.
10. Robert Moore, "From Rags to Witches: Stereotypes, Distortions and Anti-Humanism in Fairy Tales," CIBC *Bulletin,* vol. 6, no. 7, 1975.
11. Nat Hentoff, "Any Writer Who Follows Anyone Else's Guidelines Ought to Be in Advertising," *School Library Journal* (November 1977), reprinted in *Young Adult Literature: Background and Criticism* (American Library Association, 1980), pp. 454–460. See also Council on Interracial Books for Children, *Human and Anti-Human Values in Children's Books: A Content Rating Instrument for Educators and Concerned Parents: Guidelines for the Future* (CIBC, 1976).
12. Women on Words and Images, *Dick and Jane as Victims: Sex Stereotyping in Children's Readers: An Analysis* (Women on Words and Images, 1972).
13. The quotations that follow are from letters and documents in the Holt files. A copy of these files has been permanently stored in the Hoover Institution Library and Archives as part of my papers. For another discussion of the Holt files, see Bates, *Battleground.*
14. The quotations that follow are from letters and documents in the Open Court files. A copy of these files has been permanently stored in the Hoover Institution Library and Archives as part of my papers.

SEVEN: *The Mad, Mad, Mad World of Textbook Adoptions*

1. William Twombley, "Text Review's Significance Shows in Revisions," *Los Angeles Times,* August 4, 1982.
2. Jonathan Rosenbloom, "The World According to Curriculum: What Are Our Children Learning and Who Decides?" American Education Publishers Online, September 3, 2002.

EIGHT: *Literature: Forgetting the Tradition*

1. Jack Nelson and Gene Roberts Jr., *The Censors and the Schools* (Little, Brown, 1963), pp. 129, 183.

2. Noel Perrin, *Dr. Bowdler's Legacy: A History of Expurgated Books in England and America* (Godine, 1992, orig. published by Atheneum, 1969).

3. DelFattore, *What Johnny Shouldn't Read*, p. 130.

4. Barbara Cohen, "Censoring the Sources," *American Educator*, Summer 1987, pp. 43–46.

5. Dorothy Thompson Weathersby, "Censorship of Literature Textbooks in Tennessee: A Study of the Commission, Publishers, Teachers, and Textbooks," Ph.D. diss., University of Tennessee, 1975, pp. 123–42.

6. N. R. Kleinfeld, "The Elderly Man and the Sea? Test Sanitizes Literary Texts," *The New York Times*, June 2, 2002, p. 1; Jeanne Heifetz, "What's Wrong with This Picture?" (unpub., 2002).

7. New York State Education Department, "Sensitivity and Bias Review of New York State Assessments" (New York State Education Department, 2000); "New York State Sensitivity Guidelines" (New York State Education Department, 2000).

8. Dale McFeatters, "The N.Y. Regents' Improved History," *New York Post*, June 8, 2002, p. 19.

9. W. Wilbur Hatfield, *An Experience Curriculum in English: A Report of the Curriculum Commission of the National Council of Teachers of English* (Appleton–Century, 1935), pp. 25–79.

10. "Should We Create an Authorized National Literary Canon?" *California English*, Fall 1997, pp. 6–8.

11. Carol Jago, "Something There Is That Doesn't Love a List," *American Educator*, Winter 2001, p. 36.

NINE: *History: The Endless Battle*

1. Frances FitzGerald, *America Revised: History Schoolbooks in the Twentieth Century* (Random House, 1979), pp. 9, 58–60.

2. FitzGerald, pp. 26, 48.

3. The books reviewed are:

Iftikhar Ahmad, Herbert Brodsky, Marylee Susan Crofts, Elisabeth Gaynor Ellis, *World Cultures: A Global Mosaic* (Prentice Hall, 2001).

Beverly J. Armento, J. Jorge Klor de Alva, Gary B. Nash, Christopher J. Salter, Louis E. Wilson, Karen K. Wixson, *Across the Centuries* (Houghton Mifflin, 1999).

Beverly J. Armento, Jacqueline M. K. Cordova, J. Jorge Klor de Alva, Gary B. Nash, Franklin Ng, Christopher L. Salter, Louis E. Wilson, Karen K. Wixson, *A Message of Ancient Days* (Houghton Mifflin, 2003).

Beverly J. Armento, J. Jorge Klor de Alva, Gary B. Nash,
Christopher J. Salter, Louis E. Wilson, Karen K. Wixson, *To See
a World* (Houghton Mifflin, 1997).

James Banks, Barry K. Beyer, Gloria Contreras, Jean Craven, Gloria
Ladson-Billings, Mary A. McFarland, Walter C. Parker, *World:
Adventures in Time and Place* (McGraw-Hill, 2000).

Roger B. Beck, Linda Black, Larry S. Krieger, Phillip C. Naylor,
Dahia Ibo Shabaka, *Modern World History: Patterns of Interaction*
(McDougal Littell, 1999).

Miriam Greenblatt and Peter S. Lemmo, *Human Heritage: A World
History* (Glencoe/McGraw-Hill, 2001).

Elisabeth Gaynor Ellis and Anthony Esler, *World History:
Connections to Today* (Prentice Hall, 2001).

Mounir A. Farah and Andrea Berens Karls, *World History: The
Human Experience* (Glencoe/McGraw-Hill, 2001).

William Travis Hanes III, *World History: Continuity and Change*
(Holt, Rinehart and Winston, 1999).

Jackson S. Spielvogel, *World History* (Glencoe/McGraw-Hill, 2003).

World History: People and Nations (Holt, Rinehart and Winston,
2000).

4. *World History: Connections to Today*, pp. 78–79; *To See a World*, p. 186.
5. *World History: Connections to Today*, pp. 254–55.
6. *Across the Centuries*, p. 64.
7. *To See a World*, p. 187.
8. *World History: People and Nations*, p. 208.
9. *World History: The Human Experience*, p. 282, *World History: Connections to
   Today*, p. 893.
10. *World History: The Human Experience*, p. 954.
11. Barbara Crossette, "Study Warns of Stagnation in Arab Societies," *The New
    York Times*, July 2, 2002.
12. *World History: Continuity and Change*, pp. 279, 788. The editorial advisory
    board for this book consists of Theodore K. Rabb of Princeton University;
    Philip D. Curtin of Johns Hopkins University; Akira Iriye of Harvard Uni-
    versity; Ainslie T. Embree of Columbia University; and Bernard Lewis of
    Princeton University.
13. The books reviewed are:

Joyce Appleby, Alan Brinkley, James M. McPherson, *The American
Journey: Building a Nation* (Glencoe, 2000).

Joyce Appleby, Alan Brinkley, Albert S. Broussard, James M.
McPherson, and Donald A. Ritchie, *The American Republic Since
1877* (Glencoe, 2003).

Beverly J. Armento, Gary B. Nash, Christopher L. Salter, Karen K.
Wixson, *A More Perfect Union* (Houghton Mifflin, 1997).

Beverly J. Armento, J. Jorge Klor de Alva, Gary B. Nash,
Christopher L. Salter, Louis E. Wilson, Karen K. Wixson,
America Will Be (Houghton Mifflin, 1999).

James A. Banks, Barry H. Beyer, Gloria Contreras, Jean Craven, Gloria Ladson-Billings, Mary A. McFarland, Walter C. Parker, *United States: Adventures in Time and Place* (McGraw-Hill, 2000).

Daniel J. Boorstin and Brooks Mather Kelley, *A History of the United States* (Prentice Hall, 2002). This is a pre-1995 text.

Paul Boyer, *The American Nation* (Holt, Rinehart and Winston, 2001).

Andrew Cayton, Elisabeth Israels Perry, Linda Reed, Allan M. Winkler, *America: Pathways to the Present* (Prentice Hall, 2002).

Gerald A. Danzer, J. Jorge Klor de Alva, Larry S. Krieger, Louis E. Wilson, Nancy Woloch, *The Americans* (McDougal Littell, 2002).

Thomas V. DiBacco, Lorna C. Mason, Christian G. Appy, *History of the United States*, vol. 2 (McDougal Littell, 1997).

Matthew T. Downey, James R. Giese, Fay D. Metcalf, *United States History: In the Course of Human Events* (National Textbook Company, 1997).

Joy Hakim, *A History of Us* (Oxford University Press, 1999).

Lorna C. Mason, Jesus Garcia, Frances Powell, C. Frederick Risinger, *America's Past and Promise* (McDougal Littell, 1998).

Lorna C. Mason, William Jay Jacobs, Robert P. Ludlum, *History of the United States*, vol. 1 (McDougal Littell, 1997).

Gary B. Nash, *American Odyssey: The United States in the Twentieth Century* (Glencoe, 1999).

Sterling Stuckey and Linda Kerrigan Salvucci, *Call to Freedom* (Holt, Rinehart and Winston, 2000).

14. *American Odyssey*, p. 654; *The Americans*, p. 39; *Call to Freedom*, pp. 745, 900; *The American Nation*, pp. 733, 663; *The American Republic Since 1877*, p. 694.

15. David Saville Muzzey, *A History of Our Country* (Ginn, 1943), p. xi; Henry F. Graff, *America; The Glorious Republic* (Houghton Mifflin, 1985) p. 22; Brooks and Kelley, p. xix.

16. *Call to Freedom*, p. 23; *The American Journey*, p. 41; *The American Nation*, pp. 16–17; *The American Republic Since 1877*, p. 23; *World History: Continuity and Change*, pp. 441–46.

17. *American Odyssey*, pp. 23–24; *World History: Connections to Today*, p. 158; Christy G. Turner II and Jacqueline Turner, *Man Corn: Cannibalism and Violence in the Prehistoric American Southwest* (University of Utah Press, 1999); James Bishop Jr., "Bones of Contention," weeklywire.com/ww/02-07-00/tw_curr2.html; William J. Bennetta, "More Fake 'History' from Glencoe," *The Textbook Letter*, September–October 1999 (www.textbook league.org/104sazi.htm); Douglas Preston, "Cannibals of the Canyon," *The New Yorker*, November 30, 1998.

18. William J. Bennetta, "A Book of Far-Left Propaganda That Fosters Anti-Intellectualism," *The Textbook Letter*, January–February 1997 (www. textbookleague.org/76west.htm).

19. See Hugh Pearson, *The Shadow of the Panther: Huey Newton and the Price of Black Power in America* (Addison Wesley, 1994).

TEN: *The Language Police: Can We Stop Them?*

1. Ray Bradbury, coda to *Fahrenheit 451* (Ballantine/Del Rey, 1979), pp. 175–79.
2. Jonathan Rauch, *Kindly Inquisitors: The New Attacks on Free Thought* (University of Chicago Press, 1993), pp. 128–29, 141.
3. Mario Vargas Llosa, "Why Literature?" *The New Republic,* May 14, 2001.
4. John Adams, "Liberty and Knowledge," *The American Reader: Words That Moved a Nation,* ed. Diane Ravitch (Perennial, 2000), p. 26.

Bibliography

American Library Association. *Intellectual Freedom Manual.* American Library Association, 2002.

Bates, Stephen. *Battleground: One Mother's Crusade, the Religious Right, and the Struggle for Control of Our Classrooms.* Poseidon Press, 1993.

Bradbury, Ray. *Fahrenheit 451.* Ballantine/Del Rey, 1979.

Burress, Lee. *Battle of the Books: Literary Censorship in the Public Schools, 1950–1985.* Scarecrow Press, 1989.

Chadwick-Joshua, Jocelyn. *The Jim Dilemma: Reading Race in Huckleberry Finn.* University Press of Mississippi, 1998.

Chall, Jeanne. "An Analysis of Textbooks in Relation to Declining SAT Scores," prepared for the Advisory Panel on the Scholastic Aptitude Test Score Decline. College Board, 1977.

Council on Interracial Books for Children. *Human and Anti-Human Values in Children's Books.* CIBC Racism and Sexism Resource Center for Educators, 1976.

———. *Racist and Sexist Images in Children's Books.* CIBC, 1975.

Courtois, Stéphane, et al. *The Black Book of Communism: Crimes, Terror, Repression.* Harvard University Press, 1999.

DelFattore, Joan. *What Johnny Shouldn't Read: Textbook Censorship in America.* Yale University Press, 1992.

Denenberg, Dennis, and Lorraine Roscoe. *50 American Heroes Every Kid Should Meet.* Millbrook Press, 2001.

Dick and Jane as Victims: Sex Stereotyping in Children's Readers. Women on Words and Images, 1972.

Differential Item Functioning, edited by Paul W. Holland and Howard Wainer. Lawrence Erlbaum Associates, 1993.

Ellis, John M. *Literature Lost: Social Agendas and the Corruption of the Humanities.* Yale University Press, 1997.

Elson, Ruth Miller. *Guardians of Tradition: American Schoolbooks of the Nineteenth Century.* University of Nebraska Press, 1964.

Fischer, David Hackett. *Historians' Fallacies: Toward a Logic of Historical Thought.* Harper & Row, 1970.

FitzGerald, Frances. *America Revised: History Schoolbooks in the Twentieth Century.* Random House, 1979.

Glazer, Nathan, and Reed Ueda. *Ethnic Groups in History Textbooks.* Ethics and Public Policy Center, 1983.

Handbook of Methods for Detecting Test Bias, edited by Ronald A. Berks. Johns Hopkins University Press, 1982.

Hatfield, W. Wilbur. *An Experience Curriculum in English: A Report of the Curriculum Commission of the National Council of Teachers of English.* Appleton-Century, 1935.

Hentoff, Nat. *Free Speech for Me—But Not for Thee: How the American Left and Right Relentlessly Censor Each Other.* HarperCollins, 1992.

Jenkinson, Edward B. *Censors in the Classroom: The Mind Benders.* Southern Illinois University Press, 1979.

Karolides, Nicholas J. *Banned Books: Literature Suppressed on Political Grounds.* Facts on File, 1998.

Landes, David S. *The Wealth and Poverty of Nations: Why Some Are So Rich and Some So Poor.* Norton, 1998.

Last, Ellen. "Textbook Selection or Censorship: An Analysis of the Complaints Filed in Relation to Three Major Literature Series Proposed for Adoption in Texas in 1978," Ph.D. dissertation, University of Texas, 1984. Includes bias guidelines of Gablers, pp. 191–200.

Lerner, Robert, Althea K. Nagai, and Stanley Rothman. *Molding the Good Citizen: The Politics of High School History Texts.* Praeger, 1995.

Lewis, Bernard. *Islam and the West.* Oxford University Press, 1993.

Loewen, James W. *Lies My Teacher Told Me.* New Press, 1995.

Lynch, James J., and Bertrand Evans. *High School English Textbooks: A Critical Examination.* Little, Brown, 1963.

Miller, Casey, and Kate Swift. *The Handbook of Nonsexist Writing.* Lippincott and Crowell, 1980.

——. *Words and Women.* Anchor Books, 1976.

National Council of Teachers of English and International Reading Association. *Standards for the English Language Arts.* The Associations, 1996.

National Standards for United States History: Exploring the American Experience. National Center for History in the Schools, 1994.

Nelson, Jack, and Gene Roberts Jr. *The Censors and the Schools.* Little, Brown, 1963.

Orwell, George. *1984.* Harcourt Brace Jovanovich, 1949.

Perrin, Noel. *Dr. Bowdler's Legacy: A History of Expurgated Books in England and America.* David R. Godine, 1992.

Pierce, Bessie L. *Public Opinion and the Teaching of History.* Knopf, 1926.

Rauch, Jonathan. *Kindly Inquisitors: The New Attacks on Free Thought.* University of Chicago Press, 1993.

Ravitch, Diane. *The American Reader.* HarperCollins, 2000.

——. *Left Back: A Century of Battles Over School Reform.* Simon and Schuster, 2000.

Rosser, Phyllis. *The SAT Gender Gap: Identifying the Causes.* Center for Women Policy Studies, 1989.

Schlesinger, Arthur M., Jr. *The Disuniting of America: Reflections on a Multicultural Society.* Norton, 1991.

Sewall, Gilbert T. *History Textbooks at the New Century.* The American Textbook Council, 2000.

————. "World History: An Appraisal," *Education Week,* June 13, 2001.

Thompson, Michael Clay. *Classics in the Classroom.* Trillium Press, 1990.

Tyson-Bernstein, Harriet. *A Conspiracy of Good Intentions: America's Textbook Fiasco.* Council for Basic Education, 1988.

Vitz, Paul C. *Censorship: Evidence of Bias in Our Children's Textbooks.* Servant Books, 1986.

Weathersby, Dorothy Thompson. "Censorship of Literature Textbooks in Tennessee: A Study of the Commission, Publishers, Teachers, and Textbooks," Ph.D. dissertation, University of Tennessee, 1975.

Zimmerman, Jonathan. *Whose America?: Culture Wars in the Public Schools.* Harvard University Press, 2002.

Index

A Note About the Author

DIANE RAVITCH is Research Professor of Education at New York University and holds the Brown Chair in Education Studies at the Brookings Institution, where she edits *Brookings Papers on Education Policy*. A historian of education, she is the author of seven previous books.

Ravitch is a board member of the New York State Council for the Humanities, the New America Foundation, the Albert Shanker Institute, and the Thomas B. Fordham Foundation. She is a visiting fellow at the Hoover Institution, a senior fellow at Brookings, and a member of the National Assessment Governing Board.

She graduated from the Houston public schools and earned a B.A. from Wellesley College and a Ph.D. from Columbia University. She served as assistant secretary of education in charge of research for the U.S. Department of Education from 1991 to 1993. She was elected to the American Academy of Arts and Sciences, the Society of American Historians, and the National Academy of Education. Ravitch was honored as a Literary Lion by the New York Public Library. She has received honorary degrees from Williams College, Reed College, Amherst College, Union College, Ramapo College, St. Joseph's College, Middlebury College Language Schools, and the State University of New York.

She lives in Brooklyn, New York.

A *Note on the Type*

This book was set in a modern adaptation of a type designed by the first William Caslon (1692–1766). The Caslon face, an artistic, easily read type, has enjoyed over two centuries of popularity in our own country. It is of interest to note that the first copies of the Declaration of Independence and the first paper currency distributed to the citizens of the new-born nation were printed in this typeface.

Composed by Creative Graphics,
Allentown, Pennsylvania
Printed and bound by Berryville Graphics,
Berryville, Virginia
Designed by Anthea Lingeman